BEYOND A REASONABLE DOUBT

BEYOND A REASONABLE DOUBT

SANDOR FRANKEL

STEIN AND DAY/*Publishers*/New York

Copyright © 1971 by Sandor Frankel
Library of Congress Catalog Card No. 73-163452
All rights reserved
Published simultaneously in Canada by Saunders of Toronto, Ltd.
Designed by David Miller
Manufactured in the United States of America
Stein and Day/*Publishers*/7 East 48 Street, New York, N.Y. 10017
ISBN 0-8128-1403-7

SECOND PRINTING, 1972

This story happened, this way.
Some names have been changed,
to respect the privacy of
certain people involved. The
book—like justice—is dedicated
to the truth.

BEYOND A REASONABLE DOUBT

CHAPTER ONE

T HE carwash where it happened—
Mr. Wash Carwash, 616 Rhode Island Avenue, Washington, D.C.—is
larger than most automatic carwashes you've seen and charges $2.25 for
a cleaning. It is a one-story, grayish-beige building carved out in the
middle; when open for business during the day, garagelike doors raised
at both ends, it looks like a long, low tunnel from and to nowhere in
particular. You turn off Rhode Island Avenue into the large driveway,
pull around to the back, and step outside the car so the vacuum men can
give it a quick inside cleaning. Then they slip some chains under the car
and slide it through the tunnel, where it is soaped down, pelted with
showers from several directions, mechanically dried, then slid out the
other end of the tunnel.

So you can watch the process when you leave your car in the rear,
there is a glassed-in corridor running the length of the Carwash against
the left, or east, wall. You walk down that corridor, and you see other cars
being cleaned in front of and behind your own. There are a lot of men and
kids—a few dozen, it looks like, mainly black and dirty, dressed in old
clothes or blue coveralls—working inside what they call "the pit," the
place where dirty cars slide noisily by to get clean. Before you reach the
end of the corridor, you pass a bathroom you may use and a manager's
office you may not enter. At the end of the corridor, you pay the cashier,
and she thanks you and asks you to come again.

And if you're walking down the glassed-in corridor, keeping an eye
on your car, you can look across the pit to the tiled wall on the other side
and see a few closed doors. They are employees-only doors, where the
Carwash houses its boiler and spare equipment, and where the employees
can change clothing and clean up. You never get near those small, window-
less rooms off the wall on the other side of the pit if you're only there to

get your car cleaned. You just walk down the glassed-in corridor, and all you hear are noises from the pit, loud and mechanical and indistinguishable, noises that cover you all over, like when you press a seashell to your ear.

December 10, 1968, was not an unusual Tuesday at the Carwash. Irving Rosenberg, the manager, white, fifty-four, arrived shortly after 7:00 in the morning, after dropping off his niece at her job and arranging to pick her up around quitting time. John "Pop" Weaver, a fifty-six-year-old black man, spent most of the day helping clean the right side of each car before and after it slid through the noisy machinery in the pit. Gloria McDowell, an attractive twenty-four-year-old black girl, was the cashier, and for her, as for everyone else there, the day was slow: bad wintry weather, and who wants to have a car cleaned when rain is due any minute.

A few minutes after 5:00 that afternoon, Phyllis Chotner, Rosenberg's niece, called her uncle at the Carwash to find out what time he'd be driving her home. He told her Gloria was totaling the day's receipts, and he'd call back when he was ready to leave. At about 5:15 Rosenberg called her back, said he was leaving, and told her to meet him in front of the building where she worked. After waiting outside for over an hour, Phyllis called Mrs. Rosenberg to find out whether Irv had called home. But Irving Rosenberg had not called his home, and John Weaver had not called his home, and Gloria McDowell had not called her home.

Phyllis Chotner waited in the cold a bit longer, and Mrs. Rosenberg called the police.

At 7:43 P.M. Charles E. Floyd and Leslie C. Jackson pulled their police cruiser into the driveway of Mr. Wash Carwash and saw a car they recognized as the manager's parked by the front door. The large overhead garage doors were locked shut. Two lights were still burning in the driveway; some lights were on inside. There were no sounds.

Floyd opened the customers' door in front—the only unlocked door—and called out to the quiet whether anyone was there. A very slight echo. Then silence. Overhead an electric heater burned noiselessly. Floyd walked up and down the glassed-in customers' corridor. Nobody there, nobody in the bathroom off the corridor, nothing disturbed. He entered the manager's office and saw the empty combination safe, door swung

10

open, no jimmy marks. Then back to the customers' corridor, through an opening, and into the pit.

When Floyd stepped onto the motionless conveyor in the middle of the Carwash, a mouse darted out and scampered through an open door into the employees' locker room on the other side of the pit. Floyd watched it dart past some work clothes strewn loosely on the floor, then over the bottom of a woman's polished brown boot. Drawn down around the boot were a black girdle and pink panties. Above them were the smooth naked legs of a Negro female. She lay on her stomach, hands tied behind her back with a strip of blue cloth, her skull bathed in blood. Though the body was female, Floyd could not tell whether she had been pretty. Near her feet lay a thick iron pipe, three-quarters gray, one-quarter red.

Still standing on the conveyor, Floyd turned slightly to look past the locker room into a tiny adjoining bathroom. On the far wall a urinal. The tiles beneath the urinal were splattered with red, like an abstract painting. Beneath the urinal against the wall lay a white male whose face was covered with red. Beside him was some rumpled clothing. On the wall were slivers of flesh.

Without bothering to take any pulses, Floyd radioed for assistance on a double killing.

CHAPTER TWO

D ETECTIVES of the homicide unit received a radio run at 7:50 P.M. to meet a scout car at the Mr. Wash Carwash. They arrived within minutes and met Officers Floyd and Jackson.

A homicide man is a specialist, trained to react routinely in situations which are not routine. He knows, in crimes he is assigned to investigate, that the offender is by definition a killer. He knows that the case will one day culminate in court proceedings and, because one man's death at another man's hands is important, the case will be treated as important. He knows not to rely on memory when facts may be needed months, or years, in the future. So he looks, and he writes while he is looking. Since he does not know what facts will turn out later to be important, every fact becomes important.

They began with the bodies. But it is a slow process until a homicide man reaches the body he sees across the room, a slow process until the coroner, waiting at the door of the locker room, is allowed in to pronounce Gloria McDowell officially dead. First, the homicide detectives scavenge the floor inch by inch, noting absolutely everything along the floor, measuring the location of everything from two fixed points, every little object, looking for shoe prints that may be photographed, or weapons, or clues, or . . . or anything. The process is tedious because when you don't know what you are looking for, you look for everything. The bodies are observed, and everything noted, before they are touched. Other homicide detectives arrive to help, and the Mobile Crime Laboratory Unit arrives and diagrams the scene in detail and photographs the Carwash from all angles, inside and outside.

Seven feet and one-half inch from the door opening from the pit into the locker room, the dead woman lay against the west wall, head north, face turned awkwardly to the right against the ground. The blue cloth that bound her wrists behind her back was not noticeably different from the material of the blue uniforms strewn about the room. A dull yellow towel hung loosely about her neck. Her panties and girdle were completely off her left leg and pulled down her right leg to the calf; her white net stockings were off the left leg only but still attached to the girdle. A brown leather boot about ten inches high was on her right foot; a similar boot lay near the entrance door. The watch on her left wrist was intact. Hair that looked like hers, and blood, were splattered over the three-quarter-length black suede coat she wore and traces had splashed against the room's north wall. The hair on her head was matted thickly with blood near a gaping laceration on the back of her skull. Large amounts of blood were congealing beneath her mouth and nose. More blood had dripped down the inside of her left knee. Her head lay beneath a sink, the bottom of which had been doused with blood. Her head had apparently been smashed even as she lay on the ground, and the blood had spurted upward against the base of the sink.

A four-foot length of iron pipe lay parallel to the right side of her body. The bloody quarter of the pipe was near her toe. Between the pipe and her body was a book of matches bearing a telephone number. A knife with a six-inch blade broken at the end lay just inside the locker room doorway.

At 8:50 P.M. the coroner was allowed into the locker room to pronounce Gloria McDowell officially dead. When her body was finally moved for examination, a topless blue ballpoint pen was recovered from beneath her. On the floor between her legs was a single head-hair.

In the adjacent bathroom detectives slowly worked their way toward the body of a middle-aged white man, face swathed in blood, eyes and mouth open toward the ceiling, head nearly under the urinal against the north wall. He was clothed in a blue uniform, with "Irv" and "Mgr" sewn on the right chest. He wore white socks and black shoes. On his clothing were large quantities of blood and human tissue. Pieces of a plate of false teeth lay scattered near the body.

The rumpled clothing that Officer Floyd had seen to the left of Rosenberg dressed the body of a middle-aged Negro male hunched over on its left side, wearing a brown corduroy coat, dark pants, dark socks, and brown shoes. His back rested against the toilet near the urinal. The toilet was splattered with red. The men's heads were close together. The floor between their heads was thick with red fluid.

13

A homicide detective told Officer Floyd there were three victims.

From the white man's body to the west wall of the room, the floor was caked in blood. More blood was splattered on the walls and door, some in the pattern of blurred handprints. In the blood were a small clear button and visible particles of human tissue. A light bulb hanging overhead and a light fixture over the medicine cabinet didn't work. On the wash basin in plain view were a pair of lady's black leather gloves and a black leather handbag. Both were stained with blood but, oddly, the purse had not been looted. The black man's rear pocket bulged with a wallet still containing $253. And he still had his pay envelope with $77.26 in cash. The white man still had an envelope with $4.01 undisturbed in his pocket.

In time the coroner officially pronounced Irving Rosenberg and John Weaver dead.

As the search for visible clues proceeded, so did the search for invisible clues. Whether you are a killer or a saint, the palm sides of your hands and fingers contain patterns of narrow ridges and furrows, intricate designs of loops and arches and whorls. The tiny lines never shift on a person's fingers during the course of his life, and no two fingers are identically patterned. Tiny as those ridges are, the crest of each ridge is lined with a multitude of still tinier pores, which leave an impression of invisible perspiration secretions when pressed against a smooth surface.

To develop any latent prints that might be present, the police virtually repainted the Carwash with multi-colored fingerprint powder, sprinkled over a small surface and gently brushed. If fingerprint patterns existed on the surface, the powder would adhere to the outline of the ridges, sweeping over the rest of the surface. To lift the print, a piece of tape was carefully placed over the developed impression, set indirectly against the pattern outlining the ridges, and lifted straight up. The image of the fingerprint sticks to the tape, available for later magnification and comparison. Using silver nitrate—a solution sprayed onto the surface to react with the latent salt deposits and form a visible fingerprint pattern—tests for prints were run on all loose pieces of paper.

In all, latent fingerprints were developed on the desk drawer, cabinet, and safe in the manager's office, on the inside of the right front window of Irving Rosenberg's automobile parked outside, on the mirror in the bathroom from which two men's bodies had just been removed, on a pack of matches on the floor next to Weaver, on the door between the locker room and bathroom. But as for the knife on the locker room floor, and

14

the pipes strewn around inside—and everything else that had been coated with powder and gently, painstakingly, brushed—nothing.

The prints that had been lifted would be developed and retained. They might be sufficiently distinctive to lead police to the killer, but that would be unusual. Or they might be compared with fingerprints of the victims' co-workers and acquaintances to suggest a suspect. Or they might be compared with the prints of anyone who later became a suspect. If they matched, that would be very helpful.

The recovery of the physical evidence then began. As each item was picked up, it was carefully marked for later identification. Bits of paper or clothing with no apparent meaning, loosely strewn items of no apparent relevance: all were gathered and marked as evidence. You could never do too much, you could never be too thorough. Even the toilet seat, bearing some blood and a faintly perceptible boot print, was removed for tests.

As the police gathered their evidence, the bodies of Irving Rosenberg, Gloria McDowell, and John Weaver were photographed from all conceivable angles before they were moved, and were then transported to the D.C. Morgue for autopsies to determine medically the cause of death. It would not be difficult in this case. All three heads and faces were markedly deformed by severe, crushing pressure. They had died from what the coroner termed "severe comminuted, compound open skull fracture with brain laceration." That is, their heads and brains had been bashed from life to death by strong blows from a heavy object. The men had also been stabbed. Gloria McDowell's body revealed no signs of sexual molestation. There was not a single unbroken bone left in what had once been Irving Rosenberg's face. The coroner noted that on certain of the bruises, "the pattern is strongly suggestive of screw thread markings as might be found on metal pipe."

Even at the autopsy the investigative job of gathering evidence continued. Items of the victims' clothing, blood samples, hair samples, even nail samples of the victims, were collected and kept as possible evidence. You could never tell—even the loose strand of hair removed from the third finger of John Weaver's left hand might become important. Perhaps some clothing fibers could be microscopically detected under a victim's fingernail and later matched positively with a suspect's clothing. Or blood of a victim's type might later be found on a suspect's clothing, different from the suspect's own blood type. As soon as time allowed, the evidence would be sent for tests to the F.B.I.

15

Of course, simply calling those items "evidence" did not make them important or even helpful. Clothing, blood, nails, boots, pipes, a broken knife, a loose brush, even the toilet seat: many items of "evidence" but none yet a lead. Only one thing now to be sure of: someone had to visit three homes to tell the people something horrible has happened to your husband, or your uncle, or your daughter. That kind of telling is done in person.

The newspapers, of course, would run the story as front-page news; but they would be told only that a cashbox had been stolen, not that most of the money was in two bags or that one of the bags had a lot of change or that the bags were green and white. Those facts would be known only by the police, the owner, the killers, and perhaps by someone who might later come forward with some information. That way anyone wanting to appear helpful to the police later on could not weave a credible story simply from facts he had read in a newspaper.

And now, after the shreds had all been gathered, after the blood and tissue had been lifted off the walls and floors, the homicide unit of the Metropolitan Police Department began in earnest to search for the killer. Or killers.

With nothing to start with, where do you start?

They started that night with the owner of the Carwash, Robert Gordon, who had been at the Carwash the day of the murders until 4:15 P.M. Business was slow, and he had instructed Rosenberg to close the place at 5:00. There had been no apparent trouble during the day and no suspicious idlers.

They learned from Gordon, and from his bank, that on the day of the murders, Rosenberg had received and cashed his own $185 paycheck plus a payroll check for $807. They learned that a day's receipts plus petty cash usually total another $700. They learned that payday was not until Wednesday but that Irving Rosenberg often cashed the payroll check Tuesday to pay employees a day early if they wished. Someone who had worked for a while at the Carwash would have known that if you were going to hit the place, late Tuesday afternoon would be ideal. They learned specifically where money had been taken from: mostly from the manager's office—from the bags inside the safe, whose combination only Robert Gordon and Irving Rosenberg knew, and from behind removable panels over the door where some bills had been hidden—as well as from the now empty tip box.

They interviewed a long-term employee named Barbara "Sonny"

16

Craig, a white, pimply-faced, tough-talking girl, who stated that she had coincidentally called in sick the day of the murders. She had, however, telephoned several times during the afternoon and had spoken with Irving Rosenberg and Gloria McDowell. Neither had seemed unhappy, and neither had mentioned any trouble. Sonny Craig told the police that about a year ago Rosenberg had had some trouble with two Negro employees, one named Harold Briscoe, who used to steal from the tip box until he quit a year ago, and one whose first name may have been Robert, who Rosenberg had thought once broke into the Carwash before quitting a year ago. And she said that about half a year ago Rosenberg used to argue all the time with another employee until the man had finally just walked off the job. That man's name was Bishop Blue.

They spoke that night with Helen Watson, who helped wipe cars dry at the Carwash. She told them that at about 5:00 P.M., as she was leaving work, Gloria McDowell was inside counting the day's receipts and Pop Weaver was somewhere in the back. She offered to split a cab with Gloria, but Gloria had said Irv would be driving her home that evening. After Helen left, Rosenberg had locked the door behind her. She knew from personal experience that Irving Rosenberg was careful about opening the door after locking it unless he knew whoever was outside. Helen had not known that there was a safe in the Carwash. As she left, she had noticed two married employees, Alicia and Richard McKenzie, making a U-turn in front of the Carwash as if to drive off.

Alicia and Richard McKenzie were full-time employees at the Carwash. They had left work at 4:55, just as the last of the workers were leaving. Helen Watson was hailing a cab, and Jerry Richardson seemed to be pulling out of the driveway. The McKenzies usually drove a third employee home, a man named Lewis Banks. On December 10, for some reason neither remembered, Lewis Banks had not ridden with them. They had last seen him walking away from the Carwash as they drove away. When the McKenzies left, only four people remained near the Carwash. Three were now dead. The fourth was Lewis Banks.

The police now had a skeletal timetable.

But as Richard McKenzie thought some more, he recalled that there was one employee he had not actually seen leave the Carwash that night. The man's name was Arondo Coates.

The McKenzies had not noticed any strangers around the Carwash. They did, however, notice a blue and white cab pulling in as they were leaving. They did not see it pull out.

No, they did not know of any trouble any of the three victims had

had with anyone. Even though, said Alicia McKenzie, Pop Weaver used to take numbers at the Carwash. And Irving Rosenberg had argued with somebody at the Carwash, come to think of it. Just yesterday. With whom? "Just some old lady that had her car washed yesterday." No name.

And there was another man the police might want to check out. He was a white man Irving Rosenberg simply did not trust. He had worked at the Carwash until last week, when he quit, or was fired by Irv. His name was Henry Long.

There was just one last man Alicia McKenzie suggested the police might also want to investigate. Nothing specific, but the man had been employed at the Carwash, and his behavior had been strange. In fact, she said, she suspected him. His name was Bishop Blue.

The following morning, police returned to the Carwash to speak with some more employees.

They spoke with a long-term worker named William Wells, who could suggest nobody who might want to harm any of the victims. He had called the Carwash yesterday at about 5:15, and Irving Rosenberg had answered the phone. Rosenberg sounded normal. Wells had asked to speak with Gloria, but Rosenberg had said she was gone. He had asked to speak with Pop Weaver, but Rosenberg had said he too was gone.

He had called the Carwash to find out about a numbers bet.

William Wells also told the police something about Henry Long, whom the McKenzies had also mentioned. Henry had been a maintenance man at the Carwash and would always refuse to help out with the cars even when his own work was through. And Wells had once seen a picture in a newspaper of a man wanted by the F.B.I. who looked like Henry. When Wells would tease him about it, Henry would just laugh it off.

They spoke once more with Sonny Craig. She told them more about the former employee named Bishop Blue: that he was a Negro male, about forty-five years old, and that he had a violent temper. And that while he worked at the Carwash, he used to carry an iron pipe wrapped in a towel.

A named suspect.

She also remembered a younger Negro male, about twenty-five years old, dark, about 5'9" tall, about 170 pounds, with well-processed black hair, who had worked for a day or two at the Carwash a few weeks earlier. She didn't remember his name, but one detective remembered his description. Two weeks earlier the detective had driven his police cruiser in

18

for a cleaning. He had spoken with Gloria McDowell, and Gloria had pointed the man out. She had told the detective that the man was ugly, that the man was mean, and that the man kept looking at her.

Barbara Craig did not recall the man's name. He had been a part-time employee. Pursuant to Carwash policy all names and records of part-time employees were always destroyed the day following their employment.

Another suspect. No name.

Before leaving the Carwash, detectives went over the scene once more. They found Irving Rosenberg's keys in a drawer next to the cash register in the cashier's booth. Several employees on the scene told the police that Rosenberg always—always—kept his keys in his pockets. From the bathroom they recovered more pieces of the shattered denture plate. From the locker room they recovered another long, heavy iron pipe slightly stained with blood, stains they hadn't noticed yesterday evening. Several similar pipes, replacements in case something went wrong with the machines, lay scattered about the Carwash.

Outside a room near the murder scene they noticed an electrical switchbox with some red marks that nobody had noticed the previous evening. The name "Jery" was written on the box in red. The red appeared to be blood. Detectives removed the door from the box and took it for scientific testing. But before they left, they got a partial list of names of present and former employees of the Carwash. Some of the names they had seen before, and some of the names were new. One of the names was Jerry Richardson.

The police checked out neighboring businesses on Rhode Island Avenue. Nobody had seen anything unusual at the Carwash yesterday or last night. Someone said something about betting on numbers, and the police spoke with the man who took numbers bets at the company across the street from the Carwash. He told them who he turned his daily book in to.

Homicide detectives visited the homes and some associates of the three victims to see whether overnight they had remembered any useful information.

At Ben's Chili Bowl, a restaurant where Gloria McDowell had once worked, they learned that she had been very popular with men. They took Eddie McDowell, the man who had divorced her a month ago, to headquarters for some questioning. He was a suspect only because of his status as Gloria's divorced husband. Perhaps he was jealous; perhaps his relationship with Gloria would furnish some motive for him to brutalize her and anyone with her at the time.

19

He had called her regularly even after the divorce, McDowell said; they were still pretty good friends despite the divorce her family had caused. In fact he had tried to call her at home about 5:30 the day she was murdered but had been unable to reach her. She had several boyfriends, but he knew of nobody with whom she had trouble. Eddie McDowell had been at work around the time of the killings, he told the police, re-hearsing a singing group he managed. While he was being interrogated by the police, a team of detectives fanned out to check McDowell's story, to speak with the people he claimed to have been with at the time of the murders, to speak with them before McDowell could, perhaps, concoct an alibi with their cooperation. And when the police spoke with the people he had mentioned, they learned that Eddie McDowell had not murdered his ex-wife. He could not imagine who had.

At Pop Weaver's home, detectives learned that Pop normally carried a hawkbill knife, which was gone when his corpse was found. A neighbor told them that Pop Weaver seemed to know a lot about the numbers game.

The numbers game. Files of the police gambling section were promptly checked. Five years ago an anonymous complainant had reported that John Weaver was writing numbers in the vicinity of a given address. Police surveillance had subsequently observed him visiting that address on sev-eral occasions. Beyond that information John Weaver's name did not appear in connection with any gambling investigation. A check of police reports reflected very little gambling information for the neighborhood of the Carwash.

On their way to speak with Sylvia Rosenberg, a pair of homicide detectives stopped at the Carwash to speak with a patrolman who had found something in the bushes exactly 188 feet from the Carwash drive-way which he thought they might like to see. It was a towel, the same faded green of the towels used in the Carwash, and it was stained with what appeared to be blood. Homicide took it and drove out to speak with Sylvia Rosenberg.

Mrs. Rosenberg told them her husband had always carried credit cards: Central Charge, Shopping Plate, Amoco, Shell Gas. He never kept his money in his wallet, always in his pocket. And he had argued with a man about one week ago. An employee, one with a short temper, who always carried a gun or other weapon in his pocket, who had quit because he thought Mr. Rosenberg was too bossy. His name stuck in her mind. An odd name. Bishop Blue.

She also heard something suspicious that she wanted to mention to

20

the police. She had heard that her husband's black wallet had been recovered from Pop Weaver's pocket. In fact, however, police knew that the only wallet recovered from Weaver had been tan.

The first concrete, specific, false rumor.

Within twenty-four hours of the killings, the police began checking out some suspects.

Arondo Coates. The McKenzies could not recall his leaving the Carwash last night. And this was not the first time Arondo Coates's name had been on the lips of policemen:

In February, 1965, he had been arrested for burglary and had served time; in May, 1965, he had been arrested for robbery and had served time; in October, 1965, he had been arrested for larceny and resisting arrest and had served time; in June, 1966, he had been arrested for larceny and had served time; in July, 1967, he had been arrested for shoplifting and had served time; in March, 1968, he had been arrested for shoplifting and had served time.

When the police transported Arondo Coates for a talk at homicide headquarters, he told them he had worked at another carwash for a year before being fired, and had been hired by Mr. Rosenberg at Mr. Wash Carwash the day before the murders. His job was driving the customers' cars from where they were parked to the point where chains could be slipped underneath to guide the cars through the pit. He told them he had worked Tuesday until about 5:00, when he left with another employee, Jerry Richardson, and that they were the last people to leave, except for the victims. He told them that Jerry Richardson had dropped him off by the Seaton Market, where he had bought some cheese and other items and had walked home. He arrived home at about 5:10 and did not leave until the following morning. He told them he lived in Apartment 4 at 1821 North Capitol Street with a fellow named Robert Parker. He told them he had not had any trouble in his two days at the Carwash.

Two detectives responded immediately to the Seaton Market to verify Coates's story. They showed three employees mug shots—one front, one profile—of Arondo Coates, and asked whether he had been in the market the previous day. None recalled seeing him.

The detectives then responded to the address given by Coates as his home. They rapped on the door but nobody answered. The neighbors knew who lived in Apartment 4, however. A man named Robert Parker.

21

And he lived alone. None had ever seen a man matching the two photographs of Arondo Coates. They showed the same photographs to the liquor store salesman across the street. The salesman had never seen Arondo Coates.

And nobody around had seen Robert Parker for the past few days.

Jerry Richardson. The letters "Jery" had been written, apparently in blood, on a switchbox near the rooms in which three dead bodies had been found. And only last month Jerry Richardson had been arrested for assault.

Jerry Richardson's job was to help dry cars as they slid out of the pit. He told the police that he had just begun working at the Carwash the day of the murders. He told them that another new man had come on the job that day from another carwash and had bragged that he'd had to leave the other carwash because he'd been in a fight. The little white manager had overheard the other new man say, "This carwash ain't worth a shit," and had told him not to repeat it, and the new man had answered him sharply. Nobody suspicious had been hanging around the Carwash when Jerry Richardson left about 5:00 to drive the new man to the Seaton Market. He claimed not to know the man's name. Even when police showed him Arondo Coates's photograph, he claimed not to recognize the man.

One more cute little bit Jerry Richardson did remember. The little white manager had been kidding the cashier girl about the stockings she was wearing, large squares; he had teased her about how they looked like ladder stockings and how he was going to climb up her legs.

Later that afternoon the police checked out the neighborhood Jerry Richardson had given as his home. His next-door neighbor told them Jerry had been visited earlier that day by one Negro male and one Negro female. The male was about 5′9″, about 170 pounds, dark brown complexion. The neighbor had not got a good look at either subject, but the police showed him some photographs anyway. He stated that he had seen the photographed subject in Jerry's apartment on previous occasions.

The photographs were of Arondo Coates.

Lewis Banks. The last person the McKenzies recalled remaining at the Carwash near Irving Rosenberg, Gloria McDowell, and Pop Weaver.

Lewis Banks admitted he had been the last man to leave the Carwash yesterday evening, leaving behind the three people whose mutilated bodies were later discovered. But he claimed that a taxicab had pulled into the driveway just as he was leaving—a Chevrolet, late model, black, with a white stripe around it. He said he told the driver the Carwash was closed, and to return tomorrow. The driver had left, and Lewis Banks was once again the last person in the Carwash. He said that as he was about to leave, Rosenberg had shut the large overhead sliding door, and that he had therefore walked to the unlocked front door, passed by Gloria as she was counting the day's receipts, and left. And that, he said, was the last he had seen of them.

But the police would want to speak with Lewis Banks again. A print left by one of his fingers had been found on the interior door separating the employees' locker room from the bathroom. And the number on the matchbook between Gloria McDowell's body and the bloody pipe was the telephone number of the place where he was living.

In the twenty-four hours that had passed since the murders, homicide detectives had called on and interviewed many people. A sketchy list of Carwash employees had been compiled. The Carwash was a haven for convicted killers and robbers who needed a job to get probation or parole. One by one they would be checked out by teams of homicide detectives: get the man's story, keep one detective talking with him while another leaves the discussion and immediately contacts the names the man has given, the employees he was with at the time, or the friends, or relatives. Take his fingerprints and compare them with the prints that had been lifted the night of the murders. But nothing positive had come up today. Even the heel mark on the top of the toilet seat had come up too faint for comparison.

More names would be checked tomorrow and the following days. Meanwhile unsolicited information was arriving:

a suburban detective called to report that yesterday, at about 10:00 P.M., he spotted a panel truck with the name "Mr. Carwash" traveling outside Washington;
a local reverend called to report that yesterday, at about 6:50 P.M., he spotted a late-model brown Pontiac in the Carwash, and a group of five or six people pushing a light-colored 1958 Ford also parked in the driveway;
a local patrolman called to report an anonymous tip that yesterday, at about 7:45 P.M., an old blue or green pickup truck

occupied by a white male, 35–45 years old, heavy build, was parked across the street from the Carwash, backed out hurriedly into the street, barely missed hitting several cars, and sped away.

A day had passed and the police had much information, but they still did not have the killer. Perhaps, at least, they had his name. Or names.

The next day, December 12, 1968, police responded once again to the address Arondo Coates had given as his home. This time Coates was there. Police asked him to come with them to the homicide office, they had a few more questions he might be able to answer. Several detectives remained behind to look for answers elsewhere. They checked out alleys in the rear of Coates's building; they checked out the trash cans; they checked out the sewers. In fact they checked out dozens of sewers near Jerry Richardson's home, near the Carwash, and throughout different sections of the city. And they found nothing against Coates or Richardson, or anybody else—no money bags, no bloody clothing, no money: nothing. And negative fingerprint comparisons on Coates and Richardson.

Lewis Banks was brought back to headquarters for another chat. This time they let him give his answers to a lie detector. They strapped him to the instrument panel encased in a large desk frame, and hooked on the devices that would mechanically record his muscular activity and changes in his pulse, blood pressure, respiration, skin reflexes. Banks told them that he wears his coveralls when he works at the Carwash, and carries his cigarettes and matches in the top pocket. After work he would change in the locker room in which Gloria McDowell's body was found. He had recently come up from Georgia and carried around his phone number because he just hadn't memorized it yet. But he had walked out the front door of the Carwash two nights ago, and the three victims had been alive, and he had never seen them again. As for his fingerprint on the bathroom door, that, of course, was not unusual: that was the bathroom and locker room he used. He and, over the months, hundreds of other employees.

The lie detector said that Lewis Banks was telling the truth.

That afternoon detectives drove to Prince George's County Hospital, where a patient named Albert Hughes claimed to have some news for them. Hughes, a middle-aged white man, said he had been sitting in a bar near the Carwash a short time after the murders, when two Negro males he knew came in. The three had gone to the men's room to drink

24

from Hughes's bottle and while there one of the men had told Hughes he had seen Rosenberg and Weaver get killed. Hughes had first met the man several years earlier in the maximum security ward of St. Elizabeth's Hospital, the local mental institution, where the man was serving a sentence for murder while Hughes was doing time for car theft. Later, the two had worked at the Carwash. And Hughes remembered the man's name. It was, after all, an uncommon name: Bishop Blue. The other man's last name was Green.

Meanwhile, more information was arriving, from several sources.

A Carwash employee called to report that a former employee named Jeremy Carroll, Negro male, about twenty-seven, could be the murderer. No specific reason, no specific incident. Just a hunch.

A man who knew Gloria McDowell claimed to have driven past the Carwash at 5:30 the afternoon of the murders and noticed a 1957 blue Pontiac parked in the Carwash driveway, empty, parking lights on, motor running. He had seen the car on previous occasions, driven by a tall, young Negro man with medium-brown complexion who used to pick up Gloria McDowell after work. But he could not, unfortunately, recall the license tag number.

Another stranger had contacted the police earlier that day, saying he had some information. When the police stopped by his home, he told them he detected a connection between the Carwash case and a murder that had occurred about a year earlier in a park in Buffalo, New York. The stranger knew about that case because he had found the body. And the subject wanted in the case had a strange name: Sugar, or Candy, or something like that. That night, Washington police telegraphed the chief of police, Buffalo, New York, requesting all information relating to that murder and murderer.

Police questioned and requestioned dozens of employees in businesses around the Carwash: had they noticed anything suspicious recently, anyone hanging around, any incidents that seemed peculiar. Most were reluctant to talk.

They interviewed people who suspected roommates, who suspected Carwash customers and employees, who had seen Negro males of certain heights and weights standing in front of the Carwash at about 5:00 P.M. the day of the murders; they interviewed drunk and sober people, and fearful people, and people who thought they had the motive all figured out. They notified charge-account establishments to report all charges made on any of Irving Rosenberg's stolen credit cards.

25

They gave some more lie detector tests, and ran some more fingerprint comparisons. They interviewed people who had actually seen Arondo Coates and Jerry Richardson leave, and who had seen them during the early evening of the murders, and who swore their actions and manners had been totally normal. And the "Jery" written in red on the electrical switchbox turned out to be just some old paint.

Two days had passed. The police had their suspects. But they still did not have their killers. Or killer.

On the third day of their investigation, police learned some things about some names that had by now become familiar.

They learned that Jeremy Carroll, whom one Carwash employee suspected, was a nervous type, a fighter, whose brother was presently confined in a mental institution for psychiatric care. They learned that Carroll had been fired from his last job three days before the murders for threatening another employee. They knew that his behavior on the job had been peculiar. And Jeremy Carroll had a hefty arrest record: for car theft, for possession of a weapon, for housebreaking, for larceny.

They learned that Harold Briscoe, whose name Sonny Craig had mentioned as a possibility, had once beaten up and threatened his girlfriend with an icepick. That his treatment of her had resulted in summonses for hearings on criminal complaints lodged with the United States Attorney's Office. That eight months ago Pop Weaver had asked him for some money Briscoe owed him, but Briscoe told Pop he wouldn't pay just then. And that, in 1960, he had been arrested for burglary when he and an accomplice tried to break into a Washington carwash.

And they learned an interesting fact about the dead girl. They learned that her uncle teasingly called her "Cadillac Girl" because she used to be driven home in different Cadillacs. One of her boyfriends, in fact, drove a fairly distinctive Cadillac. It was a 1969 El Dorado, pink, with initial tags "AAJR." Those tags were listed to a man named Arthur Austin, Jr., who lived on one of the most crime-infested streets in Washington and whose father was one of the city's big-time gambling operators. They learned that Austin had told an acquaintance that at about 5:15 the afternoon of the murders, he had driven by the Carwash and seen Gloria McDowell standing by the window. And that the day after the murders, Arthur Austin had visited the Carwash to ask why Gloria had not met him that morning.

They spoke with another of Gloria McDowell's boyfriends, Orville Harper, whose Cadillac was black and whose phone number was listed in Gloria's memo book. Harper and Gloria had been dating for half a year—"right heavy"—until September, when she returned to an old boyfriend. They had been pretty close friends—close enough for Orville Harper to have a key to her apartment. He would occasionally see her after they broke up. He even remembered driving past the Carwash late in the afternoon the day of the murders and seeing her inside.

Orville Harper answered all the detectives' questions. It was not his first trip to homicide headquarters. He had been there when his son was arrested for killing a store owner in a holdup.

The list of names was mounting. The many names in Gloria McDowell's memo book. The names of recent escapees from St. Elizabeth's hospital—none turned out to have been committed because of criminal charges. Then the police visited the Carwash's accountants and received the names and addresses of all full-time Carwash employees for the past three years. More names. Hundreds and hundreds of them.

By the end of the day, one more lead had collapsed. Buffalo police reported that the man who had been indicted for the Buffalo park murder was named Lorenzo "Candy" Skinner. But "Candy" had also been indicted for killing his wife on August 13, 1968, and had been put in an Erie County jail. He had not killed anybody in Washington since that date.

For every new fact, a new rumor. In the afternoon, one of Irving Rosenberg's nieces called homicide to report overhearing two men speculate that the murders occurred when someone had come to the Carwash for a numbers payoff and had been laughed at.

Three days had passed. Whoever had murdered three people in Washington on December 10 was still at large.

Homicide detectives kept busy for the next several days focusing on some suspects and picking up some new names.

They visited Arthur Austin, Gloria McDowell's pink Cadillac boyfriend. He denied having dated her but acknowledged that he frequently drove her to and from work. He admitted that at about 5:20 in the afternoon of the murders, he had indeed driven past the Carwash and had noticed Gloria by the front window in her suede coat. She appeared to be writing. But when he saw Rosenberg's car in the driveway, he knew Gloria had a way to get home. So he just drove on.

They checked out one interesting name that had come up from several unconnected sources. In 1954, when he was twenty-five years old, Bishop Blue was arrested for slashing the right hand of another man. The charges were dismissed. Three years later Bishop Blue was arrested for slashing the left side of a woman's face with a knife. The charges were dismissed. Two years later Bishop Blue was arrested for shooting another man in the right upper chest with a 16-gauge shotgun. The man Bishop Blue shot had died, and Bishop Blue was charged with murder in the first degree.

For the three years preceding that shooting, Bishop Blue had been employed in a carwash located near the Mr. Wash Carwash. For the two years preceding that employment, he had been employed in another nearby carwash. For the four years preceding that employment, he had been employed in another nearby carwash.

On December 16, 1960, Bishop Blue had been sentenced to two-to-seven years' imprisonment for the shotgun homicide. Five years later he was granted release for good behavior.

Police responded to Bishop Blue's apartment. Lights were on inside, but nobody answered the knock. Police left cards on his door and in his mailbox asking him to respond to homicide headquarters.

When he walked into headquarters four days after the murders of Irving Rosenberg, Gloria McDowell, and John Weaver, Bishop Blue had what appeared to be a fairly recent bruise on his left cheek. The bruise was an obvious topic of conversation between Blue and the police. Blue gave them an explanation they could check out: he had been attacked in the hallway of his home less than two weeks ago, had been robbed, knocked unconscious, and received facial lacerations—and of all things, he had actually reported the incident to the police.

He told them also of his whereabouts on Tuesday, December 10, 1968. He claimed to have been working at the Oak Hill Cemetery, a fair distance from the Carwash, all day until 5:00 P.M. He had then bussed home, and had not even passed nearby the Carwash. In fact, he said, he had not been to the Carwash since the week after he had quit, weeks ago. He remembered another man who had quit about the same time. A wild type of person who sometimes got into scrapes at the Carwash. And when he got into those scrapes, he always picked up a rock or a pipe. The man's name was Jeremy Carroll.

While several detectives continued questioning him, others attempted to verify his story. They drove to the Oak Hill Cemetery and spoke with the caretaker, who told them that Bishop Blue was a good worker, had worked all day on the day of the murders, and had not left before 5:00 P.M. They checked files for a robbery and assault report allegedly filed by Bishop Blue a few weeks before the murders, and found it. They compared his known fingerprints with the prints lifted from the Carwash on the night of the murders, with negative results. And they tested him on the polygraph machine. Bishop Blue came up clean.

But he told police some interesting things they hadn't known. He gave the location where he would occasionally bring Pop Weaver to drop his numbers money. And he told the police that Irving Rosenberg always used to play a certain number. The number had never come up while he was alive and betting. Two days after the murders, Irving Rosenberg would have won.

Detectives spoke again with Orville Harper, one of Gloria McDowell's sometime boyfriends. His fingerprint comparison had been returned: negative. He told them where he had been at the time of the murders: looking for his younger son. Police checked the people at school whom Harper claimed to have been with, and the man at the supermarket, and the man at the barbershop. Orville Harper was telling them the truth.

They transmitted to the F.B.I. physical evidence that had been removed from the scene of the murders and from the morgue, and requested appropriate examinations, analyses, and comparisons. Nothing of any potential scientific evidentiary value could be left undone. You still could not be sure what might become important.

Anonymous telephone calls kept coming in, and the people accused were interviewed, and their stories verified, and, occasionally, their innocence proved by lie detector tests: people whose sole conceivable connection with the murders was an anonymous accusing phone call.

They received a telephone call from a man who spoke rapidly, refused to give his name, and stated that two people had killed the people at the Carwash, one named Joseph and one named George Henderson. They spoke with George Henderson and learned he had quit the Carwash a few weeks ago. He told them he did not know anybody named Joseph.

They spoke with a girlfriend of Gloria McDowell, who used to bowl with her regularly. She told them Gloria dated several men who drove Cadillacs, and she described Gloria as a heartbreaker. She knew Gloria had been making some extra money at the Carwash, though she did not know exactly how, and she knew Gloria had begun hanging around with a crowd that was pulling holdups. She also knew that a month earlier, Gloria had made a several-hundred-dollar numbers hit.

They tried to reach Henry Long at home, and couldn't. They found out the license number of the car he drove, and learned that his arrest record included burglaries and car theft.

They learned that a laundry not very far from—though not very near to—the Carwash had received for cleaning a pair of trousers with apparent bloodstains the day after the murders. The name "Jack" was on the trousers. They learned that "Jack" was Edward Jackson, a sixteen-year-old eighth-grader at Langley Junior High School. They did not have to check to know that sixteen-year-olds do a good deal of robbing and killing in Washington, D.C. And they learned that Edward Jackson had been arrested for burglary last New Year's Day after breaking a pane of glass on the north side of a store building at 1:00 A.M. and entering with some friends. Jackson's fingerprints, and even those of the three boys he had been arrested with in the burglary, were submitted to the identification section for comparison with prints lifted from the Carwash on December 10. Results: negative.

They learned from a government worker who had been in the Carwash on the morning of the murders that three Negro males and one Negro female had driven in with a gray Cadillac convertible bearing Pennsylvania tags. The driver, who wore a distinctive Fu Manchu moustache, had gone into the customers' bathroom and remained there a long time. And all four had looked suspicious, and there had been some cursing, and they all appeared to be eyeing the entire place.

They also picked up some facts about names that had, by now, become familiar.

George Henderson, anonymously accused in a telephone call to the police, had been employed by the Hecht Company Department Store on December 10, 1968. Company records showed that Henderson had begun work that day at 8:30 A.M. and had been under close supervision until leaving work at 5:30. And George Henderson agreed to take a lie detector test—and passed. He was not the killer.

Jeremy Carroll was also willing to take a lie detector test. He claimed to have been at his new job pumping gas elsewhere in town at the time of the murders. The gas station kept records also. Jeremy Carroll had arrived at work on the morning of December 10, had not driven the service truck or left the station all day, had been busily pumping gas next to the owner between 5:00 and 6:00 that evening, and had not gone home until 7:22. Jeremy Carroll was not the killer.

Arthur Austin, Gloria McDowell's boyfriend with the pink Cadillac, was reinterviewed, and told the police he had arrived at his delicatessen at 5:40 the afternoon of the murders, shortly after viewing Gloria through the Carwash window. He had no fresh scratches or bruises. His fingerprint comparison had come up negative, and the people he claimed to have been with at the delicatessen confirmed his story. Arthur Austin was not the killer.

Harold Briscoe, the man who had threatened his girlfriend with an ice-pick and who had once been arrested trying to burglarize another Washington carwash, was found, brought to headquarters, and questioned. He was a very large man, an alcoholic, and on the day of the murders, he was sitting in a rocking chair, drunk, surrounded by a large group of people. Harold Briscoe was not the killer.

After several unsuccessful attempts, detectives finally located Henry Long at home and brought him to headquarters for questioning. He was a very nervous type, and the police chose not to put him on the polygraph machine. He told them whom he had worked with at the Carwash on the day of the murders, whom he had left with, and what he had then done. And as he talked, several detectives left headquarters to check out his story. They found the people who had left with him, had dropped him off, and had spent the evening with him. Henry Long was not the killer.

One week had passed since Irving Rosenberg, Gloria McDowell, and John Weaver were hammered to death. In one week the Metropolitan Police Department had dispatched its finest, most thorough investigators to solve the crimes. In one week they had combed through records, through sewers, through blood, through pasts, through rumors, and through facts. They had come up with some names, had eliminated some, and were left with some. But the killer or killers were still on the streets of Washington, D.C. Unless, of course, they had gone elsewhere.

Into the second week after the killings, the list of suspects expanded. None of them were prime, but many were possible. And when there are no prime suspects, you check out all the possibilities.

An engineer at the Georgetown University Hospital called to report that a man he worked with named Franklin Young had started to talk about the murders the day after they happened. Young had told him a lot of details, but the engineer had read the same newspaper accounts Young had and didn't recall reading those details himself. This made him suspicious. Especially when Young had mentioned how pretty the dead girl used to be. And the engineer knew that Tuesday would have been Young's day off. A few days after the conversation, the engineer noticed two pairs of almost new gloves in Franklin Young's open locker. One of the gloves appeared to have bloodstains on the palm and thumb. The engineer had removed that part of the glove, and he gave it to the police.

Promptly, homicide detectives forwarded the piece of glove material to the F.B.I. for determination whether the red spots were blood and, if so, what type.

The same day they were given the piece of glove, another lead developed. A twenty-two-year-old man named Percy Monroe was observed acting suspiciously by a female plainclothes security guard in a large department store. She watched him place four lady's blouses under his coat and leave the store. She summoned a police officer, who arrested and searched Percy Monroe. In addition to the stolen goods, his pockets contained three needles and two syringes of the type commonly used by heroin addicts, one bottle cap used as a heroin cooker, and one belt used as a tourniquet.

In the District of Columbia a shoplifting junkie caught red-handed is likely to get a jail term. Percy Monroe tried to help himself by offering the police some information. He was interviewed by the homicide squad when he let it be known that he might be able to help solve the Carwash murders.

He told them he had been in a bar at about 7:00 the night of the murders, a bar police knew to be a hangout for criminals.

"I was standing at the bar," he told them, "and I overheard a conversation between two dudes that was standing next to me. One dude was saying that they did not have any intention of hurting anybody just to get the money, and the other dude said to him it did not make any difference to him one way or another, it's over with now. One dude said something about a station and the other mentioned about a gas station or something like that. I left that section of the bar and walked down to the far end of the bar where there was three fellows together and two of them were talking. One dude asked the other dude what do you think about the killing of the three people. The one that was doing all the talking pointed to the two dudes that were standing at the section of the bar where I first overheard the two dudes talking and said that they knew something about it or participated in it." He didn't know their names, but the first two dudes hang out with the girlfriend of another dude named Robert Williams.

Percy Monroe did not pretend to be giving information to the police out of the goodness of his heart. After he had been arrested, the security guard had spoken with him, and had asked him some questions—among others, "asked me if I knew anything about this case, saying that if I helped him, he might be able to help me. I thought it over and told him this." Monroe was quite candid about this. Not perfectly candid, though. No, he would rather not sign a statement police had typed incorporating what he had just told them.

When you've been a detective for a long time, you develop a feel for when a man is just looking for a break for himself. That was what Percy Monroe sounded like. But when you've been trying to solve a triple murder unsuccessfully, you check out every possibility.

Robert Williams, the dude Percy Monroe said was the boyfriend of the girl who hung out with the two dudes who had allegedly discussed the murders, had to be interviewed in the maximum security ward of St. Elizabeth's Hospital, where he was undergoing psychiatric treatment to determine his competency to stand trial for eleven armed robberies. Grudgingly he told detectives the name and address of his girlfriend. She was on drugs, he said. He wasn't exactly sure how she spells her last name, but the police shouldn't have too much trouble finding her. They also asked him whether he knew anyone matching the descriptions Monroe had given earlier of the two men discussing the murders: number one subject, a Negro male, 23-24, 5'9", 160-165, black bush hair, eyeglasses, neatly dressed; number two subject, another Negro male, 5'8", 22-23, 150 pounds, bush haircut, dark complexioned, dressed in tennis shoes, khaki pants, and a corduroy coat. To Robert Williams those descriptions matched two friends of his, good friends, you might even say business associates. The three of them on previous occasions had pulled some holdups together. He didn't know where they lived, but he knew their nicknames were Bo and Poochie, and he knew their last names: Holley and Monroe. Monroe, he guessed, might be the one who pulled the Carwash job.

Detectives checked the address Williams had given for his girlfriend and couldn't find her there. They checked the D.C. General Hospital, where she might be because of an overdose of pills she had recently taken. They checked with the narcotics squad for a different address, all with negative results.

Finally the woman called on the police. But she had bad news for them. She had absolutely no idea who Percy Monroe could have been referring to. And when the police ran fingerprint comparisons with all Holleys and Monroes who had criminal records, everything came up negative.

That had not been the first tip that had died, and it would not be the last. The F.B.I. had checked the piece of leather glove, supposedly bloodstained, taken from the Georgetown University Hospital locker of Franklin Young. The red stains were paint.

Again and again, police revisited the Carwash and spoke with employees, many of whose faces were by now familiar.

William Wells, who had told them previously about calling the

Carwash to place a numbers bet, now asked whether they had checked out a man named Mac who used to work at the tire company next door. Wells said he had seen Mac slip into the Carwash unnoticed a few days after the murders and walk back to the door of the locker room in which the bodies had been found. When Wells approached him, Mac had left hurriedly. Wells also remembered that Mac had worked at another carwash two years ago.

Police went next door to learn more about Mac. They spoke with the tire company garage manager and learned that "Mac" was a thirty-year-old Negro named E. L. Macklin; that Mac had been fired the weekend before the murders for being drunk on the job; that when he had been fired, Mac had threatened to shoot the manager in the head or cut his throat. He had not done either, however. Instead he had simply walked out of the tire company, walked into the Carwash, and stayed there for an hour.

Some other employees of the tire company remembered Mac, and the police jotted down additional facts and opinions: that he boasted of a .38-caliber gun he owned; that he used to carry a hawkbill knife and a large pocketknife; that he occasionally visited the Carwash next door "to see my pretty little girl," presumably Gloria McDowell; that he was suspected of being on drugs; and that the way he acted generally just seemed to be like a mental case.

Police obtained mug shots of E. L. Macklin from central criminal records and showed them to the tire company garage manager. He identified the man as Mac. They showed the photos to William Wells, and he identified them as Mac. And then they showed the photos to Sonny Craig, who had already provided so much information in their investigation. She provided more. She told them she had seen him the day before the murders near the pump room, raising the lid from a large can and looking into the can. When she approached, he had walked away quickly as if he had something to hide. And she told them that a few weeks before the murders, he had spent a day or two working at the Carwash.

Police responded to the apartment of E. L. Macklin. They knocked on the door but received no answer. His neighbor didn't know enough about him to provide them with too many facts, but she had seen Macklin often enough to form a general impression of him. She thought—she couldn't prove it, but she thought—that he was crazy.

Bashing in the heads of Irving Rosenberg, Gloria McDowell, and John Weaver had been a crazy thing to do.

34

The police dropped in on the resident manager of the apartment house in which E. L. Macklin lived. The apartment was registered to his mother, who had filed an affidavit before moving. She had sworn that her son was mentally retarded.

Then two pieces finally fit together. Detectives returned to the Carwash and spoke with Ralph Jenkins, the assistant manager. He told them a story they had first heard from other sources within twenty-four hours of the murders, about a man who had been staring at Gloria McDowell in a way that had made her mention it to some other people—to other employees of the Carwash, and once to a detective who happened to be standing nearby. Jenkins himself had seen the man's leer. Gloria had gone so far as to tell Sonny Craig that she was going to ask Irv to order the man out. Jenkins had seen the man return to the Carwash a few days after the murders and heard him mention he would soon be going to New Jersey. Jenkins could not recall the man's exact name but did know his nickname. Mac.

The police even learned some things about Jenkins himself while they were there. That he had recently made a play for Gloria that had been rejected, though they had remained friendly. That he always talked about his girlfriend Gloria. And that around Thanksgiving he had her name tattooed on his right forearm.

They responded once again to the home of E. L. Macklin. Again he was not home. His cousin Katherine was, though, and she told them Mac had not come home the previous evening. That wasn't unusual; he sometimes stayed out for several nights at a time. But his cousin had nothing to hide, and let the police into Mac's bedroom, where they noticed several blue uniforms very much like the ones worn by workers at the Carwash. They also noticed, on top of a bureau in the bedroom, a book of carwash tickets redeemable at the Sparkle Car Wash in nearby Alexandria. Police knew that a few days ago two young Negro males had robbed the Sparkle Car Wash at gunpoint and bound their victims with bailing twine they had carried in. The manager there had been held up several times before, and rated these two boys as amateurs: they were in such a hurry they missed several hundred dollars in the bottom of the safe.

Evidently, E. L. Macklin's cousin thought the police had seen just about enough. When they tried to look into his bedroom closet, Katherine stood in front of the door. They were not allowed to look inside.

E. L. Macklin was located and invited to homicide headquarters for questioning. He arrived at about the same time as Charles Gilbert, an old

35

man who squinted through extremely thick eyeglasses. While Macklin was telling one pair of detectives of his whereabouts the day and night of Tuesday, December 10, 1968, Charles Gilbert identified himself to another detective as the driver who had pulled his cab up to Mr. Wash Carwash for a cleaning between 5:00 and 6:00 on the night of the murders. Irving Rosenberg, who was standing in front of the Carwash talking to three Negro males, had waved to tell him the place was closed. Charles Gilbert described by height, weight, clothing, and complexion the three men he had seen talking with Rosenberg. And then he added, "One of them was the guy with bushy hair and sideburns that was here in your office." That would be E. L. Macklin.

An apparent eyewitness identification of a suspect is not automatically accepted by policemen searching for the truth—especially when the eyewitness's eyes are obviously bad and his witnessing made in the dark of an early winter evening. Charles Gilbert was asked many more questions, and at the end he said, "I am just about sure he was the man." Just about sure is not enough.

E. L. Macklin admitted to detectives that he often hung around the Carwash—it was a place where he knew people. He was now employed at a different carwash in another part of town, and had been for a while. He'd been at work the day of the murders until mid-afternoon, and he'd hung around with different friends for the rest of the day.

A pair of detectives were assigned to check out every detail of Macklin's story. Records of his present carwash showed he had worked there on December 10 until 3:00 P.M. The people Macklin said he'd been with were Macklin's kind of people, carwash kind of people, with criminal records, with bad backgrounds. They were sought and questioned, and their stories, pieced together, told the police that Macklin had been nowhere near the Mr. Wash Carwash on December 10. And their stories contained the subtle variations and inconsistencies, the lack of inflexible precision, that an experienced investigator regards as indicia of the truth. His fingerprints compared negatively with the prints lifted from the Carwash the night of the murders.

After four days of investigating Macklin's alibi, the police called him in again, told him they believed him, and asked whether he would consent to a lie detector test just so they could be sure. He took the test, he passed, and he was no longer a suspect.

The homicide unit picked up other wisps of suspicion:

36

Perhaps Ralph Jenkins, the assistant manager who had told them some things about Mac, was himself the killer. After all he'd been rebuffed by Gloria McDowell; was rumored to have financial problems; and had access to a duplicate set of keys to the Carwash. Police brought him down for questioning. He told them that on the day of the murders, he had left work in the early afternoon to pay a department store bill and that he had spent the rest of the day with some other people. He agreed to take a polygraph test, and while he was being hooked to the machine, other police left to check his story. His alibi was corroborated, and he passed the polygraph test. Ralph Jenkins was not the man.

Someone told them Irving Rosenberg had needed money and might have borrowed from numbers backers. Police surveilled the large apartment building where Pop Weaver was alleged to have made his daily numbers drop. They learned nothing.

Someone telephoned anonymously and told them the Carwash murderer was named Morris. Detectives checked all people named Morris who had worked at the Carwash, and employees with relatives named Morris, and came up with nothing.

Some people even claimed to be the killers—in many big cases someone will seek the glory, or the notoriety, or simply seem to suffer a compulsion to confess—but always the confession turned out false.

Sonny Craig told them of a friend whose great-grandmother had been burned at the stake for witchcraft. The friend often made predictions that came true, and had told Sonny of a vision in which she had learned that the murderer was a man named "Little Joe." Sonny told the police who "Little Joe" was, and they checked him out, and he was innocent.

Someone wrote to say that a certain named doctor had got a bad carwashing at the Carwash and had threatened to get even with Irving Rosenberg. They checked the doctor out, and he was innocent.

Someone told them that two weeks after the murders, two Negro males had driven into the Carwash in a light green Cadillac, glanced in the direction of the locker room, stared at the new cashier, and sweated noticeably from the face and forehead.

A large number of detectives had invested a great deal of time and collected a lot of pieces. Every fact and rumor and statement they had heard was duly recorded in a rapidly growing mass of files—nothing could be lost or forgotten. But now it was New Year's Day, 1969, and the mur-

37

ders still remained unsolved. The newspapers would not let Washington forget:

**TRIPLE MURDERS TOP
30 D.C. HOMICIDES
LISTED AS UNSOLVED**

On Tuesday, December 10, three persons at a Washington carwash were found beaten to death under circumstances which have left police baffled.

In the three weeks since the triple slaying—the first in Washington in more than 40 years—police have interviewed more than 500 persons in connection with the case.

But the hundreds of man-hours put into investigating the murders—at Mr. Wash Carwash, 616 Rhode Island Avenue—have yielded virtually no clues.

With each passing day, the odds on breaking the case grow longer, according to the commander of the Homicide Squad.

The three victims of the murders were Irving Rosenberg, 54, manager of the Carwash; and two other employees, Gloria McDowell, 24, and John Weaver, 56.

At this point, police are not totally certain of the motive, although robbery remains a strong possibility.

The three murders brought the Homicide Squad's total of unsolved cases for the year to 30, compared with only four open cases last year.

Looking for someone trying to hide can be a difficult job. There are thousands of places for him to go, thousands of things for him to do, thousands of people for him to hide among. It is even more difficult when you do not know precisely whom you are looking for. You check out every lead, and every rumor and suspicion. You are stubborn. You shake the dust from every irrelevancy to find a trace of something helpful. Sometimes you get lucky and shake out a diamond. And sometimes you get real lucky. Sometimes things just come to you. If you are a homicide detective, the lucky things often come to you clothed in the trappings of death.

When you are a homicide detective, a husband killing his wife is standard stuff. If you are young and inexperienced, the captain may let you cut your teeth on a few husband-wife killings before assigning you to the big cases: you can make the errors of inexperience in investigating the scene, in letting potential witnesses slip away, in handling physical evidence carelessly. You can get the first vomit or two out of your system

38

looking at an unimportant corpse, observing an unimportant autopsy, watching the coroner make the standard Y incision into the woman's torso and poke around in the goo surrounding an unimportant corpse's wet but lifeless parts.

On January 5, 1969, at 5:00 P.M., the police switchboard at the Ninth Precinct received a call from an unnamed female who said she had an unwanted guest at her home: her husband. The policeman who received the call heard her ask someone whether that someone wanted to speak with the police. Then he heard her say that the police were coming. Then he heard the phone drop, and then a lot of screaming. Alma Green was shot and killed by her husband Lawrence Green at 5:05 P.M.

In 1960 Lawrence Green had been charged with a series of gunpoint robberies, had stood trial, and had been found not guilty by reason of insanity and sent to St. Elizabeth's Hospital. He escaped, pulled some more holdups, was arrested, charged with three of those holdups, convicted of two, and sentenced to a term of imprisonment of five-to-fifteen years. He was recommitted to St. Elizabeth's Hospital as a mental patient, where he remained until March 8, 1968, when the hospital superintendent certified that, on the basis of staff examinations and observations, "It is our opinion that Mr. Green is not suffering from an abnormal mental condition at the present time, and, if he were suffering from an abnormal mental condition at the time of the offenses, he has now recovered his sanity, and in our opinion will not be dangerous to himself or others within the reasonable future by reason of mental disorder." He was therefore transferred to jail and within a few months was released on parole. That meant that on May 16, 1968, having lived as a prisoner or fugitive for all of the last eight years, Lawrence Green, now thirty-two, walked into a crisp spring day with no restraints except his conscience and moral balance.

Neither of these was sufficient to restrain him when, eight months later, he poured half a dozen .38-caliber lead bullets into his wife's body and ran. His children and neighbors, who had seen him shoot, would make convincing witnesses. Lawrence Green had reason to know he would not be treated leniently if arrested, so he ran into a nearby store, shoved his gun into the chest of a salesman, and robbed enough money for temporary support.

Another husband had killed another wife and had run away. Still, he would probably be caught one day, so homicide detectives interviewed and got statements from all witnesses. There was no question that Lawrence Green had killed her. The case had no distinctive flavor until one of Alma's brothers told the police that Lawrence Green used to work at the Carwash on Rhode Island Avenue. And that, the day after the triple murder, Lawrence Green had driven up to his wife's house with a few other Negro males and had given her $75.

He did not have a job that provided that kind of cash. For the next few days homicide detectives checked into the doings of Lawrence Green. They learned of his record and his mental history. They heard that he was pulling holdups all over Washington, and that he'd previously beaten his wife's head with a hammer. They heard that Alma Green's mother supposedly had some information about Lawrence and the Carwash. And then a woman at George Washington Hospital volunteered to an officer on duty that she knew Lawrence Green was the Carwash killer.

Detectives drove immediately to the hospital, and Arlene Singleton told them how she knew. A co-worker of hers named Malva Burnett had come to work in mourning for a cousin named Alma, who had just been killed by her husband. Malva told Arlene that Alma's husband had recently been threatening to kill her, and the family had been thinking of trying to send him back to St. Elizabeth's. And then Arlene Singleton said:

"Malva told me, 'You know those three people who were killed at the Carwash on Rhode Island Avenue?' She said she thought it was Mr. Sam's Carwash. She said 'Lawrence said he had killed them.' He had made this statement at the home of Alma, and her aunt was living there at the time. When the aunt said she wanted to call the police, Lawrence threatened her. Then he gave her $175 of a larger sum of money he had, which he said was from the Carwash. He had gone right home and said 'Guess what, I just killed three people, but I got some money for it.'" Malva had told Arlene that Alma's brothers and children were there and had persuaded the aunt not to tell the police.

Homicide detectives found Malva Burnett at her job. But she had no firsthand information, she said, she had simply heard about Lawrence and the Carwash from her sister. She gave detectives the names of Alma Green's brothers and aunt, who were supposed to have heard it all from Lawrence Green's own mouth.

Detectives spoke with the sister and the brothers and the aunt, and learned nothing.

They compared Green's fingerprints with prints lifted from the Carwash the night of the murders. Negative.

Early one morning ten days after the murder of Alma Green, a man brandishing a long-barreled revolver walked into a prominent Washington bank a few blocks from the White House, approached the manager, and said: "This is a holdup. Hang up that phone or I am going to kill you. I am going to kill all of you." He escaped with over $2,000, commandeered a nearby taxicab at gunpoint, and attempted to flee. Within minutes he was arrested by agents of the F.B.I. and robbery detectives of the Metropolitan Police Department. Recovered from his possession were the bank money, a .38-caliber revolver, and a box of .38-caliber ammunition. Lawrence Green was no longer a fugitive.

He was advised of his rights by homicide detectives and was informed that his name had come up as a suspect in the Carwash case. He said he'd heard of the case—the one where three people had got killed—but said he had nothing to do with it. The old white man and the old colored man were friends of his, Green said. And, anyway, he wouldn't have done anything like that. "I could have used three bullets instead of beating them to death," he said.

The courtroom definition of hearsay testimony is the out-of-court declaration by one person introduced by another person for the purpose of establishing the truth of the matter asserted. When police added up everything they had on Lawrence Green's involvement in the Carwash case, all they had was hearsay, plus knowing the kind of man he was, plus some strong suspicion. Plus the fact that Lawrence Green could pass in the dark for E. L. Macklin.

And that was still all they had a week later when an old friend of Alma Green's, an apparently credible woman, volunteered something to them now that Lawrence Green was in jail: the day before her death, Alma had confided that Lawrence was the Carwash killer, that Lawrence had actually returned bloody from the killings, and that if Alma tried to turn him in, he would kill her.

Lawrence Green might very well be the Carwash killer, or one of them. But with Alma Green dead, there was just no way to prove it.

Shortly after the capture of Lawrence Green, the homicide unit received reports of examinations performed by the F.B.I. on physical items—"evidence"—that had been submitted a month ago for scientific testing. Most of the loose hairs that had been recovered from the murder scene and from the victims' clothing and bodies bore Negroid characteristics, and many of the hairs were suitable for comparison purposes if the police could supply other hairs to compare. Although the loose button

41

found between the two male victims' bodies could not conclusively be established as having come from Weaver's shirt, multicolored cotton fibers adhering to the button were microscopically similar to the shirt's fibers. Weaver's fingernail clippings had contained one fur hair of rodent origin and one blue synthetic fiber; neither of the other victims' nails contained any textile fibers. Of the two traces in Weaver's nail clippings, neither could be associated with any of the other items which had been submitted for comparison. The blue cloth which had bound Gloria McDowell's wrists exhibited physical characteristics similar to those of the work garments which had been submitted, and seemed to have been torn from one.

And the items had contained large quantities of human blood. Some of the blood was group A, some group O, and some too small in quantity for scientific grouping. But that did not matter, as things turned out. The blood samples submitted from the three victims had not been adequately preserved, and therefore could no longer be classified. The police would never know whether all the blood that had been seen and gathered at the Carwash had been the victims', or somebody else's.

December 10, 1968, was now a long time past; yet not only were there no prime suspects, there were not even any genuine leads for active pursuit. Rumors drifted into homicide headquarters, were investigated, and collapsed; by now, most were too weak even to support much investigation at all.

One man boasted to a stranger of having witnessed the murders and having recovered some evidence; but when the police located and questioned the man, they learned he had only some suspicions. Just to be certain, detectives even ran a fingerprint comparison on the man himself. Result: negative.

A Carwash employee called to report receiving an envelope in her mail at home, with printed lettering. Inside was a single piece of paper, with a single word: "Carwash." Police ran a silver nitrate test for fingerprints. Finding: none usable for comparison purposes.

One woman called to say she had heard two Negro males discussing the Carwash in a drugstore and that although she did not know who they were, police might want to investigate.

One man called to say he had been drinking with another man who had brought up in a suspicious way the subject of the Carwash case and the possible murderers. The other man's name: Bishop Blue.

The circle was complete. Names and stories had come up and been investigated, and now the same names were coming up again. The frustration of not knowing where and whom to investigate was compounded by the arrest of Lawrence Green: the police could not even now be certain that the killer was still at large. Or was it killers? After all, three victims had been brutally bludgeoned. If only one man had been involved, would —could—all three have died as they died? With no more than an occasional lead to check out and dismiss, with no physical clues, with no eyewitnesses, what was there to do but wait? And if they waited, what were they waiting for, and how long would the wait last? And if the killers would ever be found, how? Who would turn them in?

Seven and one-half months after the murders, Ruby Taylor said she would.

CHAPTER THREE

T HE neighborhood around 14th and U Streets is one of several pockets of scum in the nation's capital. Actually, you can begin at 14th and R and head north on 14th up past W Street: blocks with bars and buildings and dirty cats, noise and cans and crushed cigarettes. You pass an auto-works shop, a pawnbroker, men's clothiers selling shiny suits, shells of what used to be stores but were burned down in the riots of April, 1968, and never redone, liquor stores and vacant lots and sandwich shops that specialize in chicken wings and heroin. Everybody has a hustle when the sun begins to set. You run some numbers, or turn some tricks, or run a string of girls, or pop open the trunks of parked cars, or work a con game, or gamble, or push or use drugs, or plan some hits. There are some other blocks you can hang on and get the same deals, but none is bigger or brasher or more open than 14th and U.

Ruby Taylor was born in Washington thirty-four years before the deaths of Irving Rosenberg, John Weaver, and Gloria McDowell. She was born out of wedlock to a mother with two other children and a father who worked hard and thought Ruby's mother was favoring the older children. So he insisted she be given to a foster couple who could care for her, and she was, for a few years to one set of parents, and then to another set, a minister and his wife—Reverend and Mrs. Foster—who brought her up like their own. Her real parents were not allowed to see her or give her gifts: she would not be told that she had been given away. She was a bright girl and almost got through high school, a feat in Ruby's part of town. When she was fifteen, someone told her she was not the real child of the people she knew as her parents, and she began getting a little wild. For a few nights she slept in other people's vestibules to avoid going home. Other times, she'd just stay on the streets all night long.

She got pregnant at fifteen by Darnell Taylor, a rich man twice her age who impressed the Fosters, and, at their urging, Ruby married him a year later. Only after the marriage did Ruby learn that her new husband was a drug dealer. She was too young and poor and troubled to bring up her baby daughter, Brenda, but the Fosters agreed to take the baby in. Soon Ruby Taylor was on the streets helping push her husband's heroin. Soon Ruby Taylor was hooked on the stuff herself. Soon she was alone, hustling for herself and her habit. She was still in her teens when she began getting arrested for prostitution, for disorderliness, for stealing, for the hustles that come when the monkey is on your back and you need money. Most of the time you can get it without much trouble, and the trouble, when it comes, only means a few dollars' fine or a short spell in jail. Of course, a few days in jail when you're on a habit means going through cold turkey, shaking and sweating and throwing up until you don't even think your insides are left inside. But then you get back on the street and shoot up a few caps, and maybe everything will be all right.

Ruby Taylor managed to survive. For months at a time she would get by without drugs and with an occasional job. Sometimes she'd put her baby daughter, Brenda, on her shoulders and race around the Fosters' house, the two of them laughing like loons, and sometimes she'd put her in a wicker basket on the front of a bicycle and ride her around to pick up the groceries. But then Darnell Taylor came back into her life, and the wheels came off their runners, and, in the summer of 1955, when Ruby Taylor was twenty-one and pregnant again, the man got her on a good drug rap and sentenced her to not less than sixteen months nor more than four years.

She had her second child, another girl, in jail. The Fosters agreed to take the baby even though Brenda was still on their hands. They had been good parents to Ruby, and they were good to Ruby's kids.

After Ruby got out nearly three years later, she got picked up a few times for prostitution but then stayed clean for quite a while. She moved into a house owned by the Fosters' daughter, where she helped out with the roomers and got a steady job marking clothing in a nearby cleaners. Her children stayed where they had been, but Ruby would come around to make sure they were doing well and had enough of everything they needed. Ruby Taylor would always give when she had. Like many of the people, she used to bet some dimes and quarters every day on the numbers. Some weekends she might have twenty-five or thirty numbers working at once. Not long after getting out of jail, just before Christmas, Ruby hit the number, and everyone got good presents that year.

She took up with a good man named Howard, who worked hard and kept her straight and clean. Ruby worked during those years, took things to the kids regularly, visited them often. A spat, and Howard left and she got mixed up with another man, this one not so good: a heavy drinking construction worker, high often as not, rough. And when Ruby let him go after a few years—when she discovered he'd been living part-time with another woman—Howard, the fall guy, came back, even though Ruby by now had two more daughters by his replacement. But Ruby's was the kind of life a man could shuttle into and out of and back in again, and she and Howard moved together into a new place on Wyoming Avenue, taking in three of her four daughters, though money was tight. Ruby was still working hard at the cleaners, but she was pretty lazy around the house, and it was Howard who had to clean and cook and scold the kids for her while Ruby just lazed around or read—Ruby loved to read, always had a paperback novel with her, and not a cheap one either. She'd get the kids whatever she could with whatever money she had, and do some awfully fine knitting for them, and love them as best she was able. But Ruby knew she was not as she should be to them and insisted, sadly, that they only call her "Ruby" and that they call Mrs. Foster "Momma."

It was not an easy life, and Ruby Taylor sometimes got down, real down, down enough to drive her to the needle. She split up with Howard one last time and had to work even harder to support her kids. She kept that job marking clothing in the cleaners for several years, even got her daughter Brenda a job there on Saturdays to make some spending money. Then an infection set into her hands and she had to quit, and tried to get some training in a beauty shop. Mainly Ruby just moped around, keeping to herself.

For a time she tried mixing with a straight crowd, going to parties, to clubs, just sitting in a living room talking with some people. But Ruby's talk was jail and drugs and where she'd been, and she'd been to different places from the others. They'd talk late into the night, and Ruby'd tell how she'd been farther 'round the teacup than they'd been 'round the handle. She wouldn't make up any stories, though she'd put a little yeast into some of those she had to tell. Ruby wasn't proud or ashamed of what she'd been and where, but she told them she'd probably do it all different if she had it to redo. She'd make it a little bit easier for herself, and a little bit less lonely.

Sometimes her new crowd would go to Ruby's places. One night, at one of those places, they met a man named Raymond Smith.

It did not take very long before Smith moved in with Ruby Taylor. The time was not a happy time. There'd be fighting, and Raymond would do some hitting at Ruby and at Ruby's daughter Brenda, who was living with them. Within a year—not too long after Raymond Smith sent her to a hospital operating room by slugging her in the eye—she moved out, and into the basement of a big house at 1709 Lanier Place with a woman named Emma Roland, who had once had a child by Ruby's real father. Ruby was still working some as a maid and sometimes just took welfare, but she was lazy and wouldn't clean her part of the house until, finally, she moved a few doors away into the home of a new boyfriend, JoJo. He was a junkie and a pusher—a man of the streets like so many of Ruby's men. Ruby would still come back to Lanier Place to visit the kids, but now she would have strange requests—for the sweetest kinds of candies and cookies, the sweets an addict craves when drugs cannot be found. There were other hints. JoJo would visit with Ruby at Lanier Place and lock himself in the bathroom for a quarter of an hour at a time and leave behind a washrag with red spots; or Brenda, playing with her boyfriend in the basement, would find a box of baking soda and quinine and a lump of white powder; and then, one day, Ruby's youngest daughter came to visit grandma carrying some syringes she said Ruby used to take her penicillin. Another arrest, another probation.

JoJo's baby, Ruby Taylor's fifth, was beginning to grow in Ruby's belly, but when you begin consuming heroin, it begins consuming you. Ruby Taylor, once attractive, almost but not quite plump, healthy-looking, began to shrivel up. The track marks started reappearing on the back of her hands and the crook of her elbows, her body got flabby, the dark skin around her eyes got blacker. You'd talk with her, but her mind would be around the corner and she'd only answer your question several questions later. She got to looking dirty, like you look when all you really care about is sticking a needle into your veins. That was how she looked when she entered D.C. General Hospital in the middle of June, 1969, to bring a fifth daughter into life. Ruby left the hospital and, for the time being, left her latest daughter there. She had to slip a needle in her vein.

At 7:55 P.M. on July 15, 1969, seven months and five days after the Carwash killings and a few weeks after Ruby left the hospital, members of the narcotics unit of the Washington Police Department executed a search warrant on a basement apartment. The apartment was occupied at that precise moment in time by two women, in one of those areas of town where drugs flow like water. When they entered the apartment and searched, they found in the drawer of a night table a bottle with empty gelatin capsules containing heroin traces; they found on the front mantel miscellaneous narcotics paraphernalia: a bottle-top cooker used to hold heroin being heated, a hypodermic syringe, three needle holders; they found a small green can inside a pillow on a bed, and, inside the can, they found a dozen gelatin capsules containing heroin. And they found, lying on the bed with the pillow and the capsules, Ruby Taylor.

After placing her under arrest, the police searched her purse and found even more: a crochet hook, two small books, three hypodermic syringes with needles, and an old nylon stocking used by junkies as a tourniquet to make veins bulge into accessible targets. She was charged with felonious possession of narcotics, the penalty for which is a minimum mandatory imprisonment of five years as a second offender. She was taken to court, where she admitted her addiction to the man from the bail agency who would recommend the kind and amount of bail to be set pending trial. At her arraignment, bond was set at $2000. Ruby Taylor did not have $2000. She was therefore ordered confined to the Women's Detention Center to await trial, no date for which had yet been set. Within a day Ruby Taylor was suffering from acute narcotics withdrawal.

Five days after her arrest, Ruby Taylor got word to the police that she knew the Carwash killers.

When you are a street hustler in jail, talking to the police about a murder case is not like asking a neighborhood traffic cop for directions. You always want something in return; you worry about giving something for a promise that is later unfulfilled; most of all, you worry about what will happen to you if you talk. The street is a rough place to be when you are a hustler, and word of cooperating with the Government shoots almost electrically through the street grapevines. So you get out word through someone you can trust, and you feel out the other side carefully before you deliver.

One of Ruby's friends in jail told a guard that she had a friend with some information on a big killing. The homicide unit was promptly notified, and homicide detectives Arif Mosrie and Jim Kennedy drove to the Women's Detention Center, a low brick building with crisscross metal screens on the windows, to check out one more lead. With all the possibilities that had already collapsed, there was no reason to believe that this story from another stranger would be any different.

They were ushered into a private room, where none of the inmates would know of their presence or their mission. And then the guard ushered in Carolyn Skinner, a forty-four-year-old black prisoner who was acting as Ruby Taylor's emissary. Carolyn told them that her friend—still unnamed at this stage—was afraid the police wouldn't protect her if she told them who killed the people at the Carwash. She told them all her friend wanted in return for the information was to get out on bond to see a daughter who had just been born. Mosrie and Kennedy told Carolyn they could make no promises but that they would protect her friend and, if the information was good and accurate, they would bring the fact of her cooperation to the attention of the United States Attorney's Office, the prosecuting office in the District of Columbia. They asked Carolyn how good her friend's information was, and she said: "It's like I would shoot someone and then run to someone's house."

The following day Mosrie and Kennedy met Carolyn Skinner in the same room, and she reported that her friend would speak with them. Arrangements were made with jail personnel for Ruby Taylor to approach a guard on an innocent pretext and for the guard to take her down to the room where the police were waiting.

Ruby Taylor walked in wearing a blue prison dress, with a paperback novel in the pocket. She spoke cautiously and struck both detectives as not the ordinary streetcorner addict-whore: she seemed to them articulate, a pleasant personality, a woman of some intelligence. She was, of course, a junkie; just a look at the tracks on her arms told them that. She told them she had just given birth at D.C. General Hospital, and she wanted to see the baby. The police told her they could make no promises but would do their best to help her make bond if her information was good. She was cautious and hesitated before speaking, but then she told them what she knew. And she agreed to sign a statement when they assured her she would receive police protection against the men she was accusing.

"I have known Ray Smith since 1966," Ruby Taylor began. "He was my boyfriend. I had seen Pete Pettiford several times. I met him through Ray."

She told the detectives that Smith and Pettiford had been fired from the Carwash over the splitting of tip money about three weeks before the murders. Smith was living on V Street at the time—she thought the number was 67 V, but anyway it was in a gray building on the north side of the street, one or two houses from the corner, and you could look out the rear window and see Pettiford's house on Flagler Place. She had been at Smith's apartment several times before the murders when the men would be drinking and talking about how many cars they'd washed that day and saying, "This would be a good day to hit." But one or the other would always back down.

The day of the murders, Ruby said, she had gone over to Ray's, and he'd been half high. Pettiford was there but left to get some beer. "Before he left," Ruby went on, "I heard Ray and Pete saying something about the sound of the brushes and hot water would cover the sound of what they were doing. This is when I knew what they were planning. I heard Ray tell Pete, 'Man, you don't have heart enough to do anything.' Then Pete said, 'Man, just watch me.' "

When Pettiford left to get the beer, Smith and Ruby began arguing about one of her daughters. Then a third man's voice came to the door and said, "Come on, man. I got the piece." Pettiford returned shortly, called to Smith through the window, and Smith left the house with ski masks, jackets, and some coveralls.

Ruby told the detectives that Smith had locked her in when he left and that she had fallen asleep until he returned covered with blood. She had asked him whether he had been in a fight, and he said, "No, I had to smack some bitch." She told him nobody would get that bloody from smacking somebody, and Raymond Smith told her, "If you smacked her with what I smacked her with, you would." Then he called out to Pettiford through the window and told him to put the stuff in the usual place, told Ruby to clean off one of his blood-soaked shoes, and went to wash up. Ruby took some unbloodied money out of his pocket, and left.

Both detectives asked her some other questions after she repeated her statement. She told them the reason for her fear: some time after the murders, Raymond Smith had driven a long white station wagon to the place she was staying at with her stepmother, Emma Roland. He was working for a funeral home at the time and had the body of a dead man in the car. He had told her she would be just like that if she squealed.

Of course, other people had claimed to know the identity of the killer or killers ever since the murders had been committed, and some things would have to be verified before the police would make any moves based on Ruby Taylor's information. But some things about her story seemed to check out.

First, she impressed the detectives as an obviously bright woman who told no lies about her background. She sounded like she was telling them the truth.

And after she read and signed her statement, she told them two more facts she hadn't bothered mentioning before. She told them Smith had returned on the night of the crime with two bags, one containing a lot of

50

change—this despite the fact that the newspapers had intentionally been told by the police, and had reported, that only a cashbox had been stolen.

And she told them that one bag was green and one bag was white.

Mosrie and Kennedy left to do some checking on the rest of her story.

A canvassing of criminal records gave them some precise information about the two men Ruby Taylor had accused.

Raymond Smith, Ruby's ex-boyfriend, was twenty-nine years old. In 1958 he had been convicted of petit larceny and sentenced to thirty days or $100. A few months later he was arrested and charged with over a dozen counts of housebreaking, but a federal grand jury chose not to indict. A few months later he was arrested again, this time for housebreaking and assault with intent to rape. Smith agreed to plead guilty to the misdemeanor of assault, the felony charges were dropped, and he was sentenced to four months' imprisonment. Within a year, he was again arrested, this time for felonious assault with a knife. Again charges were dropped. Again he was arrested, this time for robbery holdup. He agreed to plead guilty to petit larceny and assault, for which he received a thirty-day sentence, and the felony charges were again dropped. In succeeding years he would be arrested for rape and for housebreaking, but never convicted. The very week that Ruby Taylor told homicide police that Smith and Pettiford were responsible for the Carwash triple murder, Raymond Smith was given a suspended sentence and placed on two years' probation for petit larceny.

"Pete" Pettiford, Smith's friend, turned out to be Pierre Pettiford, Negro male, twenty-eight years old. At the age of twenty, Pettiford had been arrested for felonious assault with a knife, but charges had been dropped. A year later, he had been indicted for interstate transportation of a stolen motor vehicle and unauthorized use of the same vehicle, and his conviction was followed by a suspended one-to-four-year sentence with four years' probation. Within months, he was arrested again for unauthorized use of a motor vehicle, and his probation was revoked. He was released in mid-1966, and was arrested regularly thereafter for drunkenness and disorderly conduct, for which he occasionally served some time. Seventeen days after the Carwash murders, he had been arrested for trying to leave a store with three steaks underneath his coat, and the charges had been dismissed. Half a year later, he was again arrested for petit larceny, was found guilty, and was given two years' probation.

With a break in the case, Mosrie and Kennedy were now taken off all other assignments and detailed full-time to the Carwash case.

They contacted Carwash personnel to verify Ruby Taylor's story. It

51

was important to verify that Smith and Pettiford had worked at the Carwash around the time of the killings to corroborate that aspect of Ruby Taylor's statement, to assure that Smith and Pettiford had known that Tuesday was a good day to hit the place, and to account for the unnecessarily savage beatings that could be best accounted for under the theory that the robbers became killers when they were recognized by their victims.

Carwash records reflected that both men had worked there for a few months in late 1966. Their names did not appear on any Carwash records after that year, and because records of transient employees were not kept, nobody could say conclusively whether either had worked there after 1966.

They learned that Raymond Smith and Pierre Pettiford had lived within two blocks of Gloria McDowell. And they learned that because of the car he used to drive, Raymond Smith was sometimes nicknamed "Cadillac."

When Mosrie and Kennedy returned to the isolated room at the Women's Detention Center and Ruby Taylor was again brought down to see them, they showed her eight mug shots, front and profile, and she told them which was Raymond Smith and which was Pierre Pettiford. Two days later, Ruby Taylor was brought to the United States Courthouse, where she testified before a federal grand jury. The following day, Government authorities apprised the court that had originally set her bond that she was cooperating with the Government by giving good information in an unsolved murder case, and Ruby Taylor was released on her personal recognizance to appear in court when required or face additional charges for bail-jumping.

But you don't just stroll blithely around with information about the perpetrators of a triple murder. If Raymond Smith had threatened Ruby Taylor before her drug arrest, her safety after being released on personal bond, conceivably because of information she had supplied, would be in even greater jeopardy. The police offered Ruby Taylor any safety measure she wanted. They would, if she liked, relocate her in another city with 'round-the-clock protection by the federal marshal service. But that, she said, was not for her, that was too much like jail. She would just as soon get herself a room and not tell anybody but Mr. Mosrie and Mr. Kennedy where it was.

And she did, calling them almost daily to let them know things were still O.K. and she was still alive. She got herself a job as a clerk in a small store selling cheap clothing and trinkets, and every few weeks changed

52

her home address just to be sure, telling only Mosrie and Kennedy where she was living. She was especially afraid of Smith, the man she said was the more vicious of the two. He used to get real mean sometimes, she said, and would brag about the man he had killed in California and got away with, and how he'd served time already in some big places.

In the weeks they spent checking out her story and seeking information on Raymond Smith and Pierre Pettiford, Mosrie and Kennedy met her regularly, just to let her know protection was there if she should need it. Her story never changed. Not once in all the hours Mosrie and Kennedy spent listening to Ruby Taylor tell about Smith and Pettiford and about herself did they hear a lie they could detect, the one lie you can usually spot if you are a trained detective talking with a junkie. They would pick her up in an unmarked cruiser somewhere far from her home, and drive off to a parking lot where they could talk. She told them she was just using methadone now, she used heroin only when she got depressed. She described for them the first great high she got years and years ago and the thousands of injections since then in filthy hallways trying to recapture it, the retching in jail during cold turkey, and the attempts to get off by taking methadone, and then the depression, the depression you try to fight finally by slipping a needle underneath your skin just one last time. She told them about standing in the rain and seeing the rich drug man who sells the junk drive past in his big new car, the man who would not even look at Ruby and the others even though they're the dirt who put him in the big car. She'd sit in the police cruiser in a darkened parking lot and look at one or the other detective, and then down at the scabbed track marks on her arms and quietly say, "Mr. Mosrie, it's a shame a junkie like me lets a little white powder ruin them."

When you've been a policeman for so many years, you get a kind of savvy that lets you sense when people are telling you the truth or telling what they think you want to hear. To the detectives during those intense sessions parked alone in the isolated night, she seemed a sincere woman, finally spewing up the honest, sordid details that accompany a life of puncturing veins with needles and lying with strangers for money to hustle some more capsules. She told them she knew all the dealers but would not tell them who: for Ruby Taylor would not be an informant against bad people who'd been good to her. Smith and Pettiford, though: those two, she said, had killed some people, and just might kill some more.

Police asked questions about and showed pictures of Smith and Pettiford to various potential witnesses who, over half a year earlier, had given whatever information they had: Sonny Craig; Charles Gilbert, the cab driver; Gloria McDowell's friends; even Bishop Blue. None could state that either Smith or Pettiford had any association with the Carwash or the victims subsequent to late '66. They checked with the security guard who had arrested Raymond Smith a month ago trying to leave a supermarket with two cooked hams and four packets of bacon under his raincoat. They spoke with Pettiford's current probation officer and learned that Pettiford was an alcoholic and that charges would soon be brought for violation of his probation. Of all the people they spoke with, nobody had a kind word to say about Raymond Smith or Pierre Pettiford.

Then they came upon an application Pettiford had made for employment with the National Press Club, where he had worked for ten days as a dishwasher just last month. He had written, in a space reserved for previous employment, "Carwash, Rhode Island Avenue, Irv Rosenberg," from January, 1967, to June, 1968. As his reason for quitting he had written: "Too cold." The man police spoke with at the Press Club told them Pettiford had acted strange, like he was on narcotics or something.

It would be nice, of course, if there were more evidence, or more witnesses, or scientific corroboration of Ruby Taylor's statement. It would have been helpful if comparisons of Smith's and Pettiford's fingerprints with prints lifted at the Carwash on December 10 had not been returned negative. But there comes a time when you're sure in your own mind you've got the right men, when you think you've got a good, believable witness, and you make a decision to go. Maybe, after you make the arrest, after the suspects are in jail, other evidence will develop, other witnesses will come forward. Meanwhile, the more time you allow to pass, the harder it gets to make your case, the greater the chance of something happening to your witness. So you make your move.

On August 25, 1969, eight and one-half months after the killings, one month and four days after Ruby Taylor had come forward, police obtained arrest warrants charging Raymond Smith and Pierre Pettiford with murder in the first degree.

In the attempt to locate and arrest the two men, police learned that Smith had a violent temper when drinking, that he'd get "insane" when refused money, and that on one occasion he had used a shotgun in his own hallway. From Smith's and Pettiford's probation officers they learned the schedules of their visits.

54

Early in the afternoon of Thursday, August 28, 1969, Mosrie and Kennedy stationed themselves in the second-floor hallway of the government building in which Pettiford was scheduled to visit his probation officer. They had never seen Pettiford in person but had studied the mugshots that accompanied his criminal record. Just before 2 P.M., two black men walked up the stairs and started down the hallway in their direction, and Kennedy immediately recognized the tall slender one. He and Mosrie approached.

"Mr. Pettiford?" Kennedy began.

"What do you want?" the man answered.

They were face to face when Kennedy showed him a warrant and informed him that he was under arrest for first-degree murder. Pettiford's companion left, and Pettiford was immediately searched. Kennedy reached into his own wallet and withdrew Police Department Form #47, and read it slowly to Pierre Pettiford:

"You are under arrest. Before we ask you any questions, you must understand what your rights are. You have a right to remain silent, you are not required to say anything to us at any time or to answer any questions. Anything you say can be used against you in court. You have a right to talk to a lawyer for advice before we question you and to have him with you during questioning. If you cannot afford a lawyer and want one, a lawyer will be appointed for you. If you want to answer questions now without a lawyer present, you will still have the right to stop answering at any time. You also have a right to stop answering at any time until you talk to a lawyer."

Pettiford was then escorted across the street to the homicide bureau for processing, where he was given the form containing advice of his rights for him to read and sign. Pierre Pettiford said he was innocent and asked for an attorney.

Mosrie dialed the Legal Aid Agency and asked them to send over an attorney for a newly arrested accused murderer. As they waited for a lawyer to arrive, Mosrie asked where Pettiford had been on December 10, 1968. "Man," he answered, "I don't remember that stuff, I don't keep a diary."

When the call from homicide reached the Legal Aid Agency, Sanford Berman, a twenty-six-year-old lawyer who had been with the Agency for less than a year and happened to have a free afternoon in his office, was sent over to assist on some kind of a murder case. He didn't want to get tied up too late: it was a pretty summer day, and the apartment house pool would be open until the early evening. He began the two-block stroll to homicide headquarters.

When he arrived, Mosrie and Kennedy briefed him on the charges and showed him a copy of the arrest warrant and supporting affidavit containing the allegations of an anonymous informant. Berman recognized the case as a big one. The detectives took him to a room in the rear where Pettiford had been sitting waiting, and Kennedy introduced him to Pettiford. The detectives left the room so that Berman could speak privately with his new client.

Berman explained to Pettiford the relationship between a client and attorney—that Berman was on his side and that anything Pettiford might say to him was a privileged confidential communication that Berman would not and could not be ordered to disclose to anyone. He explained all the rights which the detectives had gone over several times already. They chatted alone for an hour, and all Pettiford had to say was that he did not—could not—recall exactly where he was on December 10, 1968, but he knew he wasn't robbing and killing people at any carwash.

When Berman left the room to tell the police he had finished speaking with his client, they asked him if Pettiford would take a lie detector test.

Berman returned to the little room and explained to his client what the police wanted; he explained that Pettiford did not have to take the test and that any refusal to take it could not be used against him in court. He informed Pettiford of the options, and told him that perhaps, just perhaps, if Pettiford passed the test the charges would be dropped.

Pierre Pettiford said he had nothing to hide and agreed to take the test.

Sergeant Crispen Preston, a large pleasant man with blue-gray eyes that never seem to blink, was the lie detector expert. He had tested hundreds of accused murderers and hundreds of accused robbers, and was usually right.

The room in which the polygraph examination would be given is small and high-ceilinged. The walls are tiled with pale blue holed cork, bare. The polygraph machine itself is a large desklike instrument. On one side would sit Pierre Pettiford; on the other side, Sgt. Preston. Nobody else could be present. Overhead a lighting fixture of four long fluorescent bulbs. A mirror on one wall is actually a one-way viewer from another room. Berman could either look through that viewer, a position from which he could not hear anything, or sit near the door, which would be cracked open a few inches, to hear. He chose to listen, and sat outside in the hallway sipping coffee with Detective Mosrie, listening to the two voices inside.

When he meets you to give a polygraph test, Preston shakes your hand. It's not that he's a gentleman, but sometimes you can tell something about a person from the way he shakes hands: limply or firmly, with sweaty or dry hands. And Preston looks and listens to everything you do and say, from that first instant. The polygraph test really begins as soon as he sets eyes on you, when he begins deciding the questions he will ask.

Before hooking a suspect to the machine, you find out some things about him, things bearing no direct relationship to the case. A polygraph examination isn't designed to trick you. Before hooking up Pettiford to the contraption that separated them, Preston told him what the questions would be. And then Preston slipped the rubber tube around Pettiford's chest, put a blood pressure cuff around Pettiford's left arm, placed two thin attachments to the third and first fingers of Pettiford's hands—all devices connected to the instrument recording physiological changes within the body—and began asking the questions for real. And as Pettiford answered, chart paper flowed out of the machine with a series of patterned lines reflecting the way Pierre Pettiford's body was responding to his own answers.

Preston asked him the same set of eleven questions three times, in virtually the same order. Some were questions designed to ascertain that degree of Pettiford's general guilt complex, if any, in order to learn his reactive pattern to alleged crimes of which he could not be guilty: to do that, Preston fabricated a carwash crime at another location. Some other questions were irrelevant, and some were control questions, questions designed to elicit some emotional response, to show how Pettiford's body would react when it did react to something—questions which Preston constructed out of the several facts Pettiford had told him in the short interview that had preceded his attachment to the machine. But three of the questions, sprinkled among the others, were relevant: Did you do the Carwash killings? Do you know who did? Do you know what was taken? And Berman, listening outside, noticed that one of the questions had something to do with a green bag.

When it was over, Pettiford left the room in Mosrie's custody and

Preston studied the charts for a few minutes. Then Preston gave Mosrie and Berman the results. The first set of responses had been ambiguous. But the last two were clear. The "big blurpers" told Sgt. Preston one thing: Pierre Pettiford had participated in the Carwash murders.

The charges would not be dropped. Pettiford told his lawyer that the test was simply wrong. Berman thought the man might very well be lying when he handed Pettiford his card. Then Pettiford was taken for fingerprints and more booking preparatory to appearing in court.

That night police hunted for Raymond Smith. Because word had probably hit the street by then of Pettiford's bust, Smith's immediate arrest became essential. The longer he was at large knowing the police were looking for him, the longer he would have to prepare himself for his own arrest, and to hunt for Ruby Taylor. A local lookout was broadcast within the police department: Look for Raymond Smith, male, Negro, d.o.b. 10-22-39, 5'8", 148 pounds, medium complexion, thin moustache and goatee, stained teeth, black hair with receding hairline, tattoo of a heart with the letter "A" on his right forearm, homemade tattoo of "Ann" on left forearm. Consider armed and extremely dangerous.

The next morning Raymond Smith called his probation officer to say he'd heard the police were looking for him, and he was coming in to surrender. The police were notified, and Mosrie, Kennedy, and a third detective stationed themselves in the same hallway in which Pettiford had been arrested the day before. As with Pettiford they recognized Smith from mugshots. He entered the probation office and sat down before being arrested. Immediately he was searched, his wallet, cigarettes, and loose change were removed from his pockets, and the police department form containing his rights was read to him. Raymond Smith's eyes grew wet, and he said he hadn't done a thing.

The detectives escorted him to the homicide unit across the street, where they followed the same preliminary procedure they had used the day before with Pettiford. Unlike Pettiford, Raymond Smith told them he did know where he had been on December 10, 1968. He had been in Durham, North Carolina. He said some papers in his wallet would back up his story: a form from the North Carolina Employment Security Commission dated in Durham on December 12, 1968, and some tickets for a dance in Durham dated November 22, 1968. Eight and one-half months had passed since December 10, and it was difficult to remember that precise day. But he did remember returning from Durham to

Washington on New Year's Day, and he did remember that he had been in Durham for four months previous to that. He even gave police a few names they could check against his story: Ruth McCallum, with whom he had lived in Durham. Or his father, with whom he had stayed for a while in Durham. Or a man named J. C. Bennett, who lived on the same street in Durham as his father. Or the Holiday Inn Motel, where he had worked for a week or two in Durham. Or the North Carolina Employment Security Commission or The American Tobacco Company, or Hertz Rent-a-Car—they could all say where he had been.

When Raymond Smith finished his story, Mosrie asked whether he cared to give a written statement, but Smith declined. They finished processing him, and he was taken that morning to court for arraignment.

That same day Pierre Pettiford was arraigned on charges of first-degree murder, and Berman was appointed by the court to represent him. In the cell block three flights below the courtroom, Berman stressed that Pierre Pettiford was to speak to nobody—nobody—about the case. There might be other people in jail, after all, who would like to make a bargain with the Government if they could claim some information about the triple murder. Pettiford assured him he had talked with nobody but Berman and would talk to nobody else. And he told Berman that he had seen Raymond Smith that morning in the cell block, and Smith had said he had been arrested for the Carwash murders.

In court, when the judge was informed of the charges against Pettiford, he set bond at $25,000. Pierre Pettiford did not have $25,000 and was returned to jail.

That morning a young privately practicing lawyer named Thomas Fay was in the office of the administrators of the Criminal Justice Act, the statute under which attorneys are appointed to represent indigent defendants in criminal cases. The official he was speaking to mentioned something about a new murder case and asked Fay if he'd like the assignment. Raymond Smith now had a lawyer.

Fay went down the elevator to interview Smith in the cell bock before arraignment. Smith told his new lawyer what he had already told the police. And he told Fay he vaguely recalled the Carwash, remembered it was owned by a guy named "Bob," but that he himself hadn't worked there for a couple of years. After chatting awhile, Smith was taken up to the courtroom, where he pleaded not guilty and heard bond of $25,000 imposed. Raymond Smith did not have $25,000 and was returned to jail.

59

Within a few days of the arrests of Smith and Pettiford, Detectives Mosrie and Kennedy drove to Durham, North Carolina, in an unmarked police cruiser to check out Raymond Smith's alibi.

Police check out the alibi of a man they have arrested for a number of reasons. He may be telling the truth and be innocent, though that seemed most unlikely to the police in the face of Ruby Taylor's statement, the defendants' records, and the results of Pettiford's lie detector test. More important, checking out an alibi may also "freeze" defense testimony. Perhaps Smith had not yet told his family and acquaintances in Durham what his story would be at trial. If the police could get to them before Smith or his friends did, they could get truthful answers to some questions. The testimony of those potential alibi witnesses could not then be changed at trial. Unless, of course, they later chose to lie. And for that we have juries, to reject lies and accept truth.

When they reached Durham, Mosrie and Kennedy checked in with the commanding officer of the detective division of the Durham Police Department and explained their mission. As a courtesy to them, Durham detective Henry Hayes was assigned to help in their investigation. Hayes was a big, good-looking black man, born and raised in Durham, and he knew the city and the people. He even knew the Smith family, and most of the people Raymond Smith had named as possible alibi witnesses; in parts of the black section, everybody seemed to know or be related to everybody else. As the three men spoke with each person, they took notes from which they would type out a running résumé of each conversation when they returned to their motel room late each evening. With three men present, they felt no need to get signed statements from the witnesses.

The police called first upon the manager of the Durham office of the North Carolina Employment Security Commission. Their records showed that Raymond Smith had indeed filled out an application there on December 12, 1968. But it is less than half a day's drive from Washington to Durham, and Smith's application form contained one glaring fact inconsistent with what he had told the police: on December 12, 1968, he had stated that he had last worked at a place called Curtis Chevrolet in Washington during November, 1968. He had not been in Durham for four months.

Vera Bullock, Smith's half-sister, told them she recalled seeing Smith in Durham around Thanksgiving, 1968, when he drove by in a rented car. She said Smith had been staying with Ruth McCallum on Fargo

60

Street. She also recalled that Smith had asked her for money sometime around Christmas, 1968, so he could return to Washington.

But Vera Bullock could not definitely say that Raymond Smith had been in Durham on December 9, 10, or 11, 1968. Perhaps, she said, the police might want to check with J. C. Bennett, a good friend of Raymond's. She thought her brother eventually got the money to return to Washington from the Welfare Department—perhaps they'd want to check there.

At the Welfare Department, they discovered that Smith had appeared there two days after the murders and said he'd just come from Washington. He had applied again on December 31, 1968, this time for transportation money to return to Washington, and had stated that he'd only been in Durham for about a month.

They spoke with Sara Magnum, a cousin of Smith's Durham girlfriend, Ruth McCallum. Sara Magnum, like Vera Bullock, remembered seeing Smith in Durham in late November, 1968, and she remembered seeing him in Durham around Christmastime. Between those dates she had not laid eyes on the man. Sara Magnum could pinpoint the dates because on November 30 a friend of hers named Bill got arrested for rape, and she hadn't seen Raymond from that day until Christmas week.

They spoke with Ruth McCallum, who had known Raymond Smith since 1961. She had seen him on Thanksgiving Day, 1968, when Smith drove by her house and she was sitting on the front porch. And she had seen Smith on Christmas Day as well. But between Thanksgiving and Christmas, 1968, Ruth McCallum had not seen her boyfriend, Ray Smith.

They spoke with Viola Fuller, whose address Smith had given on one of his Durham applications. She told them she had rented a room to Ray Smith for about three weeks, beginning around Christmas, 1968. He had paid only one week's rent. Sometimes he'd be gone for days at a time when she tried to catch up with him for the rent money. He offered to help her out in the store she ran in the building, she said, but there was just something about Raymond Smith she didn't trust. When she discovered some stolen clothing in his closet, she had insisted he move out.

They checked with some local businesses to see whether their records reflected anything about Raymond Smith. They visited the Holiday Inn and learned that he had worked there for the last six days of October, 1968. The personnel man at The American Tobacco Company said he had nothing on a Raymond Smith, and the Jack Tarr Hotel had nothing, and the Durham Sun-News had nothing. Raymond Smith had, however,

61

rented a Hertz car on October 31, but he had returned it November 4; in fact, he had never bothered paying half the rental costs.

Claude Smith, Sr., Raymond Smith's stepfather, remembered Raymond staying with him in Durham for about three weeks in October when Raymond was working at the Holiday Inn. He also remembered Raymond moving back in for a few days after Christmas, just before leaving Durham on New Year's Day. And he suggested they might speak with his daughter, Cora Young.

Cora Young corroborated much of what others had told them. Raymond Smith had come to Durham in October; she had also seen him in November, but she was quite certain she had not seen him in December, because in October he had taken two of her guests' wallets and hadn't bothered to come back. They spoke with Claude Smith, Jr., who remembered Raymond working at the Holiday Inn just before Thanksgiving. And he remembered seeing Raymond a few days before and a few days after Christmas. But as for December 9, or 10, or 11, he just could not be sure whether or not he had seen Raymond Smith.

Finally, after several attempts, they found J. C. Bennett, the last name Raymond Smith had given as an alibi witness, and the man others in Durham had named as a good friend of Smith's. Bennett told them he had seen Smith in Durham in October, and after Christmas, 1968, when Smith had asked around for money to return to Washington.

But Bennett remembered something special: Bennett claimed to have seen Smith nearly every day in December, when he and Smith had done a good deal of drinking and gambling together. In fact, Bennett could even recall seeing Smith in Durham on December 10, 1968. The detectives pressed him on the date. How could he recall it? Did something unusual happen that day? Or perhaps he had been told by someone else that Washington police had been in Durham for a couple of days asking questions about Raymond Smith's whereabouts on December 10, 1968, and perhaps J. C. Bennett was trying to be of some assistance to his friend Ray Smith? In a flurry of questions, police asked Bennett whether he had spoken with Smith's sister, Vera Bullock. "Yes," he answered, "she talked to me on the phone. She told me the date." The police probed further, and at last J. C. Bennett told them, "I can't say that I saw him on December 10 because I was working, but I know I saw him about that general time." J. C. Bennett was asked a few more questions. And he remembered that just before Christmas Raymond Smith had told him he had just come down to Durham from Washington, D.C.

Mosrie and Kennedy had now spent three days in Durham checking out Raymond Smith's alibi. Not a person they had spoken with could place Raymond Smith in Durham on December 10, 1968. No public records or official business records reflected Smith's presence in Durham between the end of October and December 12, 1968. The police pieced their information together: Raymond Smith knew Durham pretty well, had some family and personal ties there, had arrived in the city some time in October, had worked for a while at the Holiday Inn, had stayed around until some time in November, and, around Thanksgiving, had left Durham. He hadn't reappeared in Durham until around December 12, 1968, a day on which his presence in Durham was conspicuously documented by records from the Employment Commission and the Welfare Department. It looked to the police as if Raymond Smith had come back to Durham after the murders to establish an alibi.

When they returned to Washington, Robert Coleman, without knowing it, told them they were right.

Robert Coleman was a black man, twenty-eight years old at the time of the Carwash murders.

He was born in a fair-sized seaport town in the South, the youngest child and only boy in a family of four children. His father was a sometime truck driver and sometime merchant seaman, his mother was a substitute school teacher. For the most part, they lived together when Coleman was a little kid and when his father wasn't at sea. But for reasons he never knew, his parents split up when he was just five, and Coleman and his three sisters moved into their grandparents' dairy farm in another state down South. In a year, his parents got back together, and Coleman and two of his sisters moved back with them. They lived in one of several apartments surrounding a small courtyard in the colored part of town. The neighborhood was not very elegant, not very clean, and tough, and poor. Coleman went to a school for black kids and didn't do particularly well. Sometimes, when nobody was looking, he would cry because he couldn't read well. Some things he just didn't understand. When he was a kid during the war, he used to throw away little red chips his mother got from the man. They were ration chips, and it was the last time Robert Coleman would throw away money so readily.

When you are a black boy in a bad neighborhood without much money, and a nigger to many of the white folk you meet, you sometimes begin doing things that maybe you shouldn't do. When there is a fuel

63

given six months apiece. So he looked for something better. He went back to safes, and this time he was the teacher and his buddy the pupil. The two of them began pulling burglaries, dozens of them. Late one rainy night, they emptied hundreds of dollars of merchandise from a hometown clothing store into their car. On the last trip into the alley back of the store, a policeman stopped them and asked what they were doing in the alley. Coleman told him they had ducked in to take a leak, and the policeman drew his gun, ordered them to face the wall of the building, checked the side door of the store, and placed them under arrest. Months later he got to court and was seated on a bench with others who were locked up for alleged crimes. The D.A. walked from man to man, pointed at each, and offered a certain number of years if they wanted to plead guilty without an attorney or trial. Coleman thought he couldn't do any better than one to four years and took it.

When you have been running and hustling most of your life, jail can become unbearably dismal. One day while Coleman was working on the road with other inmates, the armed guard turned his head and Robert Coleman raced into the woods. He did not have much of a chance. The black road camps worked in a white area so the black men could be easily spotted. After running for hours, Coleman ran into some of the state troopers who had surrounded the woods. He was given another year in jail, to run consecutive to the term he was already serving for burglary.

He never tried to escape again, but never became a model prisoner either. Working for hours and hours clearing rocks and leaves out of a highway ditch only to see the armed guard let a road-grader push it all back in didn't make much sense to Robert Coleman, but when you just take your shovel and toss it into the woods and refuse to go on, the man puts you in the hole for weeks on end, solitary confinement, where all you eat is bread and water plus two meals a week, and they make you sleep on the freezing cement floor with a half-blanket they give you at midnight and take away at six in the morning. It gets very cold there in the mountains on that cement floor, and your bones begin to ache; they ache for the rest of your life. There is no one to talk to, and you play tic-tac-toe with yourself and just feel the time pass, for weeks, slowly. At last, they let you out of the hole and back to working the ditches until one day you refuse to eat a piece of fatty uncooked meat, and back you go into the hole, back onto the cold cement, and weeks and weeks pass again before you can return to the road with the other men and dig in the ditches and crack rocks and see a white farmer sidle up to the armed guard to ask to borrow fifteen niggers for a day.

So Robert Coleman learned how to crack rocks and cut bushes, and how to box. He thought he might be able to make it as a boxer when he got out. In one of the road camps, he met a guy who said he used to be a professional boxer, and told Coleman about a friend in Washington, D.C., a ranked light-heavyweight, who might be able to get him started. Coleman had been earning the standard fifteen cents a day in jail, a dime of which he could spend on candy and cigarettes and a nickel of which he was forced to save. After three years and eight months, he was released, given forty dollars for his labors, and, with nowhere else to go, he took a bus to Washington, D.C.

In Washington the friend he had met in prison helped Coleman locate an apartment and introduced him to some local boxers. Coleman did well boxing, traveling around the country, keeping clean except for some under-the-table pay for his boxing. A contract to fight regularly in Philadelphia seemed likely. Everything was going well.

Until Robert Coleman decided that he would pull just one more job. Masked and with loaded pistols, he and two buddies barged into a D.C. liquor store, fired a shot into the ceiling, and drove away two minutes later with $3,000. After a while, Coleman left his friends at their girls' house and rode off in a taxi. In the evening his friends too drove off in their own car. As they were driving out of an alley near the girls' house, the driver spotted a cruising police car, panicked, and, with his friend, abandoned his own car in the middle of the street, lights on, guns and $2,000 inside. The men got away, but the police approached and inspected the car, traced it to its owner, and arrested him for the liquor store holdup. His friend gave them Robert Coleman's name, and within a month Coleman was back in jail. He was sentenced to one to five years this time, learned about furniture refinishing and upholstery, and did some more boxing. Mostly he just sat and let time pass. Nearly three years passed before he got back onto the street.

When he got back out, Coleman kept straight for a time. A few construction jobs, a job with the government—hard work, but the pay was pretty good, three or four dollars an hour. Then he began looking around and seeing other dudes making big money and buying things he wanted and couldn't have. So he began to supplement his income.

First, boosting—shoplifting from department stores, close to $1,000 a day, later fenced to a man for several hundred dollars daily. You make a lot of money that way, but seems like the more you make, the more you need. For a time Coleman was "all together," wearing diamonds on his fingers. Life on the street is strange, but if you hustle right, you can step outside any night and pick up a few hundred dollars. Clothes, women, thousands and thousands of dollars lost through an addiction: to the crap games. The pots are big in hustlers' crap games, and you can win big if you have enough to enter. You don't get street money by working in an office.

But there were other addicts in town whose addictions were even stronger than Coleman's tie to the crap table. In early '67, after half a year of profitable boosting, one of Coleman's friends offered an even more profitable way to supplement the income from his government job. Be my lieutenant, the man said, and I'll give you $500 a week. That was all the man said, but Coleman knew what he meant. Drop off a few packages of heroin here and there, collect some money for me, just keep the weight off my shoulders so I can clear my daily grand. Drugs is a rich but risky business, and Robert Coleman said no.

And then he thought of the man's big house and new car and the things the man was doing and the possibility of starting his own bankroll, and he changed his mind.

He took the job, met a lot of people, and soon he had his own customers. Instead of $500 a week selling heroin and cocaine, he'd make $300 daily. Early in the morning, off to the job with the government. Then back to the streets by mid-afternoon, talk with the whores patrolling 14th Street, bet on a few numbers, and stand on the sidewalk and sell. He and his friend, who had the direct line to a wholesaler, would stand near each other on the street. The friend carried the pills, hundreds at a time, selling them for $2.50 each. Coleman carried a loaded gun just in case someone tried to get dishonest. The two would buy the drugs in packet form with empty gelatin capsules and dilute it and fill the caps. Coleman tried the stuff himself: empty the capsule into a wine top, add some water, heat it, fill the syringe, tie a sock around your arm tightly to bulge the vein, then pop it in. Or sometimes pour some cocaine on a torn matchbook cover and hold it to your nose and sniff. But it was not very good, and it could make you an addict, so Coleman popped his veins just a few times, for the experience, and quit.

If you are doing $1,000 a day for yourself, as Coleman's friend was, the police will probably get you. Perhaps it will be a new police cadet who goes undercover, makes a buy from you, and later arrests you on a warrant. Or perhaps it will be a regular customer who has been arrested and is cooperating with the police to get a deal. You meet many people, and it is a risky profit. If you are making a few hundred a day, and dealing with someone clearing a thousand, you may get caught up with him.

When one business gets good, others develop. Whores work the area around 14th and U, Coleman's major narcotics neighborhood, like bees work a honeycomb. Some of them work for men, some work for themselves, some even work because they like it and it isn't tough work. They are strange people, the young whores in high boots and ugly wigs and short dresses who flag down the cars cruising 14th Street. They can be tough if you're a buyer, but putty if you're an owner. If you are Robert Coleman—personable and good-looking and kind of tough—you walk down the street on a night when heavy rains have driven most of the girls into the bars, and you hear a man force his girl to give him the full $500 her body has earned her that night. When he leaves, you go up to her and tell her she wouldn't be treated that way if she was your woman. She knows you hustle in the area—street people often know what's happening, who's doing and who's done what, where, and when—and she doesn't mind talking to you, so you take her to a room and make her your woman and go get her clothes at the other guy's house. He doesn't want to give them over, but he is a dandy with shiny clothing and greasy hair and you slap him around a little until he lets you take her clothes. The girl is yours then. That means she does whatever you want her to do.

She goes onto the streets for you and gives you a few hundred dollars a night, and you put her up in a place, and she brings a few more girls, and soon four or five of the girls waving to the men who drive slowly up and down 14th Street are yours. If they do well, you give them a party, you bring some drugs, and you all get high. Sometimes a strange girl will come to town and phone to tell you she knows about you and is looking for a friend, and you meet her and party with her.

On July 9, 1968, one of those girls flew in from Boston to have a party. Coleman met her on the corner that night and began walking toward a hotel where he kept a room and where they would meet another couple. But at 13th and U, in the heart of Washington's whorehouse district, officers of the narcotics squad of the Metropolitan Police Department suddenly arrested Robert Coleman for a heroin sale he had allegedly made on the street two weeks earlier to an undercover policeman. He was searched, incidental to the arrest, and the police found several dozen capsules of heroin in his pockets.

The penalties for federal heroin offenses are severe. For selling there is a mandatory minimum of five years' imprisonment, and a possible twenty-year maximum. For mere possession you must get two years and can get up to ten. In addition to the two narcotics raps now on his head, Coleman had been picked up several months earlier in a sweep arrest during the riots of April '68 and charged with curfew violation, rioting, and burglary. Robert Coleman knew the drug charges would be tough to beat.

And Robert Coleman had met a college girl at a play one night, a good clean girl, and they had fallen in love, and a few months later got married. He had told her of his string of girls, and that he loved her, but that she had to accept what he was, and she had cried a little bit and accepted him. He knew that something very special was happening to him, and he didn't want to give it up. So he posted the required percentage of his bond, thought things over for half a year while waiting for a trial, and then, with his wife, skipped town. When he failed to appear in court as required, bench warrants were issued for his arrest on each charge.

They went to Albany, New York, where Coleman got a government job and gave up the hustle. Drug dealings were handled severely up there, he had heard, and after an arrest you can't just post a percentage of your bond to get out. Between his salary and his wife's as a nurse's aide, they got along. But when you are a wanted man, you begin to feel a hand over your shoulder, ready to tap at any moment. Everyone is looking at you everywhere you go.

After half a year, Coleman and his wife returned to Washington so he could give himself up. One of his women there was rich, and he looked for her for a week to get some money. Legal fees were high, and maybe someone had to be paid off. But before he could find the woman, the police found Robert Coleman on August 29, 1969, and he was back in jail, charged with narcotics sale, narcotics possession, burglary, riot, and now, fugitivity. And having jumped bond once, it would be difficult for Robert Coleman to get out on bond again.

Robert Coleman did not want to stay in jail. Within a week of his arrest, he told a guard that he had information about some robbery and murder cases, and that he wanted to speak to the police.

Detectives Mosrie and Kennedy were in Durham, so engrossed in investigating Smith's alibi that they had not bothered to call Washington headquarters to learn what, if anything, had developed back home.

When the homicide unit of the Metropolitan Police Department was notified that Coleman wanted to talk, Detectives Bernard Crooke and Otis Fickling responded to the D.C. jail to listen to him. He told them he had information on a number of cases—several holdups, including a $15,000 parking lot hit one year ago, and an unsolved shooting. And he told them he knew Pierre Pettiford pretty well and had met Raymond Smith and that he knew the police had the right men in the Carwash case.

But before Coleman would talk about the Carwash case, he wanted police assurance that they would help him in his pending cases. One thing Robert Coleman stressed: he was not asking to be put on the street to dig up information on Smith and Pettiford. He had enough on them already, and he was willing to testify in court.

Gradually he and the police began their bargaining. Coleman tossed a taste—just a taste—of facts to them: a day or two after the murders, he had talked to both Smith and Pettiford, and they had told him all about the job, told him things had got out of hand during a robbery, told him they needed money to get to North Carolina to prepare an alibi.

Coleman had just given them bits and snatches, but the police knew he was ready to deal. Crooke and Fickling told him that if the rest of his information was good, they would try to help him. They told him they would arrange for him to be brought to homicide headquarters or the courthouse to speak with the detectives in charge of the case—somewhere away from prisoners who have nothing to fill their time but notice one among them huddling with the man.

One week later Mosrie and Kennedy, back in Washington after what they considered a successful trip to Durham, sat down with Coleman in an isolated room in a remote corridor of the federal courthouse. Again both sides began warily at first, a slow feeling out between strangers. Two white detectives in their suits and ties looking for evidence of the truth, and a black man in loose prison blues asking to see the sun again. Neither side sure of the workings of the other's mind and heart.

Then Coleman talked. He told them that on the night of the murders— he knew it was the night of the murders because he read about it the next day in the newspapers and recognized the name of Gloria McDowell as the girlfriend of a buddy he had met at Ben's Chili Bowl—Smith and Pettiford had come up to him on 14th and U Streets and asked him for money and a little dope. And he had heard them discuss beating some

71

people and doing some robbing, and they had told him they trusted him not to tell anyone. They needed to borrow some money for Raymond Smith to get to Durham, North Carolina, to establish an alibi.

Coleman gave Mosrie and Kennedy detailed answers to their questions. When they asked him to sign a statement Mosrie would type out for him, Coleman refused: a piece of paper can get into the wrong hands, a leak can spread to the street, and the street can be rough. But he wasn't backing down; he was prepared to cooperate. In fact, he would tell it to the grand jury—a secret group—any time they wanted. Which Mosrie and Kennedy arranged that morning.

Eight days later Robert Coleman was released in the custody of his wife pending his own trial.

CHAPTER FOUR

O N the day Robert Coleman met with Mosrie and Kennedy and testified before the grand jury, the case of United States against Raymond Smith and Pierre Pettiford was scheduled for a preliminary hearing.

By that time Fay and Berman had met with their clients several times, and both defendants kept protesting their innocence. Though they had read of the murders and had worked at the Carwash several years ago, they denied any connection with the crimes. Only after a few meetings could Fay convince Smith that the police, after having checked his alibi in Durham, were not about to drop the charges. And despite their backgrounds and their instability, despite Pettiford's alcoholism and lie detector test and Smith's admitting his guilt of the petty crimes that filled his past, Raymond Smith and Pierre Pettiford seemed to their lawyers too small-time to pull a big robbery accompanied by a spectacular triple murder. Fay and Berman thought their men were innocent.

Neither defendant could say for sure who'd want to turn them in on a phony murder charge. Smith could imagine only one person, a woman he used to live with and whom he'd left. Raymond Smith was a man who had a lot of women, and this particular one used to throw herself at him. She was, in fact, the only person he could imagine who might hold a grudge against him. She'd once got a few thousand dollars in settlement for an injury received in a cleaning store, and Ray had taken half of it. She'd once accused him of trying to have sex with her oldest daughter and trying to make the girl into a prostitute. And he had knocked the woman around quite a few times, occasionally in the presence of her own daughter. Ruby Taylor was the only person he could imagine who would want to stick him with these charges. She had a big lying mouth, he said, and she was mean.

73

A preliminary hearing is a courtroom session in which a judge or magistrate determines whether probable cause exists to believe a crime has been committed and the defendant has committed it. Whether or not the preliminary hearing results in a finding of probable cause, the grand jury may later choose to indict or not to indict. But if the judge at the hearing does not find probable cause, the defendant must be immediately released unless and until an indictment is returned. If the judge does find probable cause, the defendant is either released or committed to jail on conditions of bond previously imposed, pending action by the grand jury, which will then hear much of the same evidence.

The hearing is not really much of a safeguard. The rules of evidence are grossly relaxed, and the judge need not determine whether or not he believes the defendants are guilty, only whether there is "probable cause" to so believe. Exactly what that phrase means is an enigma; in practice, "probable cause" is what exists when one apparently credible person claims under oath to have witnessed another commit or admit to a crime. The witness's account is often introduced into evidence by hearsay testimony: by the policeman in charge of the case simply reciting what the witness has told him, corroborated by the policeman's own account of any factors which support the accusation. The finding of probable cause is generally so pro forma that the defense simply uses the hearing as a forum to discover as much of the Government's case as possible, putting on no defense at all, while the Government reveals as little of its case as possible but enough to justify a finding of probable cause.

Although the only court in Washington with jurisdiction to actually try murder cases is the federal District Court, the local Court of General Sessions, situated in an old red building two blocks away, handles most of the preliminary hearings. And it was in one of the musty hallways of the Court of General Sessions that Detective Mosrie approached Berman to say that one of Rosenberg's sons had called the police and said Mrs. Rosenberg might be bringing a gun to the hearing to take care of the men who had killed her husband.

By the time the judge took the bench, the courtroom was jammed, mostly with people who were there to watch the first stages of the Carwash case. Sylvia Rosenberg had arrived by the time that case was called. Before the defendants were brought out from behind the green door leading from the cell block to the courtroom, Berman and Fay asked permission to approach the bench to speak with the judge. Berman related what Mosrie had told him and asked that the courtroom be cleared. The motion was denied, but the judge decided that all other preliminary hearings scheduled for the day would be called first to help empty the courtroom—and that although Mrs. Rosenberg would not be searched, policemen would be stationed on both sides of her.

While waiting for the other cases to be disposed of, Fay and Berman entered the cell block to speak briefly with their clients. They informed Smith and Pettiford of the possible danger in the courtroom and of security measures that the judge would and would not take. They explained that the day's proceedings were pretty much a formality, after which Smith and Pettiford would doubtless be held for action by the grand jury. As in most preliminary hearings, there would be no sense in the defendants' testifying: nothing they could say at this stage would prevent a finding of probable cause, and anything they did say could later be used against them in the trial itself.

When the case was again called, Smith and Pettiford stepped into the courtroom in their loose-fitting prison blues. Smith was visibly shaking, and Pettiford kept looking around. Fay and Berman again approached the bench and requested that the courtroom be cleared to prevent possible violence. This time their request was granted, and all spectators, including relatives of the victims, were asked to leave the courtroom. Only marshals —for security—and newspaper reporters—to assure the constitutional protection of a public trial—were allowed to remain inside. With Mrs. Rosenberg and her son peering in through the rear door window pane, the preliminary hearing began.

The defense argued in support of a written motion they had previously filed for production of the witness who had turned the defendants in. They were certain the request would be denied and only the police would testify, but a defense attorney builds as formidable a record as possible for appeal, and Berman believed they would have strong grounds to contest in federal District Court the validity of the ruling and would stand a good chance of persuading that court to reopen the hearing and to order the Government to produce its key witness. There was no conceivable way, they argued to the judge, to test the validity of the unknown witness's accusations without confronting him or her under cross-examination on the witness stand.

The motion was denied.

The only witness called by the Government was Arif Mosrie, who testified briefly that three people had been murdered and that an unnamed witness who feared for his or her life had detailed the circumstances under which Smith and Pettiford had planned the robberies and that the witness had seen Smith return bloodied from the scene. The cross-examination was designed simply to have Mosrie disclose as much information as possible. He disclosed that no photographic identifications of either defendant had been made by anybody but the unnamed witness, and that the defendants could not be linked to the crime by any fingerprints, or by hairs, or by fibers.

It seemed like a fairly skimpy Government case so far: Mosrie said nothing about Robert Coleman. But there was simply no effective way to explore the validity of the accusation of one person through another person's mouth. When Mosrie was through, the defense put on no witnesses, but argued to the court the self-contradiction in the Government's concealing the identity of its key witness: if what the witness reported was true, then Smith and Pettiford must already know the witness's identity, and thus no useful purpose could be served by denying the defense the opportunity for cross-examination. But the witness was in fear, said the judge; the motion was denied, probable cause was found, and the defendants were remanded to jail to await action by the grand jury.

Berman and Fay stepped into the cell block with their clients to explain the next step: a motion in the District Court for an order reopening the preliminary hearing to afford the defendants a meaningful chance to confront their accuser. The motion would be made promptly, they explained, because no right to a preliminary hearing exists following an indictment, and the defense could expect a fairly speedy indictment. Though probable cause would no doubt be found even if the witness were produced and cross-examined, extensive interrogation could provide useful leads for investigation and for subsequent impeachment of the witness at trial.

Smith and Pettiford listened. Pettiford calmly asked some questions in his slow, deep monotone—a voice of calm unconcern, resentful because, as he kept telling the lawyers, "I didn't do it." Raymond Smith was very nervous, sweating, quietly sobbing as he repeated that he had been in Durham, North Carolina, on December 10, 1968. The lawyers left for the day, and their clients returned to jail.

Within days the defense filed its motion in District Court for an order granting them the right to confront and cross-examine the person who had accused Raymond Smith and Pierre Pettiford of a triple murder. Exactly two weeks after the hearing in the Court of General Sessions, the chief

76

judge of the District Court granted the motion. The lawyers related the ruling to Smith and Pettiford, and both men were pleased.

Because the Court of General Sessions was now stripped of jurisdiction, the new preliminary hearing would be held in the federal courthouse, a large, clean-looking, squat building on Pennsylvania Avenue between the Capitol and the White House. When the case of U.S. v. Smith and Pettiford was called, every bench in the small first-floor magistrate's hearing room was filled, and the hall outside the room was crowded with people hoping for a chance to see. A tape recorder in front would preserve all testimony.

Smith and Pettiford were escorted through a side door to seats at their lawyers' sides in the front of the small hearing room. Before any testimony, the Government asked that the room be cleared of spectators because of the imminent divulgence of its key witness's identity. Both Fay and Berman, still fearing for the safety of their clients, consented. The magistrate denied the request.

Detective Mosrie was called first for the Government, and he repeated much of what he had said at the original hearing, with the defense again attempting to keep him talking as long as possible. When his questioning was over, the Government renewed its request that the room be cleared. Despite the presence of half a dozen marshals and policemen, the next witness's conception of her own security—apart from the security itself— was essential to the Government's case. Again the motion was denied.

The Government does not generally prepare its witnesses for testifying at a preliminary hearing. The Government attorney at the hearing may be handling dozens of hearings that day and has only a sketchy outline of each case. After the hearing and indictment, the case will be assigned to one prosecutor for thorough preparation and trial, but until then it will pass through the hands of several experienced professionals who have learned to handle matters of life and death and human passion clerically. So Ruby Taylor's only preparation was a brief chat with the Government attorney who would ask her a few questions at the hearing and never see her again.

The Government called its next witness. From the rear of the hearing room came a short woman, wearing a two-piece blue suit, low heels, and a burned-red wig. She had been waiting in a tiny room with a detective who, after handing her a copy of her signed statement to read, was trying to put her at ease. "I'm a little nervous," she said, "but I'll go in and tell the truth."

77

As Ruby Taylor walked to the front of the hearing room, Fay asked Smith in a whisper whether he knew her. Smith said yes, her name was Ruby Taylor. Pettiford whispered to Berman that it was an old girlfriend Smith used to live with.

Ruby Taylor stepped up to the witness stand, just a few feet in front of the table where Smith and Pettiford sat with their lawyers, and swore on a Bible to tell the truth. Seated within a foot or two of her was Detective Kennedy, just so she would feel secure.

Before Ruby Taylor began her testimony, the magistrate told her that security precautions had been taken and there was nothing to be afraid of. When he finished and the Government attorney asked his first question, Raymond Smith put his right hand to the side of his mouth, almost shielding Kennedy's view of his lips, and mouthed the words, "Don't do this, Ruby."

Direct examination by the Government was brief: the more a witness talks, the greater the chance of his saying something that will later be disproved or contradicted when he testifies at trial. For that very reason the cross-examination of Ruby Taylor was designed not to prove her a liar—for the finding of probable cause was a foregone conclusion—but simply to have her talk and talk, the more words the better. Cross-examine her gently to encourage her, and then, at trial, destroy her.

So Ruby Taylor's testimony lasted for a very long time, over several Government objections that the purpose of her testimony at this stage was simply to determine probable cause. Fay and Berman questioned her politely, and Ruby Taylor sounded like a good witness, calm, unruffled, composed. The Government's objection to divulging her present address was sustained, but she was permitted to tell in matter-of-fact detail about the planning of the robberies and return from the murders, and about the subsequent threat from Raymond Smith. It was all so routine that only the defense took any particular notice when Ruby Taylor stated that the only money bag she had seen Raymond Smith return with was white.

Finally the defense had asked just about enough— enough to disprove by subsequent investigation, sufficiently detailed so that Ruby Taylor could not possibly keep it all consistent by the time she would testify at trial. She was excused from the witness stand. As she stepped down, Smith whispered into Fay's ear, "She's a goddam liar, and a bitch." Before she left the hearing room, the magistrate reminded her that she had no reason to fear for her personal safety.

When she left the room, the defense argued that her testimony had failed to establish probable cause. The magistrate spoke again: "I think the totality of facts and circumstances here are such, and the detail of the witness's testimony is such, that she is a credible witness, that not only is probable cause established here, but on the testimony here a jury could indeed find guilt beyond a reasonable doubt. I therefore hold these defendants for action of the grand jury." Then, before adjourning, he looked at an old lady seated in the crowded room and spoke to her: "Rumors have come to my attention, Mrs. Rosenberg, that you may have had some ideas of perhaps doing harm to the defendants in this case. I don't know whether that's true or not, but let me tell you now: if you had any such ideas, abandon them, and let the law handle this case." The hearing was over.

After the magistrate had ruled, Fay and Berman returned to the cell block with their clients to learn what else they knew about Ruby Taylor: she didn't like Raymond Smith one bit; she was an addict and a whore; she hung out at 14th and U and at 7th and O, and 7th and T; she had an older relative named Emma Roland who lived somewhere on Lanier Place. And she was lying about their having committed the Carwash crimes, about Smith's threatening her by driving a hearse past her, and about where Smith was living at the time she allegedly heard them plan the robbery.

The lawyers explained the next stages: the grand jury would indict them, they would be rearraigned on the indictment, the lawyers would continue investigating, and then the trial would be held. How far off would the trial be? Probably about four to seven months. That seemed like a long time for innocent people to spend in jail, Smith and Pettiford said. The lawyers said they would do their best.

While the defense was agreeing that Smith and Pettiford would probably stand or fall together on the basis of Smith's Durham alibi, Detectives Kennedy and Mosrie and Ruby Taylor drove out to 67 V Street, the address Ruby had given as the scene of the planning and of Smith's return. The detectives had been around there several times before, and the place just didn't seem to match Ruby's description. When they arrived, Ruby immediately told them they were one block off, and took them to the house at 137 V. That, she said, was the building in which Smith had lived, in a rear apartment with a view of Pettiford's home on Flagler Place. The place matched the description she had been giving all along. They tried to find the landlord, couldn't, and left a homicide number for him to call.

79

Soon after the second preliminary hearing, the defense of Smith and Pettiford officially became a public charge. Both men filled out affidavits of indigency, swearing that they were presently incarcerated, had no jobs, no property, no debts, no cash, no cars, no stocks, no bonds. In a capital case, every indigent defendant is entitled by statute to two attorneys. For Smith, a soft-spoken, white-haired man named Charles B. Murray was appointed as Fay's co-counsel. Murray, the only lawyer over thirty in the case—he was sixty-nine—was a former director of the Legal Aid Agency and a former Assistant Attorney General in the Department of Justice. He had been involved in Washington's last triple murder forty years earlier, as a law clerk in the U.S. Attorney's Office assisting in the preparation of the Government's appellate brief following a conviction. He'd recently retired from retirement to become a partner of his younger son, Charlie J. Murray, who had just graduated from law school. The elder Murray requested of the court that his son be allowed to join him without compensation on the Carwash case, and the request was granted.

One of Berman's colleagues in the Legal Aid Agency was appointed co-counsel for Pierre Pettiford: John Perazich, who had been defending accused criminals since being admitted to practice two years earlier. Perazich visited Pettiford shortly after being appointed and asked him about failing the lie detector test. Pettiford said the reason was the way the questions were asked. Perazich knew the unimpeachable reputation of the sergeant who had administered the test and knew Berman had been sitting right outside the polygraph room. But a criminal defense lawyer is concerned not so much with the question of guilt or innocence as with the question of whether the Government can prove a man guilty beyond a reasonable doubt—and his job is to do everything within the bounds of ethics to ensure that the question is answered in the negative.

One month after the second preliminary hearing, a federal grand jury, having heard testimony from Ruby Taylor, Robert Coleman, and Arif Mosrie, returned an eight-count indictment charging Smith and Pettiford with murder and armed robbery. Six of the counts charged murder: three counts of murder "purposely and with deliberate and premeditated malice" and three counts of felony-murder, murder committed "while perpetrating and attempting to perpetrate the crime of robbery." Each of the two types of murder is first-degree and a capital offense. The seventh count charged robbery "while armed with a dangerous weapon, that is, a pipe," and the last count simply charged robbery "by force and violence and against resistance and by putting in fear." Certified copies of the indictment were mailed to each defendant at the D.C. Jail. They were arraigned on the indictment two weeks later, and entered pleas of not guilty. Fay and Berman told Robert Shuker, the Assistant United States Attorney to whom the case was now permanently assigned, that they'd drop by his office soon to discuss it with him.

Smith and Pettiford were still being held in jail without an adjudication of their guilt or innocence. The law requires that conditions for pretrial release be set in most criminal cases, conditions designed only to ensure a defendant's presence at trial and otherwise taking no account of the likelihood of his committing other offenses if released. The one exception is a capital offense, in which case the law allows the amount of bond to reflect a judge's conception of the defendant's potential dangerousness—to the extent that the judge may refuse to set any bond at all. In the case of a triple murder, especially where the life of the Government's key witness is allegedly in jeopardy, the risk of danger may seem too great to allow the defendant release pending trial. When the Government moved for revocation of even the $25,000 bond that had originally been set on Raymond Smith and Pierre Pettiford, the motion for revocation was granted.

In Pettiford's case the issue soon became moot: his probation for his most recent larceny conviction was revoked not only for his arrest on the triple murder charges but for failing to report for probation conferences as required, occasionally reporting drunk, and failing to maintain steady employment. Though Smith's probationary status still stood, his lawyers, certain that probation would be revoked because of his arrest for the triple murder in the unlikely event that a realistic bond were set, did not bother appealing the revocation of his bond. Pettiford was now being held in a different jail from Smith, a jail for service of the larceny sentence rather than a jail for awaiting trial in the Carwash case. But both places, whatever the names or locations or theoretical purposes of confinement, were jails, and bad ones.

A criminal defense attorney doing the job right files a lot of papers. For every reasonable motion filed, either he gets something that may be helpful in trial or he gets a built-in issue to support an appeal in the event of conviction.

A week after the second arraignment, the defense filed a motion for the court to order mental and physical examinations of Ruby Taylor to

81

determine, if possible, whether she was addicted to or used drugs on the day of the murders, on any of the days on which she spoke to the police about Smith and Pettiford, and on the day she testified at the preliminary hearing; and to determine, if possible, whether any such addiction or drug use could have impaired her ability to observe and recollect events.

A few days later they filed some more papers, this time a comprehensive motion for discovery and production of evidence from the Government. In a criminal case, the defense is entitled to learn much of the Government's case before trial. If the charge is first degree murder, the Government must even provide a capital list, divulging the names and addresses of all Government witnesses, at least three days before trial.

The defense made motions for discovery of the substance of all statements made by either defendant to the police or to anyone else; for the names, addresses, and any written statements given by everyone the police had interviewed in connection with their investigation; for all photographs that might have been shown to anybody, and transcripts of all grand jury testimony, and results of all scientific tests that might have been performed in connection with the case; for the criminal records of all potential Government witnesses, and papers, documents, and photographs the Government intended to introduce at trial. They requested access to any tapes of electronic surveillance the Government might have employed and all medical records the Government might have relating to Ruby Taylor and her addiction. They asked for the numbers, amount, and denominations of the bills and coins allegedly stolen from the Carwash, the names of the companies and account numbers of Irving Rosenberg's stolen credit cards, the dates police had issued stop orders on the use of those cards, and any existing information about their use or recovery after December 10, 1968. They asked for a summary of all negotiations and promises between the Government and Ruby Taylor in connection with her testimony and, finally, for "all material now known to the Government, or which may become known, or which through due diligence may be learned from the investigating officers or the witnesses in this case, which is exculpatory in nature or favorable to the accused or which may lead to exculpatory material, or which tends to negate the guilt of the accused as to the offense charged or would tend to reduce the punishment therefor."

Before the discovery motion was resolved, an earlier motion for funds allowing the defense to investigate Raymond Smith's Durham alibi was granted. In early December the Murrays drove to Durham to check out what Smith had told them.

They spent two days there, searching for and interviewing the dozens of people and places Ray Smith had suggested as proof he was in Durham on December 10, 1968. They spoke with a lot of the people Mosrie and Kennedy had interviewed a few months ago, most of them poor country types, and went to many of the same places. Unfortunately several of the places where Smith said he had applied for employment destroyed application records after a month. And because private defense attorneys do not have the aura of authority that surrounds detectives, several places refused to provide any information, despite releases the Murrays had obtained from their client. Those records would have to be subpoenaed. But within two days they had documentary proof that Raymond Smith had worked in Durham at the Holiday Inn during the last week of October, 1968, and that he had been to two different government agencies on December 12, two days after the murders. A number of people also recalled seeing him in Durham around the time of the murders, though nobody could say for certain whether he had been there on December 10. There were some more Durham people and places to contact—Smith's stepfather, Claude Smith, J. C. Bennett, the Jack Tarr Hotel, the S & W Restaurant, The American Tobacco Company, a few others—but the defense already looked pretty strong to the Murrays when they began their drive back to Washington.

Shortly after returning from Durham, the elder Murray had a lengthy talk with Smith in the jail. He told Smith generally the result of the interviews in Durham, though the defense had not yet decided whether or not to discuss with Smith the exact dates the records had reflected: perhaps if he were not an overly precise witness at trial, his alibi would appear more credible. And they discussed Smith's present status: he had been in jail for nearly four months without a trial. Murray promised to file an application for his release on bond pending trial, though he was not optimistic about its chance for success.

Pettiford, who had been around the criminal law for quite some time and knew a number of intricate legal terms, kept writing letters to his attorneys suggesting legal ploys and motions they should pursue. They pressed him for information of his whereabouts around the day of the murders or the weeks or months preceding that time. He supplied some names of people he'd seen and been with and of odd jobs he'd held for a

83

couple of days. But he just couldn't think of any place he'd worked or any one person who could say that Pierre Pettiford had been living a pretty normal life around December 10, 1968.

And when they checked out his people, the attorneys learned that his life was always far from regimented. He was known always as a heavy drinker, an alcoholic; but as his sister Yvette said, he'd be real gentle when he got to drinking a lot. And his aunt told them, "When he is drunk, he is as limber as a rag, and about as harmless." Still, it would be nice to have some evidence of his harmlessness and, if not, at least some evidence of his stability. Constantly Berman pressed Pettiford to try to recall any employment forms he might have covering the time-span in question, any applications, any W-2 tax forms. Pettiford couldn't recall a single one.

The defense lawyers gave the case to the chief investigator at the Legal Aid Agency, with a summary of Ruby Taylor's preliminary hearing testimony, for detailed investigation of everything she had said. The elder Murray himself went to 137 V Street, Smith's old address, to see whether it matched the description Ruby had given of the place Smith lived when he had allegedly planned the Carwash robbery. It did. But the old landlord told him that Smith hadn't been living there at the time of the murders, best he could recall. Another investigator was sent to find Charles Gilbert, the cabbie who claimed to have seen three men talking with Rosenberg just before the crimes. But Gilbert was simply too old and his glasses too thick to put much credence in his statement that the pictures the police had shown him of Raymond Smith and Pierre Pettiford didn't seem to be the guys he'd seen that night.

Nearly five months after the arrests, a trial date was finally set: April 27, 1970. The date had some importance for the lawyers: a jury panel sits for one calendar month, and by the 27th most of the April panel would already have heard a number of cases. They would presumably be able by then to separate fact from fiction. To Raymond Smith and Pierre Pettiford, still in jail awaiting trial for crimes they claimed to know little about, the importance of the trial date was that it was still three months away.

The Government does not sit still while the defense investigates, but sometimes its wheels grind more slowly.

"The Government" by now meant Robert Shuker, the prosecutor who would actually try the case. At twenty-eight he had been a prosecutor less than two years but had proved himself to be as tough and fair as any lawyer in the courthouse, and he usually won. Before joining the U.S. Attorney's Office, Shuker had been a criminal defense lawyer in Chicago. He had decided to become a prosecutor after defending a kid who had butchered someone in a notorious case there, a bludgeon murder with a heavy instrument. The kid was guilty, had confessed—and Shuker had got him off on the basis of some pretrial motions. It left a somewhat foul taste in his mouth because the kid was the type who'd probably kill again; so Robert Shuker had become a prosecutor.

When the file bearing the names "Raymond Smith" and "Pierre Petti-ford" found its way to Shuker's desk, he had about sixty other cases assigned to him. All were felonies, most of them important. For now there was time only for a brief examination of the newest file.

It was a triple murder. It had gone unsolved for some time. A junkie woman had turned in her ex-boyfriend and his pal, and another man had later corroborated her accusation. The file did not indicate that man's name, and there was no real reason to learn it at this stage: it was obviously a secret, and when you pick up a name, you may let it drop somewhere. All Shuker knew was that he had Ruby Taylor, that he had a drug dealer who'd been arrested himself, and that he had not a shred of scientific corroboration of their stories.

When he found some free time, Shuker called Mosrie and Kennedy to his office to talk briefly about the case. They'd been working on it since the arrests, but it was now just one among the many killings to which they were assigned.

Mosrie and Kennedy were still keeping in regular contact with Ruby Taylor, letting her know they were available should she need any help. She'd still change her address every few weeks for safety and always let Mosrie and Kennedy know where she was. She began to trust them. Just before Christmas she gave Mosrie her $50 work check to keep for her, so she wouldn't spend it or lend it to her friends. At Christmastime she took it back to buy the kids some presents. Often Mosrie and Kennedy would meet her at the courthouse to talk to her alone where nobody could be watching. On those trips they explained to any prosecutor around that Ruby had come down in connection with the Carwash case and she'd be given a $20 witness fee, the standard fee the Government gave witnesses who came down to the courthouse for interviews. It was inexpensive compared to the thousands of dollars the Government would have had to pay to relocate her if she chose to move out of Washington for safety.

85

They had intentionally not maintained close contact with Coleman. He told them he didn't need protection; if they needed him, he'd be available. There was no point keeping tabs on him until the prosecutor was ready to interview him. Nobody knew of his status as an informant, and any police contact with him could just arouse suspicion.

Neither Coleman nor Ruby was told about the other's existence or involvement in the case. No reason for one to know other areas of corroboration that would be helpful, no reason for either to suppose the Government gives out the name of one key witness to another.

Mosrie outlined the case to Shuker in his office and told him what Smith's alibi would be and that Pettiford would rely on Smith. Shuker suggested concentration on some major areas for investigation, some associations that should be established: show that Smith had been close to Pettiford in '68, that Pettiford had been close to Coleman, that Coleman had known Smith, that both defendants had worked at the Carwash around the time of the robbery—and find somebody believable who could say that in the latter part of 1968, Raymond Smith had been somewhere in the District of Columbia. Except Shuker did not yet know the name Coleman because he still did not want to know it. There would be a time for that. Until he could devote concentrated effort to the case, it was up to the police to continue investigating for independent corroboration of the two main witnesses. In the meantime Shuker would read over as many of the hundreds of pages of police investigation on the case as time allowed.

Even at first glance it looked like a difficult case to prosecute. No independent eyewitnesses, only two people who claimed to have heard admissions and who themselves had obvious and powerful motives to lie. Shuker had not met either of them yet, but no matter how honest they might seem in face-to-face private talks with the police, it would be difficult to convey that feeling to a jury in the impersonal question-and-answer sessions of a criminal trial.

But even a quick look at his file convinced Shuker that the men named Smith and Pettiford were probably guilty. The two defendants were either both guilty or both innocent—either Ruby or Coleman was telling the truth or was not—and if nothing else, Pierre Pettiford had flunked the lie detector test badly. Unfortunately polygraph results are inadmissible in a criminal trial, and the jury would never learn what Pierre Pettiford's body may have told of Pierre Pettiford's past.

There might be some other problems as well. As Shuker skimmed through the macabre photographs that had been taken at the scene, he noticed something unusual about two photographs of Gloria McDowell's body. They were almost identical shots in which her body was in the same position and the blood covered her face and head in the same patterns. In one picture, however, the iron pipe by her side rested on top of her stockings. In the second picture the pipe was partially covered by her stockings. Somebody had obviously moved the pipe. It didn't seem too important, but if the defense noticed it, they might be able to suggest that the police had handled the scene carelessly.

Mosrie and Kennedy, like Shuker, had dozens of other cases to work on, every case a homicide. No matter how many people they spoke with, nobody could establish any of the associations Shuker had suggested. They returned to 137 V Street in search of the landlord, who kept ignoring their messages to call. They finally found old Ennis Wilkins, a man without much in the way of memory and with nothing in the way of records or receipts. He just couldn't recall any dates, though he knew Ray Smith had once lived in the apartment Ruby Taylor had described, and it seemed to be around the time the police were asking about. The old man never did know what Smith's source of income was at the time. He let them into Smith's old room, and it fit Ruby's description.

Occasionally Mosrie and Kennedy dropped by the Carwash to see whether anything new had developed, whether anyone had recalled anything about Smith or Pettiford working there—to no avail. And for months Mosrie and Kennedy simply did not have enough time to speak with Ruby Taylor's stepmother, whose name had come up in the preliminary hearing, or with any of Ruby's relatives, who might know something about Raymond Smith.

And almost daily Irving Rosenberg's widow called to find out when the men who killed her husband were going to stand trial.

In mid-January, when the April trial date was set, all the lawyers met in Shuker's office to discuss informally the various defense requests for discovery. Shuker was bound by law to provide much of what was requested, and there would be no point consuming the court's time in argument over issues not in dispute.

Shuker agreed to allow defense inspection of all documents and physical objects that the Government might introduce at trial, all photographs that had been shown to any Government witness and all photographs that had been taken at the crime scene, results of all physical examinations and scientific tests, and all information in the Government's possession concerning the stolen money and credit cards—none of which had been used after the crimes. He agreed to inform the defense of the substance of all bargains that the Government had struck with Ruby Taylor: none. Although the Government would be obligated at trial, after the testimony of each of its witnesses, to provide the defense with copies of any written statements previously signed by that witness or simultaneously recorded, most of those statements would be provided a few days early so that the trial might proceed with a minimum of interruptions. And any information which could conceivably suggest the defendants' innocence or reduce the degree of their culpability would be provided forthwith to the defense, though Shuker was aware of none at present.

Several of the defense requests, however, would not be honored and would be submitted to the court for resolution. Shuker would not voluntarily provide written statements by people the Government did not intend to call as witnesses unless those statements were conceivably exculpatory —for when citizens talk to the police, they do not like the idea of their statements being unnecessarily circulated. Medical records of Ruby Taylor would not be disclosed until such time as the defense could demonstrate by medical testimony any possible effect her narcotics condition might have exerted on her capacity to perceive, recall, or relate relevant events accurately. And although the defense would be provided with the substance of any statements either defendant might have made to the police, the Government would not disclose whether either defendant had made statements to anybody else. The name or even the existence of Robert Coleman as a possible witness would be withheld for security reasons until the last allowable minute.

From the defense Shuker requested only what the law entitled him to receive: nothing.

The defense attorneys kept in regular contact with their clients. After Smith had been in jail five months awaiting trial, his lawyers filed an application for his release on bond. In the latter part of February, the elder Murray visited him at the jail to seek the names of more possible witnesses. By this time many relevant documents had been located and sent up from Durham, and Murray felt the defense was a strong one. But it was still important that the defendants not know how strong, that they not appear cocky at trial; and just to be certain that Smith would not appear to have fabricated an alibi, the Murrays finally decided that he would not be told what records they had found and what dates those records reflected of his whereabouts in Washington and Durham.

In the months he had been in jail, Smith had been picking up rumors which he related regularly to his lawyers. This time he told Murray that a friend of his had just been busted and had told Smith that Ruby Taylor was bragging to her crowd of having got Smith into trouble. Smith's friend had said Ruby was hustling for drugs, and when he had asked her to repay some money he had loaned her, she told everyone he was threatening to kill her. To Smith's friend, Ruby was acting like she was absolutely crazy.

While Murray and Smith were talking, Berman dropped by for a few moments. He wanted to investigate something Ruby had claimed at the preliminary hearing, and he learned from Smith the address of Ruby's stepmother.

Before Murray left, he explained to Smith that although the attorneys had decided not to prime him for trial by giving him specific dates, the records of the North Carolina Employment Security Commission did confirm the information contained on the card he had shown the police on the day of his arrest: Raymond Smith had definitely been there on December 12, two days after the murders, and on December 19. The defense had some other good information, information they would have to present to the court to get Smith released on bond pending trial, information which would thus be disclosed prematurely to the Government—allowing the Government enough time, possibly, to gather evidence in contradiction. Smith was delighted. So delighted, in fact, that he told Murray to forget about trying to get him out on bond.

A few days after seeing Smith, Berman and an investigator visited Ruby's stepmother on Lanier Place. They knocked on the door and explained their purpose and, reluctantly, Emma Roland invited them in. She told them she didn't consider herself "connected" in any way with Ruby Taylor because Ruby was a drug addict. Though she was often referred to as Ruby's stepmother, the only real relation, if you could call it that, was that Mrs. Roland had a child by Ruby's father.

She told the men some things about Ruby and Raymond. She remembered once going with Ruby for a hearing at the U.S. Attorney's Office when Ruby brought a complaint against him for beating her, but all that had happened was that the man told Raymond not to bother Ruby any more. She answered all of Berman's questions. Emma Roland was obviously not very articulate and could probably be cross-examined effectively by a skillful lawyer, but she did seem sure about the things she told Berman. He told her he'd keep in touch.

When he left her house, Berman thought Ruby Taylor's testimony would not stand up in court. And one thing surprised him: the police, knowing what Ruby had said at the preliminary hearing, had not yet bothered to check out Emma Roland.

By the end of February, arguments were scheduled for the disputed areas of the defense motions for discovery. On the day arguments were to be heard, the defense lawyers spoke again with their clients in the cell block behind the courtroom. Smith, who claimed not to have seen Ruby Taylor even once during 1968, suggested a way to prove at trial that she was lying about having seen him almost daily in November and December of that year. Sometime in the fall of '68, before going to Durham, Smith had had some hair woven into the bald spot on the back of his head. Though it hadn't held and the bald spot was now back, Ruby would know about his having had long hair if she'd been seeing him then. And since she hadn't been seeing him, said Smith, she couldn't know. The attorneys told him it was an interesting point. But when you are defending an accused murderer, you try not to ask interesting questions unless you're absolutely certain of the answers. And what if—just on an off-chance—Ruby Taylor happened to know all about the way Raymond Smith was wearing his hair just before the time of the murders?

The attorneys walked through the green door to the courtroom and met Shuker there, awaiting the judge's arrival. One last matter they requested of him: a chance to interview Ruby Taylor. Shuker told them he would produce her at some designated place in the courthouse one week before trial.

Then the judge came in, heard arguments on the pending motions, heard the extent of the discovery that the Government was willing to provide, and sustained each objection Shuker made to the defense requests that were still unsatisfied. The motion to order an examination of Ruby Taylor was also denied when the defense was unable to proffer medical testimony in support of the theory that Ruby's narcotics habit could affect her ability to perceive or recall past events accurately. After the hearing the lawyers adjourned to Shuker's office, where he gave the defense everything he had promised.

Two days later all the defense lawyers met at the Legal Aid Agency for their first formal conference in anticipation of trial. They discussed the witnesses who had been interviewed, the records that had been checked, the materials the Government had provided, and some documents that

90

had arrived from Durham. The dates on the documents were extremely helpful in establishing Smith's alibi, and Berman suggested they be reviewed with Smith even at this stage so that Smith would be thoroughly perpared for trial. But Smith was Fay's and the Murrays' client, and the Murrays had decided that Raymond Smith's alibi and testimony would be more credible if he did not have any precise dates. Fay had agreed, especially since Smith seemed to him to be something of a liar even if he was innocent of murder. Reluctantly Berman and Perazich agreed not to provide the information to Pettiford, in order to prevent Pettiford from communicating it to Smith.

Most criminal cases are disposed of when a defendant agrees to plead guilty to the indictment, or to counts within the indictment, or to lesser included charges. Even if he maintains his innocence, he is allowed to plead guilty if he acknowledges the overwhelming strength of the case against him—a strange kind of justice, but a rule that prevents, or at least postpones, a fatal overloading of the criminal justice system. Not one of the five attorneys representing Raymond Smith and Pierre Pettiford felt that copping a plea would be necessary; and the possibility of ending the case by negotiating some kind of guilty plea was never discussed, either with the prosecutor or the defendants.

There is a lot of killing in the District of Columbia. In parts of the city, everyone seems to have a gun, and kids on drugs walk with loaded revolvers into stores and shoot nervously and needlessly, and friends and spouses pick up butcher knives when their arguments get hot. Every time one person kills another, detectives from the homicide squad are immediately dispatched to the scene, must investigate and generally make an arrest, must prepare the case for indictment and assist the prosecutor to whom the case is then assigned in preparing the case more thoroughly for trial.

And each Assistant United States Attorney has more than one case to worry about. The thousands and thousands of criminal offenses that result in arrests are distributed among a small number of prosecutors. Each of them, like the police, is responsible for dozens and dozens of cases. When you are good, your cases are big.

Periodically Robert Shuker checked with Mosrie and Kennedy to learn whether any new developments, new leads, new witnesses had materialized. Nothing had.

A month before trial, he would be able seriously to prepare the case.

That would be time enough to meet Ruby Taylor and the second witness and to prepare them for trial. For now occasional checks with the police would have to do.

The defense investigation continued. They checked the court files and learned the full circumstances under which Ruby Taylor had come forward to the police: after an arrest for charges carrying a substantial minimum mandatory sentence, charges subsequently reduced and ultimately dismissed.

They measured times and distances. On a typical weekday at 5:00 P.M., Fay drove .95 miles from the Carwash to 137 V Street in exactly four and one-half minutes.

They spoke with all the people Pierre Pettiford could suggest concerning his activities for the months preceding the murders. They checked out Smith's Washington addresses and work record for the entire year of 1968. They tried as best they could to recreate the lives two men had lived in 1968.

They pored over their notes of Ruby Taylor's preliminary hearing testimony, outlining for investigation dozens of facts she had alleged. They visited and revisited the Carwash, learning everything they could about its practices, its employees, their habits and clothing and backgrounds. They heard a rumor that Lawrence Green, now in jail for killing his wife, had actually confessed to the Carwash killings; they sought to contact all the attorneys representing him in various proceedings to get permission to interview him. They talked with one of Green's relatives who, although disclaiming any first-hand knowledge, figured Green was the Carwash killer "because that's just the kind of thing Lawrence would do." They studied the results of the dozens of scientific test Shuker had given them and realized the Government had nothing concrete, nothing physical, nothing measurable to connect either defendant with the killings— though they were certain the Government was relying on something or someone besides Ruby Taylor. They spoke with several of Ruby Taylor's daughters to try to learn as much as they could about her.

Most of all they tried to locate Ruby Taylor, to get somebody to speak with her, to find out why she had accused Raymond Smith and Pierre Pettiford of crimes they denied—perhaps to hear her admit to somebody that she was sticking them with a bad rap, perhaps to have that somebody wired to record her confession. They checked regularly with D.C. General

Hospital and with the Women's Detention Center to see if she was there. Drug addicts represented by the Legal Aid Agency were asked to keep an eye out for her, perhaps at 14th and U, or 7th and O, or 7th and T. Fay himself would occasionally cruise by those corners in the early evening after work, looking for her. Friends of Smith were asked to seek her out. But she could not be found.

She kept calling in to Mosrie and Kennedy and telling them where she was and saying everything was still all right.

The defense attorneys interviewed and reinterviewed their clients. Occasionally they'd drop in to chat with Shuker, to try to learn whether the Government was really relying exclusively on Ruby Taylor to convict two men of a triple murder. But Shuker's answer never changed: they'd get a capital list three days before trial.

About six weeks before the trial, Shuker began preparing for the prosecution. There were dozens of other cases that needed at least his part-time attention, and several would go to trial before this one, but the Carwash case would now take precedence.

He reviewed as thoroughly as time allowed the hundreds of pages of homicide files, beginning with December 10, 1968. He subpoenaed copies of all conceivably relevant documents in Durham and Washington. He studied what the people in Durham had told Mosrie and Kennedy. He called the two detectives in for long discussions. Then he added up all the evidence and crystallized a theory of the truth: Raymond Smith had been in Washington until early October, 1968, had gone to Durham, worked there at the Holiday Inn, rented a car at Hertz, perhaps looked around for another job, and stayed in Durham until some time in November. At which time he nad returned to Washington, not to return to Durham until immediately after the murders. It looked to Shuker as if Raymond Smith had returned to Durham to establish an alibi.

Shuker finally learned the name of Robert Coleman. As he read through the homicide files, he noticed an interview summary prepared by one of the homicide detectives who had originally interviewed Coleman while Mosrie and Kennedy were in Durham. The summary of what Coleman had said then, at a time when Coleman was being extremely cautious about what he would divulge to the police, was somewhat inconsistent with what he had told the grand jury. The inconsistent police interview would have to be turned over to the defense.

93

Try as they might, Mosrie and Kennedy had been unable to locate any other witness who could honestly testify that Raymond Smith was in Washington in any of the last few months of 1968, or that he was seen with Pettiford or Ruby Taylor at any time in 1968, or that Smith or Pettiford was with Coleman at any time in 1968, or that Smith or Pettiford was seen at the Carwash any time in 1968.

As the time for trial grew near, Shuker began issuing subpoenas for records he still had not received and for prospective witnesses to appear for interviews: the important ones like Ruby Taylor, minor ones like the owner of the Carwash, the victims' relatives, all the police who had responded to the horror on the night of December 10, 1968.

The defense attorneys thought their case was exceptionally strong. The younger Murray even visited Smith in jail to suggest the possibility that by disclosing its case the defense might be able to persuade Shuker to drop the charges—though that would entail the risk of giving the Government time to try to combat the specifics of the defense. Smith said he'd rather wait in jail until trial than run that risk.

Rumors kept floating into the defense attorneys' offices. Someone named Robert Williams might have been the killer. E. L. Macklin might be, or Lawrence Green. As best they were able, the defense tried to locate those people and investigate their activities on December 10, 1968.

One rumor in particular struck Berman as important enough to mention to Shuker. Shuker passed it on to Detective Kennedy. Several days later Berman dropped by Shuker's office to see whether the rumor was true. While they were talking, Shuker's telephone rang. Detective Mosrie was on the line. Kennedy had just called Mosrie to confirm the rumor. Ruby Taylor had walked into a hospital a few days ago complaining of a stiff neck, headaches, and difficulty breathing. Fifteen hours and thirty minutes later, she had died. Her death resulted from massive infections that had circulated in her bloodstream, settling in her lungs and the lining of her heart. The infections could have been caused by an injection with a dirty needle or by a thousand other things. There was simply no way to know for sure.

That would be the reason Ruby Taylor had not responded a day ago to Shuker's subpoena.

The defense had thought for some time it could beat the Government's case. Now, viewing Ruby's death in a cold, practical light, there was no Government case they could see. Unless, as the younger Murray ventured offhandedly to Berman in the street one day, the Government as usual

94

came up with a man with pending drug charges who claimed to have heard the defendants discuss their murders.

Four days after learning of Ruby's death, Shuker walked down to the magistrate's hearing room to listen to the tape recording of her testimony at the preliminary hearing. A clerk handed him the tape and explained how to operate the machine. Shuker switched it on and listened for several minutes, but the words were muddied. He called in the clerk, who gave him another machine. The words were still unclear. The fault was in the tape and not the machine.

For four hours Shuker played the tape over and over to pick up every word he could. Ruby Taylor sounded like a magnificent witness as he listened to her voice for the first and only time, alone, in the small, silent room. To Shuker, the voice sounded like a sad, tired, sincere, and unavenging woman who was simply listening to some questions, thinking for a moment, and then answering as best she could remember.

Ruby's testimony obviously could not be followed during one quick listening. Shuker decided to order the tape transcribed by a court stenographer and to file a motion with the trial court to allow into evidence the transcript of Ruby Taylor's testimony. Admission of the transcript would obviously provide the defense with a strong appealable issue in the event of a conviction, but if you worry too much about the court of appeals, you never get there. With Ruby Taylor alive, the Government's case had not been overpowering; without her, it would be hopeless.

The tape of Ruby's testimony suggested other leads, which Shuker promptly pursued. He subpoenaed Emma Roland for an interview. When she arrived, the old woman had trouble understanding the questions asked her, didn't seem to recall anything too precisely, and wasn't really the kind of witness whose credibility the Government would want to vouch for. The old cab driver was subpoenaed, and various Carwash employees, and others among the hundreds of names listed in homicide files.

Shuker prepared a confidential memorandum for his superiors describing the crime, the accused criminals, and the case against them, and inquiring whether the Government would ask the jury to impose a sentence of death. The Government infrequently asks for capital punishment. In a few days Shuker received the answer: no.

After reading through all the Government's files on the case, Shuker filed a motion in open court. Although a multitude of loose hairs had been removed from the Carwash locker room and adjoining bathroom the night of the murders, nobody had bothered taking hair samples from Smith and

95

Pettiford for comparison. Shuker's motion requested that the court compel the defendants to submit to removal of hair samples.

Over opposition of the defense, the motion was granted. The law, while recognizing a man's privilege against self-incrimination, nevertheless allows "nontestimonial" or "noncommunicative" evidence to be taken from a defendant against his wishes—and hair samples, like blood samples or handwriting samples or fingerprints, are considered "nontestimonial." Though the distinction is sometimes made merely on the basis of the label applied, the real distinction behind the labels is the degree of intrusion upon a man's liberty. And snipping some hair, when weighed against society's interest in establishing innocence or guilt, is not considered unreasonably intrusive.

And so a few weeks before trial, Raymond Smith and Pierre Pettiford, hands cuffed in front and wearing prison blues, were escorted by marshals and Perazich to Shuker's office, where Detective Kennedy was waiting with a pair of scissors. Raymond Smith smiled as Kennedy snipped a few hairs off his head and his chest and combed some hairs out of his groin. Pettiford just stared out the window at the clear blue sky of an early spring. When it was his turn, he refused until Perazich told him to get it over with, and Kennedy quickly snipped and combed out some of his hairs. When the marshals escorted them away, Raymond Smith was still smiling, and Pierre Pettiford was talking and talking about how he was being framed and how he'd beat the charges anyway. Their hair samples were promptly sent to the F.B.I. for testing and comparisons.

And Shuker gave the police a date to bring in Robert Coleman.

Before the date set for Coleman's interview, Shuker decided to drive out with the police to the scene of the crime. On the way there one rainy afternoon, they passed by the address Coleman had earlier given as the place he'd gone to with Smith and Pettiford the night of the murders, 1337 1/2 U Street. The address didn't match Coleman's description, so they left the car and walked one block west to 1437 U. That was the place Coleman had described.

While Shuker and the detectives were getting back into their car at 14th and U, Berman and Perazich were at the Carwash speaking with Robert Gordon, the owner. They explained who they were, and Gordon allowed Ralph Jenkins—the man with Gloria McDowell's name tattooed on his arm—to show them around. Jenkins took them into the employees' locker room and bathroom, where heavy bloodstains still covered much of the walls and floor. As they walked through, Berman sketched the lay-out of the Carwash. They were talking with Gordon and an employee named Sonny Craig when a car pulled up in the front driveway, and Shuker, Mosrie, and Kennedy stepped out.

Gordon showed Shuker around. He showed him the rooms and some heavy iron pipes identical to the pipes removed as evidence on the night of the murders; he took him into the manager's office and pointed out the safe and the panel over the door and took him to see where the tip box had been broken open. He told him what fine workers Irving Rosenberg, Gloria McDowell, and John Weaver had been. And he asked why defend-ants always seem to get all the breaks in a criminal case.

Shuker tried talking with the employees as they worked. He showed them the knife that had been found on the locker room floor the night of the murders and asked whether anyone recognized it. But nobody knew a thing. He decided to show the employees pictures of the defendants to determine whether or not they knew anything about Smith and Pettiford. Showing photographs of defendants to prospective witnesses is a pro-cedure governed by precise rules. Other photographs of people bearing some resemblance to the suspect must also be shown, in a manner and order which does not suggest to the witness which photograph to identify; each witness must view the photographs outside the presence of other witnesses; and if the suspect has already been arrested, his lawyer must be present at the showing to ensure that it is properly conducted.

Shuker told Berman he intended to show some pictures to the em-ployees. The detectives had brought with them mug shots of both defend-ants as well as numerous other shots of other men. The lawyers and detectives crowded into Gordon's small office, and Shuker handed Berman the half-dozen mugshots. It was a fair sample.

Most of the workers didn't recognize—or claimed not to recognize—any of the photographs. Gordon pointed out two girls, one white and one black, who had worked at the Carwash longer than most. The white girl was called into the office, where Kennedy silently showed her the photo-graphs, one by one, and Shuker asked whether she recalled any of them as ever having worked at the Carwash. She pointed at one picture and said the man had worked in the pit and used to wear his sleeves rolled up. Did she recall when? Around the fall of '68. She pointed to another picture and said that man had worked there about the same time. Then she left.

The man in the first picture was Raymond Smith. The man in the second picture was Pierre Pettiford.

Shuker then called the black girl, and Kennedy showed her the same series of mugshots. Did she recall any of the men in the pictures ever working at the Carwash, asked Shuker. Yes, she said, this one, pointing. When? It was sometime around early October of '68, as best she could recall. She remembered the man because of a small incident. He had been vacuuming cars in the rear, and one day he cut himself on a cab and asked Irving Rosenberg for a Band-Aid, but Rosenberg said there was none around. She couldn't identify anyone else's face among the mugshots, and she left the office.

The man whose photograph she had identified was Pierre Pettiford.

The two girls' names were Sonny Craig and Edith Dean. They told Shuker they could recall none of the men's acquaintances. But they were quite positive about their identifications. Shuker would subpoena them for a more detailed conference in his office before trial, but now at least he knew he could present evidence that Raymond Smith and Pierre Pettiford had worked together at the Carwash in the latter part of 1968.

Even without Ruby's testimony the Government would still have something of a case. Two weeks before trial Shuker finally met Robert Coleman.

He came to Shuker's office in his street clothes: a colored tee-shirt, khaki pants, a small brimmed hat. His arms were large and muscled. Mosrie was in the office with Shuker: an experienced prosecutor always has another witness present during an interview.

Shuker would speak with Coleman almost daily from now until the trial began, and there was no need to grill him too thoroughly at this first meeting. Just talk a little, ask a few questions, try to get the man to trust the Government at least for this case, to tell the truth without worrying that he will be ignored when the case is over and the street learns that Robert Coleman became a stool. But make sure he knows that all you want is the truth.

Because what Coleman had to say was not very complicated, there was no compelling reason to take notes—notes which the Government, under the law, would be required to turn over to the defense when Coleman testified. So Shuker just asked his questions.

Why had he waited so long before giving his information to the police? Because Pettiford and Smith were sort of his acquaintances, said Coleman, and, quite frankly, there's really no reason to help out the police unless something is in it for Robert Coleman. Smith and Pettiford had never done him any harm—Coleman had, after all, known them well enough for them to discuss their crimes in his presence—and Coleman

98

didn't much like the thought of sending anyone to jail. He'd actually forgotten about the murders when he skipped town with his wife in January, 1969; when you are a street hustler, you know a lot about other people's robberies and killings, and there's nothing really so special about any particular one. He hadn't thought about it, Coleman told Shuker, until he saw Smith in jail after Coleman was picked up on the bench warrants, and Smith casually asked him once not to mention it. When Coleman learned Smith had already been charged with the triple murder he decided there might be something in it for him if he told the police what he knew.

What did Coleman think was in it for him? Well, he didn't expect his own charges would be dropped, but he did hope that he might be able to cop a plea to lesser charges and get away without serving time. The Government was not making any deals, Shuker told him. Did he still want to testify, and did he still claim his account was true? Robert Coleman answered yes to both questions, and there was just something about the way he talked and looked and listened that convinced Shuker that Robert Coleman, who always looked him straight in the eye, was telling the truth.

Shuker asked whether Coleman knew a woman by the name of Ruby Taylor. He didn't, but when Shuker showed her picture, Coleman recognized her as a prostitute he'd occasionally say hello to on the street. Coleman asked why Shuker wanted to know. No reason. No reason for Coleman to know that his statements corroborated what Ruby Taylor had said.

Shuker handed Coleman a transcript of his grand jury testimony to refresh any fuzziness in his recollection—sixteen months had elapsed since Coleman had overheard the conversation between Smith and Pettiford. Coleman sat back in his wooden chair, lit a cigarette, and read. Then he looked up at Shuker and said, "That's right." Shuker told him that was all for today, come back in two days for some more talk.

Just one more thing. Did Coleman know of anybody else who might know something about Smith and Pettiford pulling the Carwash job? No, said Coleman. Nobody he could think of.

Two days later, when Coleman came to Shuker's office again, the questions became somewhat more aggressive, more detailed. Coleman's answers were always consistent. For the first time since the police had originally spoken with Coleman eight months ago, Shuker suggested that he allow the Government to relocate him and his family, at least until the trial was over. But Coleman was unconcerned about his safety. He could take care of himself and, anyway, Smith and Pettiford didn't have any friends.

Did anybody know he would be a witness, Coleman asked. Not yet, but three days before trial Shuker would have to provide the defense with a list of all Government witnesses, and Coleman's name would have to be among them. When the trial began, Coleman agreed, he would allow the Government to move his family and himself to a hotel just outside Washington until the trial was over. He still didn't think it was necessary, but if that was what Shuker wanted, O.K.

Other witnesses were subpoenaed. Precinct officers Floyd and Jackson, who had been the first to respond to the Carwash and whose recollections of the scene needed refreshing, were reinterviewed. The families of the victims were interviewed, could contribute nothing, were asked whether they wished to be subpoenaed to trial, and said yes. The two girls from the Carwash visited Shuker's office together, and repeated what they'd said. But there are certain things you want to know about a witness who looks like Edith Dean before you put her on the stand in a murder case.

"Are you a lesbian?" Shuker asked her.

"Yes," she said.

There was no need to ask Sonny Craig that question. She needed persuasion even to identify herself as "Barbara" Craig when she testified, and not to get angry when called "ma'am." Nor was there any reason to instruct her, like the other witnesses, to dress a little specially for trial. Sonny could wear her Carwash uniform to court, her jacket and pants, if she wished.

Raymond Smith's family and friends and alibi witnesses would be arriving in Washington soon. The defense lawyers hadn't mentioned who they were, but from the police notes of their interviews in Durham, Shuker had a pretty good idea who they would be. There was no real need to speak with them before the trial. They were obviously friendly with Smith or his family, they'd already given their stories to Mosrie and Kennedy nearly eight months ago, and nothing they'd said could really help Smith or Pettiford very much. But when he learned that Raymond Smith's stepfather was in town, Shuker subpoenaed him in for an interview. The man seemed honest, and didn't seem to like Raymond very much. He really had very little to say that could be helpful to his stepson.

Most important was Robert Coleman. He was brought to Shuker's office almost daily by Mosrie and Kennedy for continued grilling. Shuker asked the toughest prosecutor in the office, an older man named Vic Caputy, to assist with Coleman's preparation by putting him through mock cross-examinations. When Caputy questioned, he'd shout and point at you and tell you you were lying if he thought you were, and you could never guess what a sweet old man he really was.

Coleman didn't like Caputy from the beginning. Caputy would press him to recall a fact, an exact time, precise denominations of money that nobody could possibly recall, and press and press until Coleman would give an answer, any answer, just to get off the topic. And then Caputy would scream that he was lying, and Coleman would scream back, "Nobody calls me a liar," and Caputy would point at him and shout about how all anyone wanted was the truth and that Coleman should tell only the truth, and if there was something he couldn't remember or wasn't too sure of, then that uncertainty was itself the truth and shouldn't be concealed. And Coleman would get indignant and tell him, "I wouldn't be going through with this if it wasn't the truth," and after a while he no longer had an easy answer for every question. And after a few days Coleman began to like "the tough old guy."

Coleman would never be brought to Shuker's office when other witnesses or lawyers were present. He would be kept in another, vacant room playing solitaire until everyone else was gone, and then be brought in for more questioning. The Government could not afford to let anything happen to Robert Coleman, for anyone—the defense, the witnesses, the defendants—to learn of his role. He showed some signs of beginning to trust the people he was dealing with, to trust the Government for the first time in his life. He began to understand the reasons for the constant grilling, and thought carefully before each answer. He began talking about some personal things, about not being able to get a good job, about having been a drug dealer, about being guilty of most of his pending charges. He informed Shuker that since his release on bond he'd been doing undercover work for the Justice Department's Bureau of Narcotics and Dangerous Drugs, though he hadn't yet testified in any of the drug cases he had helped make. Coleman didn't trust the BNDD, they'd been demanding he do too much. Shuker told Coleman his testimony in the Carwash trial would appear more credible if the jury learned that he was working for the BNDD and had been treated leniently following his arrest primarily because of his help in making drug cases. But when Coleman told Shuker that if that came out during the trial, he might be killed, Shuker told him he'd do his best to keep it out.

The defense investigation and preparation continued. Smith and Pettiford provided names of Carwash employees who might recall their working there in 1966 and how well they'd got along with everybody. The Legal Aid investigator sought out all the people mentioned. Some couldn't recall either man, some could vaguely, most were of no help. One man did recall working with Smith and Pettiford in late '66, and even recalled how they'd got along with everyone just fine and didn't seem to have any grudges against anyone. The name of that man was Bishop Blue.

The defense located Sonny Craig, but she refused to be interviewed. They spoke again at the Carwash with Edith Dean and learned that she, like everyone else who worked there, idolized Irving Rosenberg and zealously wanted a conviction. Irving Rosenberg would do you a favor, lend you some money, give you a ride, pay a doctor's bill, give your sick kid a little gift.

The defense lawyers were shown the Government file on Ruby Taylor's narcotics arrest. The prosecutor who had filed those charges had noted, "Defendant is an addict, marks all over her; defendant on probation to 8/1/69."

They learned that Ruby Taylor had been paid $20 every time she came to the courthouse for the Carwash case.

They filed motions and received authorization for traveling and housing funds for several witnesses from Durham. The Murray's had sent several of them letters shortly after speaking with them in Durham, recapping for them the substance of the statements they had made, to eliminate the need for any pretrial preparation beyond brief refreshers in the hallway before they testified in court.

The defense attorneys constructed their own theories of the murders.

The younger Murray thought it was an act by someone sexually sick, possibly one of the dozens of fags and lesbians employed by carwashes; that it was not simply a robbery but a depraved beating, a beating beyond death. Or maybe Ruby really had heard the Carwash robbery planned; but if she had, Pettiford had probably been the only one she'd heard—after all, he'd flunked the lie detector test—and she knew Pettiford knew Raymond Smith, and she hated Smith. But whatever the guilt or innocence of Pettiford, Raymond Smith was certainly innocent.

102

Perazich believed it was a sick act of vengeance; otherwise guns would have been used, without wasting the time to bash three skulls beyond recognition.

Berman thought that Ruby Taylor had not lied maliciously but had mixed some things up in her narcotics delirium. Smith had told his lawyers of living with Ruby in '66 at 137 V Street, of returning home one night covered with blood from a street fight, and of having a lot of money at the time. And he was also working for the Rinaldi Funeral Home at the time and occasionally drove their hearse. And Berman assumed from what he had learned about the defendants that "Cadillac" Smith had in fact been pulling some holdups. It was precisely because all those things were probably jumbled in Ruby's mind that the defense had requested that she be examined: because though Ruby Taylor might not be intentionally lying, she was wrong.

As a matter of strategy, however, the defense attorneys decided on a simple defense if Ruby's transcript was admitted. To present all the factors that Berman believed had been mixed kaleidoscopically in Ruby's mind would introduce facts of Smith's background detrimental to the defense. To show Ruby's real motive for accusing Smith—his beating her, his several women—might turn female jurors' sympathies against him. The Government's case seemed sufficiently weak, and the defense sufficiently strong, to allow a straightforward explanation for Ruby Taylor's story: she was simply a desperate junkie who would do anything to stay on the streets. So she had lied.

Shuker believed what Ruby Taylor had said. He had spent hours listening to Robert Coleman and knew how persuasively yet subtly he corroborated Ruby's testimony, testimony whose existence was unknown to Coleman. And although Ruby Taylor's sense of time was undoubtedly somewhat confused, everything she said was basically the truth.

The oral argument over the admissibility of the transcript of Ruby Taylor's preliminary hearing testimony lasted for an hour.

Shuker argued that Ruby had testified under oath; that she had been cross-examined at length on the same issues that would be presented at trial, by the same counsel who would represent Smith and Pettiford at trial; that her unavailability was due to no fault of the Government. To which the defense responded that she had not been cross-examined at the preliminary hearing at the same length, to the same degree, with the same aggressiveness, as she would have been at trial; that questioning at the preliminary hearing had been designed simply to learn rather than impeach what she claimed to know; that she had not been questioned about the facts subsequent investigation had revealed; and that the Government had compounded the prejudice by not allowing the defense to interview her.

Constitutional protections of men accused of crime are not, for the most part, a series of hard and fast rules prescribing courses of procedure for all conceivable contingencies. "The law" is an assortment of value judgments, a balancing of conflicting interests, a series of evaluations of paired benefits and risks, of ideals and their limitations by opposing ideals —it is essentially the ideal reconciliation of conflicting ideals, the practical resolution of ideal goals. And after motions and arguments and citations of authority, after hearing every value on both sides, after taking the matter under advisement and distilling those values into a final value judgment, the court was ready to rule.

The jury would hear the words Ruby Taylor had once spoken. The defense would be allowed to impeach her testimony by outlining her circumstances as of the time she had implicated Smith and Pettiford and how the Government had disposed of her charges.

The strategic victory Berman and Fay had achieved eight months earlier—persuading the District Court to reopen the preliminary hearing in order that Ruby Taylor might testify in person under oath—had backfired. Even before a jury was impaneled, the Government and defense would edit copies of the transcript, eliminating extraneous comments and questions to which objections had been sustained, and Ruby Taylor's testimony would be fully packaged and ready for a reading to the jury by an impartial third party.

Three days before trial, Shuker provided the defense with a list of the month's jury panel and a capital list. Because the law prohibits the Government from calling any witness not named on the list, except under special circumstances, the list contained names of many people who would never actually be called—31 names spread over three pages. The sixth name on the second page was Robert Coleman.

The younger Murray visited Smith in jail one last time before trial and reviewed all the names on the capital list. When they reached the sixth name on the second page, Murray asked whether he knew anyone by that name.

Smith thought for a moment. "Coleman, Coleman, Coleman," he murmured. Then: "Wait a minute. I know that dude. I knew him in jail, about six years ago."

104

Had he seen him since then, Murray asked. Only when Coleman had passed through the jail shortly after Smith's arrest in the Carwash case. Had Smith discussed the case with him? Never. Murray had a prediction for Smith: the Government had dredged up a dope dealer looking for a break and would have Coleman testify about overhearing an alleged conversation in which the defendants admit murdering someone.

"That's a lot of bullshit," said Raymond Smith.

Before leaving the jail, Murray told Smith the kinds of questions he'd be asked at trial, both by his own lawyers and by the Government. He asked Smith to recite again his recollection of his whereabouts during 1968, and Smith told Murray as best he could remember—gave dates and then asked, "Is that right?" Murray told him that if it's the truth, then it's right, and never mind about the exact dates we have on the documents. His lawyers believed they could prove that on the day that Irving Rosenberg, Gloria McDowell, and John Weaver were murdered, Raymond Smith had been in Durham, North Carolina. They had some evidence, Murray said, that even Smith didn't know about.

Pettiford's attorneys increased their contacts with him during the final days before trial, arranging for him to be brought to the cell block almost daily for conferences. To each conference Pettiford brought a manila envelope stuffed with papers: copies of motions his lawyers had filed and sent to him, copies of letters, administrative papers from jail.

Perazich asked whether he knew the name Robert Coleman. Vaguely, from the street, Pettiford answered. They'd also met in jail the last time Pettiford had served a sentence. He'd also seen him briefly in jail after being arrested for the Carwash murders, and Coleman had pumped questions at him. He had figured Coleman was a Government plant and had not, of course, said anything incriminating: he had nothing incriminating to say. Perazich warned him that Robert Coleman would probably come up with something.

Berman and Perazich put Pettiford through a practice cross-examination, asking him some of the questions that probably would be asked at trial. They thought Pettiford would make a good witness. His appearance was good, almost like a college student: thick glasses, a low quiet voice, and a memory of his activities sufficiently vague as to be virtually unimpeachable. If Pierre Pettiford could not honestly recall a fact, he was instructed, then simply say just that. But one question in particular he might very well be asked, perhaps by his own attorneys. He might be asked why, having been in jail for eight months, he was still unable to recall his whereabouts around the date of December 10, 1968—and what would he answer to that? "I'll answer that I don't remember," said Pettiford. It might be more effective, Berman suggested, if the answer were a little more elaborate. If and when the question arose, the answer was to be more like: I have tried and tried and tried to remember, every day since I've been in jail, but I just can't honestly recall.

They told Pettiford that above all he was to show no agitation during his own testimony or while listening to others testify. Then they left the cell block, and Pierre Pettiford was taken back to jail.

The defense dispatched two investigators to the address given on the capital list for Robert Coleman. They knocked. He opened the door. They told him who they were. He closed the door. Berman dropped by Shuker's office and asked about this name "Coleman" that had appeared on the capital list. Was the man expected to testify to some conversation he claimed to have overheard in the jail? Shuker told him the trial would begin in a couple of days. The defense would learn then what, if anything, Robert Coleman had to say about the Carwash case.

Seventeen months after the murders and eight months after the arrests, Raymond Smith and Pierre Pettiford were given a trial.

Rarely does a defense lawyer like the jury to see his client in prison clothes; Smith's and Pettiford's lawyers had called the defendants' friends and relatives to make sure civilian clothing was available when the trial began.

Pettiford's sister Yvette brought a dark green—almost black—suit, narrow tie, and white shirt for her brother to wear during trial. This morning and every morning of the trial, Pettiford would arrive in the cell block in his prison denims, change into his trial outfit, and at the end of the day, change back. The trial outfit would be left on a hanger strung from the wire mesh enclosing his cell block cage behind the courtroom.

Smith's girlfriend made a mistake and brought one of his favorite outfits: a black shirt with a long pointy collar, and a yellow jacket. Pettiford laughed when Smith put the shirt on in the cell block—made him look like a hoodlum, Pettiford said. Fay promised Smith a sports jacket and a clean white shirt and tie by tomorrow. For today Smith would have to wear the black shirt and look a little like a hoodlum. But because of something Ruby Taylor had said at the preliminary hearing, Fay told Smith not to bother wearing the yellow jacket in the jury's presence.

The lawyers stepped into the courtroom, the judge entered and walked up a few steps to her elevated seat, the defendants were brought out of the cell block in their trial clothing, and the case was officially called for trial.

Before the jury panel was summoned, several preliminary matters had to be discussed. The judge was informed by lawyers on both sides, and the court record would now reflect, that the Government and the defense had agreed upon several stipulations concerning the identity of the bodies about which the coroner would testify, certain documented records, the final resolution of criminal charges that had been pending against Ruby Taylor, and the editing of the transcript of her testimony.

The defense submitted a list of all materials received from the Government, to establish a record in the event they were convicted: if they subsequently discovered exculpatory evidence that had not been provided, they might be entitled to a new trial. They submitted to the court a list of proposed questions for the judge to ask the jury panel during the selection of the jury, most of which were granted. They requested that after the panel was asked whether anyone had read about the case, those members who responded affirmatively be asked to approach the bench before elaborating on their answers. They asked that the jury be instructed at the beginning of the case that Raymond Smith and Pierre Pettiford are presumed innocent. The judge ruled that that instruction would be given, with all other legal instructions to the jury, at the end of the case.

The Government had just a few requests before the jury panel was brought into the courtroom. Numerous photographs had been taken at the Carwash the night of the murders, Shuker stated, and handed them all to the judge. The Government, he said, did not want to inflame the jury's passions by offering them all into evidence but did request that one photograph—of an iron pipe lying near the bottom of Gloria McDowell's legs—be allowed in simply to show the precise location of the murder weapon at the time the bodies were discovered. The defense objected, but the judge ruled that the jury would be allowed to view that one photograph.

The Government also asked that the jury panel be allowed to view facial photographs of the three victims taken before their murders, to ensure that no member of the panel knew any of the victims. The request was granted. It was unlikely that anyone would recognize the people in the three photographs. But when you are prosecuting accused murderers, you try to make sure that the jury realizes that the men on trial are not the only people involved. You try to make sure they never forget that although you are sitting alone at the Government's table while live defend-

107

ants are seated with their attorneys, there are silent clients at your table, now dead. You want the jury to know that not only is the life of each defendant before them but the death of each victim.

The judge made two more rulings, as she was bound by law to do. The jury panel would see a photograph of Ruby Taylor to make sure none had known her. And the jury would not learn the extent of the criminal records of Raymond Smith or Pierre Pettiford. They would not learn, in fact, that either man had ever before been arrested.

CHAPTER FIVE

A t the conclusion of the preliminary matters, a group of seventy-eight people entered the courtroom and filed into most of the dozen long rows in the rear reserved for spectators. Facing them from fifty feet away was a robed woman judge, set starkly against the backdrop of the tall marble wall behind her. In the well of the courtroom—the main area separated from the rear pews by two low railings that met at a swinging wooden gate in the middle—were two long tables set lengthwise, each parallel to the jury box flush against the right wall. Seated around the long table to the left were seven men, five of them white. Their large table was cluttered with papers. Behind each of the two black men at the table sat another man with a badge flapped over a breast pocket. They were the marshals for each defendant — each marshal motionless, expressionless, staring straight ahead at the man in front of him. Seated at the end of the long table on the right, alone, was a white man with a lot of papers in front of him. The only sound in the courtroom was the shuffling of the jurors filing in. Then there was total quiet. The judge turned her thin half-smile toward the clerk in front of her, who rose and, in a voice that filled the courtroom, announced:

"Criminal Number 1805-69, United States of America versus Raymond Smith and Pierre Pettiford." The white men at counsel tables stood and announced to the court that each side was ready.

For the first time the jury panel heard Judge Green, who asked each lawyer to stand, and each defendant, and identified them by name. She asked the panel as a whole whether anyone knew any of the people so far introduced. No member of the panel responded.

This was the beginning of the *voir dire,* the examination of the prospective jurors in which they are called upon "to speak the truth." In a criminal trial, both sides are entitled to an impartial jury, able to decide

109

the case fairly and objectively and based only on the evidence presented in court, with no preferences or animosities toward either party, with no preconceptions of the defendant's guilt or innocence. If any juror examined during *voir dire* fails to satisfy these criteria, he may be challenged "for cause" by either side or the judge—that is, he will be excused from service on the case. There is no limit to the number of jurors who may be struck for cause. In addition, each side is allowed peremptory challenges, by virtue of which a juror may be struck without the striking party being required to state any reason whatsoever. A lawyer may peremptorily strike a man whose tie offends him. In a capital offense, the defense is allowed twenty peremptory challenges, the Government ten.

When a jury panel is questioned on *voir dire,* each response or non-response is noted by the lawyers. For the most part, it is a guessing game, even for an experienced trial lawyer. All you have is a list of the name, age, address, and occupation of each prospective juror. Beyond that they are all unknowns until the *voir dire* examination begins. Three days ago, the Government had served the defense with a list of each jury panelist's name and address, as provided by statute, but the defense had conducted no independent investigation into any panelist's background.

You can sometimes spot something about a juror simply by watching. Perhaps he is joking with a neighbor; you don't want him on a serious case. Perhaps he is a young Negro male carrying a black beret and wearing sunglasses. A prosecutor will not want him. Perhaps he is staring angrily—already—at the defendants. The defense will not want him. Perhaps he is carrying a book which reflects a particular bias about law enforcement, or about law and order. Perhaps anything. You can't be sure, so you watch carefully.

"In this case," the judge said, "the defendants are charged with committing felony-murder, first-degree murder, armed robbery, and robbery on December 10, 1968, at approximately between 5:00 P.M. and 7:00 P.M. at the Mr. Wash Carwash located at 616 Rhode Island Avenue, in Washington, D.C. Specifically the defendants are charged with a robbery while armed and murder of Irving Rosenberg, John Weaver, and Gloria McDowell with a pipe. Does any member of the panel have any information from whatever source of this alleged incident?"

The bludgeon murders of three human lives is an "alleged incident" because the Government has the burden of proving not only that the defendents were guilty of the crimes but that the crimes actually occurred.

110

The fact of the crimes would never be seriously disputed by the defense, but the defendants were entitled to every protection that the law allows.

Several jurors stood, to indicate they had read about the case.

Questioning a prospective juror in court who acknowledges having heard about the case out of court is a sensitive process. It can be handled in a number of ways. Each jury panelist, whether or not he acknowledges prior knowledge of the case, can be summoned individually into court or called individually to the judge's bench and interrogated by the judge and lawyers, out of earshot of the rest of the panel, regarding possible outside influences to which he may have been exposed. Or the panel as a whole can be asked whether anyone knows or has read or heard anything whatsoever about the case, and each juror who does admit to prior knowledge can approach the bench for a determination of his capacity to decide the case solely on the evidence he will be exposed to in court. Those are the slow ways of maximizing the possibility that the question of guilt or innocence will be decided on the basis of courtroom evidence only.

Or each juror acknowledging prior knowledge can be asked a series of questions in the presence of the rest of the panel. That is the speediest way to select a jury, but there are dangers. The questions asked can be too broad, or the answers broader than the questions, and the juror may admit knowing something which disqualifies him from sitting as a juror and may say what that something is, or may express an opinion which the rest of the panel should not be exposed to, and thus taint the rest of the panel.

Most of the jurors standing to acknowledge having read about the murders told the court they could nevertheless decide the case solely on the basis of the evidence to be presented. But a cog slipped when the judge asked a man named Albert Simmons whether he had formed an impression of the defendants' guilt or innocence because of newspaper articles he had read. The proper answer would be a simple no, he had not, or yes, he had. In the latter event, he would be asked to approach the bench, out of earshot of the rest of the panel, to state what his opinion was—whereupon, for having any opinion whatsoever, he would probably be challenged for cause. But Albert Simmons did not simply say yes or no. Instead, he said "I am afraid from reading the paper I formed an opinion of guilt." He had been candid and was immediately excluded from service on the case, but the collective mind of the jury now had an improper imprint: one among them had read about the case, perhaps knew some

111

facts that they would never learn for one reason or other, and thought the defendants were guilty. And everyone in the courtroom had heard it.

Defense counsel immediately asked for and were granted permission to approach the bench. They asked the judge to excuse the entire panel and swear in another one. Parazich told the judge: "My fear is he is conveying to the jury that he has an independent basis for forming an impression." But the pool of jurors for the month had already been depleted by this and other cases, and the motion was denied. It had not been a frivolous motion, however. If Smith and Pettiford were convicted, they had an automatic right to court-appointed attorneys for appeal, and the United States Court of Appeals for the District of Columbia Circuit guarded with special diligence all defendants' rights. The convictions—if there were to be convictions—could be overturned for a reason just like Albert Simmons' candid answer. Perhaps there was some way to minimize its impact. Shuker did not oppose the defense's renewed request to interrogate individually at the bench all jurors who acknowledged having heard or read about the case. The judge honored the request.

The process took time but was necessary. Seventeen more jurors approached the bench for whispered conferences with the judge and counsel after conceding they had read on earlier occasions about the case. Smith and Pettiford remained at their table with sheaves of their lawyers' papers.

At the bench the judge began the brief interrogation of each prospective juror, allowing all counsel to supplement her questions with any of their own. Most of the jurors who approached the bench, when asked to evaluate the possible effect public media reports may have had on their attitudes toward the defendants, were certain the articles or television stories they had seen or heard had not prejudiced them in any respect. Those who were not certain were dismissed from the panel. Through the series of bench conferences, the rest of the panel sat silently, staring sometimes at the bench, sometimes at their laps, sometimes at the walls, and sometimes at Raymond Smith and Pierre Pettiford. Neither defendant's seat faced the rear of the courtroom, toward the prospective jurors, and neither looked for more than an instant toward them.

Finally, no more jurors came forward to disclose having read about the case. The judge asked once more:

"Has anyone else in the group ever heard from any source at all anything about this alleged incident?"

No response. The lawyers returned to their tables.

112

"Ladies and gentlemen of the panel," the judge said to the prospective jurors remaining, "you should disregard the comment made by one of the jurors who spoke out in court." Albert Simmons's comment still weighed on the minds of everybody concerned with the possibility of injecting reversible error into the trial, and the judge was trying to erase whatever damage had already been done: "You will have to decide this case on the evidence brought out in court and not from any other source whatsoever, as I am sure you are aware." They were to forget having heard what they had heard.

The judge asked the jury panel a number of other questions, aimed not so much at isolating clearly ineligible jurors as at providing some information about the jurors which each side might like to know in exercising its peremptory strikes: Was any member of the panel a lawyer or related to one, or employed by a law enforcement body? Would anyone give more or less weight to a policeman's testimony simply because the testimony was a policeman's? Had anyone ever served on a grand jury? Had anyone ever had his car cleaned at the Mr. Wash Carwash? Several had: it is a very large place.

"Now to this question, if your answer is yes, please come forward again and line up in front of the box, if you would, please," said the judge. "Has any member of the panel or any member of your immediate family been the victim of any kind of crime, or have you ever been arrested for any kind of crime, or any member of your immediate family, or ever been a witness in a criminal case? If your answer is yes to any of those questions, please come forward."

The law provides that an indictment is not evidence, but is merely a charge used to bring a defendant into court for a determination of his guilt or innocence. A juror is not allowed to infer guilt from a defendant's mere presence in the courtroom; he is presumed innocent. But what the law tells a person to presume may be quite different from what he presumes in fact. So a defense attorney wants to know whether a prospective witness has ever been victimized in any manner that might dispose him toward vengeance against anybody accused of a crime. It is the same wariness of transferable vengeance that prompts a prosecutor's concern about prospective jurors who may themselves have been involved with the law, arrested justly or unjustly, treated fairly or unfairly, or in such a manner as to leave a sour taste and disinclination to accept the processes of government.

In Washington, D.C., many prospective jurors have been victimized

113

by crime, and many have been arrested. Sixteen prospective jurors paraded one by one to the bench to tell the judge and lawyers of their experiences with crime: of having been robbed, occasionally at gunpoint, or burglarized, or having had cars or wallets stolen, or having witnessed killings, or having a brother who once killed a man, or a son presently charged with robbery, or being the nephew of a man who had been murdered. Most stated the experience would not prejudice them one way or the other. Occasionally one of the jurors who came to the bench would be excused from service after admitting that his experience might predispose him against anyone accused of a violent crime. One old man walked slowly to the bench, said he was born in 1888 and was retired, said he had never been victimized, and walked slowly back down to his seat. The judge and lawyers looked at one another, silently.

A bench conference with individual jurors can sometimes be an effective vehicle for an attorney to establish a rapport, asking a pleasant question with a pleasant smile, just being nice. But for the most part, the questions were put by the judge. When no other jurors had any incidents to report, the judge again addressed the group. She announced the names of all prospective witnesses for both sides and asked whether any of them were known to any member of the panel.

Occasionally the witness would be in the courtroom and stand, the jurors would look in that direction and shake their heads negatively, and the names would go on. The jury panel was allowed to see photographs of four people they would not see alive in court: Ruby Taylor, Irving Rosenberg, Gloria McDowell, and John Weaver. Each juror looked at each photograph individually, lengthily, carefully, before passing it on. The courtroom was still as the photographs were passed from hand to hand, from row to row. Occasionally a juror holding the victims' pictures would look up at Smith and Pettiford.

Finally the judge came to the part of a first-degree murder case that holds most jurors' attention. She explained to the jury panel that first-degree murder was a capital offense, which meant that the jury might be called upon to decide not only the question of guilt or innocence but the question of punishment as well. Although the Government had already decided not to request capital punishment, that issue was still within the jury's province. And the defense had not bothered asking whether the Government would seek the death penalty. If the jury were to return a verdict of first-degree murder, they would then be required to decide

114

between alternative punishments: life imprisonment or death by electrocution. To impose either sentence, the jury's verdict on punishment would have to be unanimous. Otherwise that matter would be finally decided by the court. Thus, at the time each juror would be voting on the first issue—of guilt or innocence—he could not be sure that a vote of guilty might not eventually result in the imposition of capital punishment.

After explaining, Judge Green asked the panel members to stand if they were opposed to capital punishment on general principles. Seven people acknowledged opposition on religious or philosophical grounds. General opposition to capital punishment does not disqualify a prospective juror from sitting on a case. But if, because of that opposition, a juror does not believe he can fairly decide the issue of guilt or innocence —knowing that a vote of guilty might later result in the judge's imposing the death sentence—he may be dismissed from the panel for cause. Of the seven who opposed capital punishment, one prospective juror admitted that her opposition would prevent her from deciding fairly and impartially the question of guilt or innocence on the first-degree murder charges. She was excused for cause.

The judge asked one final question.

"Is there any reason whatsoever why any one of you would prefer not to sit on this case for whatever reason, or that you feel that you would not be able to decide it fairly?"

Sometimes that question will elicit frank requests to be excused from people who are afraid, or awed, or nervous about a murder case. Several jurors asked to be excused for personal reasons. One simply stated, "I just don't feel that I would prefer to sit on this jury if I am chosen." Those jurors were excused. Seventeen jurors had been struck for cause. The remaining sixty-one were still eligible for selection, but the hour was late and that process would take place tomorrow. Judge Green addressed the panel as she would address the jury daily until they returned with a verdict at the conclusion of the trial:

"Be very sure you do not read anything in the newspapers having to do with this case or listen to anything on radio or television. Don't discuss anything you have heard here with anyone else until you return, please."

Newspapermen were in court, and articles would certainly appear daily throughout the trial. But the jurors must remain isolated from any sources of information outside the courtroom. A newspaper or television

115

story can emphasize one side against another, or report information which had purposely been kept from the jury, or misinform. None of that is fit for a juror's eyes and ears.

At 10:30 the following morning, the jury panel returned to the courtroom and resumed their rows of seats in the rear. Their names were called at random until twelve had passed through the low swinging gates to the cushioned seats inside the jury box. In turn, Shuker and the five lawyers for the defense exercised their peremptory challenges, with Shuker eventually striking nine prospective jurors, and the defense seventeen. Each challenged juror left his seat in the jury box and returned to the crowd of waiting jurors seated in the rear of the courtroom, to be replaced by another. Finally both sides announced they were satisfied with the jury as constituted. They knew very little about the four men and eight women who would decide the guilt or innocence of Raymond Smith and Pierre Pettiford. They knew that most were black; that they averaged forty years of age; that among them were a vocational rehabilitation counselor, a gasoline salesman, a maid, a government budget analyst, two secretaries, two housewives, a boys club official, two government administrators, a laborer; that two opposed capital punishment, and one's brother was a policeman, and one had been a victim of a car theft, and one had been a Government witness in an unsuccessful robbery prosecution ten years ago. But that was all. Twelve unknown faces to try to read, isolated in that jury box.

Four alternate jurors were then called. They too would hear all the evidence but would not actually help decide the case unless any of the first twelve became unable to continue as a juror. They too were unknowns, except for the first alternate. Earlier that month he had sat on a jury that had returned a verdict of guilty as charged against a defendant indicted for five separate robberies. Shuker had prosecuted the case and remembered the juror.

All sixteen jurors were asked to stand. Each placed his left hand on a Bible and raised his right hand, and the courtroom clerk asked the group if they all swore to well and truly decide the case now pending, so help them God. The group mumbled and nodded affirmatively. "You may be seated," said the judge.

Immediately the elder Mr. Murray asked permission to approach the bench. Out of earshot of the jury, he asked the judge to instruct the jury, before any testimony was taken, that Smith and Pettiford were

116

presumed innocent. Procedurally, in most courts in the District of Columbia, only at the conclusion of all the evidence is a jury instructed concerning its own role, the presumption of innocence, different types of evidence, the elements of the crime, and related matters. In a way it is a curious habit, allowing the jury to absorb—or fail to absorb—various types of evidence and procedures without having learned the rules, presumptions, and prerequisites that are supposed to govern their consideration. Nevertheless, that is the procedure generally followed, and when Shuker objected to the judge's isolating this one of a large number of instructions which would be given at the end of the case, his objection was sustained. As the lawyers were about to withdraw from the podium in front of the judge's bench and return to counsel tables, however, Berman urged one reason peculiar to this case for the judge to change her mind.

"In light of the fact that during the *voir dire* one of the prospective panelists stood up in the presence of the entire panel and stated to the effect that he thought in his mind from reading the newspaper accounts that these men were guilty," Berman argued, "this particular instruction would be appropriate at this time." Shuker, still concerned with removing any prejudicial effect from Albert Simmons' casual observation, immediately withdrew his objection. If the judge instructed the jury as requested by the defense at this particular instant, he thought, the effect of Simmons' comment would be mitigated. The lawyers returned to their tables, and the judge, addressing the jury for the first time as a select group, told them the defendants were presumed to be innocent throughout the trial. The judge then invoked the rule on witnesses, excusing all witnesses on both sides from the courtroom and into the witness room down the corridor until it was their turn to testify. The trial was under way.

First the opening statements. Robert Shuker stood in the silent, crowded courtroom and turned to the jury. It was important that they be immediately impressed by the savagery of the crimes charged, that they always have that savagery in the back of their minds just in case any one of them thought for a moment that Raymond Smith or Pierre Pettiford might not be guilty.

"In this case, the grand jury charges," he began, speaking slowly, looking from juror to juror, and occasionally glancing deliberately down at the indictment he held, "in the first count, that on or about December 10, 1968, within the District of Columbia, Raymond Smith and Pierre Pettiford did kill Irving Rosenberg while perpetrating and attempting

117

to perpetrate the crime of robbery, as set forth in the seventh and eighth counts of this indictment.

"In the second count, the grand jury charges that on or about December 10, 1968, within the District of Columbia, Raymond Smith and Pierre Pettiford, purposely and with deliberate and premeditated malice, did strike Irving Rosenberg with a pipe, thereby causing injuries from which the said Irving Rosenberg did die on or about December 10, 1968."

Each word came out slowly, distinctly; each word was important, and as the words came out, carefully measured, juror number six, a young black woman, slunk lower in her seat and winced just a little. The indictment went on, Shuker reading it relentlessly, methodically, thoroughly, reading the legal language used to describe relentless, methodical, thorough murders. Each word was a hammerstroke. The courtroom remained silent as Shuker read through the end of the indictment.

"And in the seventh count of this indictment, the grand jury charges that on or about December 10, 1968, within the District of Columbia, Raymond Smith and Pierre Pettiford, while armed with a dangerous weapon, that is, a pipe, by force and violence and against resistance and by putting in fear, stole and took from the person and from the immediate actual possession of Irving Rosenberg, property of H and C Carwash, Inc., a body corporate, of the value of about $100, consisting of about $100 in money.

"In the eighth count of this indictment, the grand jury charges on or about December 10, 1968, within the District of Columbia, Raymond Smith and Pierre Pettiford, by force and violence and against resistance and by putting in fear, stole and took from the person and from the immediate and actual possession of Irving Rosenberg property of H and C Carwash, Inc., a body corporate, of the value of about $100, consisting of about $100 in money."

Shuker paused, placed the indictment on the table in front of him, and looked up at the jurors. Every one of them had been listening; every one of them was now looking at him.

That had been the legal language. Now, speaking without notes, he would tell them the facts he expected the evidence to prove. Witness by witness, he outlined for them specific facts they would hear about the Carwash, about the victims, about the police response, about the pipes and the causes of death and the stolen money. He outlined for them the substance of Ruby Taylor's testimony.

118

Although an opening statement provides the opportunity to present an overview to the jury of facts that will later be presented strand by strand, there are certain dangers. One among these is a rule of evidence that prohibits either side from introducing testimony or evidence that has not been referred to, at least tangentially, in the opening statement. But Shuker still did not want to disclose the substance of Robert Coleman's testimony. So he closed simply by telling the jury: "The Government expects that you will hear testimony corroborating the testimony of Mrs. Taylor." Shuker was finished, and sat down. It had been a restrained opening.

Shuker's fleeting reference to "corroboration" of Ruby Taylor's testimony did not pass unnoticed. The defense asked to approach the bench, where the elder Murray asked casually whether Shuker might elucidate. "I am as uninformed as the jury is as to the nature of the corroboration Mr. Shuker referred to," he whispered to the judge. "Is there anything you can tell me," he said, turning to Shuker, "which I might comment on in my opening statement?" Charles Murray had tried many cases, but so had Shuker. Specifics of the corroboration, he answered, would have to wait until the testimony. The bench conference was over and the lawyers filed down to their seats. Judge Green nodded in the direction of the defense table, and Murray, for Raymond Smith, stood and faced the jury.

The defense realized they would have to blunt the impact of Shuker's emphasis on the savagery of the murders. The best way to accomplish that would be to acknowledge the savagery and persuade the jury to consider only the question whether Smith and Pettiford were the men responsible. They would have to confine the jury's outrage to the crime rather than to the accused. Murray began:

"Ladies and gentlemen of the jury: Mr. Shuker did not describe to you and could not, with all of his ability, describe to you the horrible crimes that are charged in this indictment. The cold reading of an indictment could not picture the nature of these offenses. I think it appropriate to put you on notice that you will hear things that will revolt you to the innermost." However, he reminded them, "You are to presume these men innocent until otherwise proven beyond a reasonable doubt." He spoke then with notes, referring in detail to portions of Ruby Taylor's expected testimony that the defense would disprove, and referred sketchily to documentary evidence that would place Smith in Durham, North Carolina, during late fall and early winter of 1968.

119

When Murray sat down, Berman rose to deliver the opening statement for Pettiford. He was brief and to the point. He told the jury Pettiford's defense would be twofold. First: the jury would be shown what type of person Ruby Taylor was and her circumstances when she first accused Smith and Pettiford of the murders. And secondly: well, perhaps the jury might expect an affirmative defense, but Mr. Pettiford simply did not remember where in Washington he was on an inconsequential day nearly nine months before he was arrested. He did know, however, that he was not with Ruby Taylor, he was not with Raymond Smith, he was not at the Carwash, and he did not rob or kill anybody.

Berman sat down, and the court recessed for lunch. Shuker stopped by his office to tell his secretary to send a forthwith subpoena to the one Durham company Smith had mentioned at the time of his arrest which had never responded to subsequent subpoenas for records on Smith: The American Tobacco Company. In his opening statement Murray had mentioned documentary evidence that would exonerate Smith and Pettiford, and Shuker simply wanted to cover all the possibilities.

The Government called Lewis Banks, who had once, like dozens of Carwash employees, been a suspect himself. Through Banks, Shuker set part of the death scene. He was a good witness for what he had to say: direct, short answers, certain of his facts. Banks testified he had worked at the Carwash on December 10 and that at 5:05 P.M., when he left, Rosenberg and Weaver were in the rear of the Carwash, and Gloria was at the cash register in front. As Banks was leaving, a cab pulled up, and Banks waved it away because they were closing. He went home, leaving the three victims behind.

None of that testimony was directly damaging to Smith or Pettiford, and cross-examination was brief. The defense knew, however, much of what the Government's case would be, and preliminary foundations could be laid for impeachment of subsequent Government witnesses by asking questions of an inconsequential witness like Lewis Banks.

"Mr. Banks," Perazich began, "in the six months or so prior to December 10, 1968, when you were at the Carwash, did you have an opportunity to observe what color uniforms were worn by the employees of the Carwash?"

"I think it was blue," answered Banks.

"Now, to your knowledge, Mr. Banks, did you ever see any employee of the Carwash with a set of white coveralls on with red letters on the back?"

"Not to my knowledge."

Although the jury did not know it, the attack on Ruby Taylor had begun.

Phyllis Chotner, Rosenberg's niece, a short, slight woman with deep black hair, followed Banks to the witness stand. Again, she could paint only some of the background for the case; the main figures would come later. Mrs. Chotner's voice occasionally became inaudible, but at Shuker's sympathetic but persistent questioning, she testified that Rosenberg had dropped her off at work on the way to his own job at the Carwash the morning of December 10 and had promised to pick her up that evening. At 5:10 he had called to tell her to wait out front, he was leaving immediately. She had waited out front, and waited, and waited, but her uncle had not come. Finally she had called her aunt, Mrs. Rosenberg, several times. Mrs. Rosenberg had phoned the Carwash and got no response. The police had then been called. Shuker asked her one last question. "Did your uncle, Irving Rosenberg, ever pick you up that night?"

Phyllis Chotner looked at the microphone in front of her and spoke softly into it: "No, sir."

Before cross-examining a witness, a good trial lawyer evaluates aspects of the witness's personality and testimony. If the witness appears to have been fabricating on direct examination, cross-examination may be designed to demonstrate deliberate falsifications in his testimony, or contradictions between his testimony and another witness's. If the witness appears to have been honestly mistaken, cross-examination will be designed to demonstrate not willful fabrication but inadvertent error, or to establish other facts not elicited in the direct testimony, or to corroborate or discredit other witnesses. But if the witness has been honest, and his testimony has not been particularly damaging, and if the witness's uncle has been murdered, it might be best not to antagonize the jury by unnecessary probing, or, sometimes, by any probing at all.

None of the defense lawyers had any questions to ask Phyllis Chotner.

The rest of the background would be sketched by the police who had responded to the scene following the call from Irving Rosenberg's wife. Officer Floyd, the policeman who had first come upon the bodies, told the jury that shortly after seven that evening, he entered the unlocked front door of the Carwash, called out, walked through one side of the

121

Carwash, through the pit in the middle, and saw some corpses in the locker room and adjoining bathroom. He briefly described their positions and the very bloody iron pipe lying beside the body of Gloria McDowell, not far from a second, less bloodied pipe. Shuker showed him the photograph Judge Green had earlier ruled admissible and asked whether he could identify the scene it depicted. When Floyd told him the photograph fairly and accurately depicted the Carwash as he had first seen it on the night of the murders, the photograph was introduced into evidence, a highlight of the horror Floyd had described. Again Shuker had elicited the testimony only to set the stage. The names Smith and Pettiford had not yet been mentioned by any of the witnesses. Again the defense chose not to cross-examine.

More background. Shuker called Officer Donald Cherry to the stand, a young white policeman with a steady voice, a good witness. Cherry was assigned to the Mobile Crime Laboratory Unit of the Metropolitan Police Department. He had responded to the scene that Tuesday night in December and had walked through, diagraming the layout and items found inside. For trial Cherry had prepared a large chart of the Carwash itself, with markings showing the locations of the dead bodies. Again simply some background, just to ensure that the jury had an accurate picture of the scene. It was unexciting but necessary testimony with little protest or cross-examination from the defense beyond Perazich's objection to the officer's reference to "killings." "At this time," Perazich objected, "that is a conclusion, as to whether the killings took place." The objection was sustained.

Detective Edward Dezon replaced Cherry on the witness stand. Dezon was a precise man, light black, with a minutely trimmed moustache and a deep, clear voice. He had been the first homicide detective to arrive at the Carwash the night of the murders and had taken notes of the scene as he walked through. He testified from those notes of meeting Officer Floyd inside the Carwash; of being directed to the battered bodies of McDowell, Rosenberg, and Weaver; of the rooms in which those twisted bodies lay. His testimony was a detective's curious mix of cold, business-like reporting of brutal horror. He stepped off the stand and walked to the diagram Cherry had drawn.

"In the first room, where the single body is," he testified, pointing to the diagram, "this was a woman's body on the floor of the first room face down. There was hair and blood plastered on the north wall of this room. That would be the wall to your right as you look at the diagram."

122

He described her clothing in detail—the pink panties pulled down around the calf of the right leg, the black girdle, the half-removed white knit stockings, the suede coat, the boots.

"There was a long metal pipe," he continued, "laying near her right boot toe, extending north and toward her waist. A portion of this pipe was just laying across the edge of the clothing that she was wearing. There was what appeared to be blood on one-fourth of the pipe, nearest the toe, the lower end of the pipe. The woman had a laceration to the rear of the head and coagulated blood from under the mouth and nose."

Perazich interrupted the witness and asked to approach the bench. "Your Honor," he began, whispering an objection to Shuker's examination of Detective Dezon, "all the gory details is something we are trying to keep out. All it does is add, if you will, blood and gore which I feel is unnecessary." Perazich claimed Dezon's testimony could serve no purpose but to inflame the jury and thus prejudice them against Smith and Pettiford. Shuker disagreed, reminding the judge of Perazich's objection minutes earlier to Officer Donald Cherry's reference to "killings" having taken place in the Carwash. He argued, straight-faced, that the Government was merely proving that some murders had taken place, and where.

"Your objection is overruled," the judge told Perazich, and the lawyers returned to their seats.

Shuker instructed the witness to continue his description of the scene. Dezon described walking into the adjoining bathroom and seeing the two bodies. Again he read from his notes, coolly reciting what he had seen the night of December 10: the door, a pair of lady's gloves in the bathroom, two male bodies together on the floor. Again he referred to Cherry's diagram:

"To the left of the basin is the urinal and to the left of the urinal is the toilet. All of these were located on the north wall of this room. All of the objects and part of the wall is splattered with blood and human tissue. I observed the bodies of two men in this room on the floor. The first body, unidentified at this time, was that of a white male in a blue uniform with the name 'Irv' stitched on the uniform. He was lying on his back with the head in a northwesterly direction with his mouth open, and false teeth were scattered and broken on the floor. Also, blood and tissue all over his clothes. His head was battered in.

"There was a second man who was a Negro male lying to the left of the first man, also in a northerly direction. He was laying on his left

123

side. His body was doubled up, knees under the chest. The back of the head was battered in."

Dezon spoke calmly, looking now at Shuker, now at the diagram, now at the jury. He did not look at Smith or Pettiford. He was simply, unemotionally, telling the story of a night at his job.

Dezon had two other facts to tell the jury. Gloria McDowell's pocketbook containing $82 had not been taken though it was in plain view on the bathroom basin. And John Weaver's right rear pants pocket was bulging with an apparently untouched wallet containing about $240. Whoever had robbed and killed in the Carwash had apparently left in a hurry.

There was no cross-examination. By the end of the first day of testimony, the Government had proved, at least, that three people had been killed in the Carwash.

The first witness the following morning was the pathologist who had performed autopsies on the bodies of the three victims the night of their deaths. He entered the courtroom carrying under his arm the medical records concerning the deaths of Rosenberg, McDowell, and Weaver.

Dr. Marion Mann testified that Irving Rosenberg had received a deep stab wound — half a foot deep — in the back — so deep that the weapon had entered his left lung. The actual cause of death, however, had been "a severe comminuted, compound open skull fracture with laceration of the brain." Dr. Mann explained it more simply: "The type of skull fracture that we call comminuted means that the force was so great that it broke the bone into many fragments." Shuker made it even easier for the jury to understand.

"Doctor," he said, walking to the front of the Government's counsel table and picking up one heavy metal pipe, "'I show you now what is Government Exhibit Number 4, a pipe. I ask you to examine the end of that pipe, if you will." The doctor examined it without speaking. Were the wounds on Irving Rosenberg's skull consistent with the pipe marked Government Exhibit 4, Shuker asked. The pipe was big, and heavy. Eleven thread marks rimmed the end of the pipe. Yes, the doctor said, that pipe was consistent with Irving Rosenberg's wounds. And, asked Shuker, was the pipe consistent with the wounds accompanying the deaths of Gloria McDowell and John Weaver? Yes, said the doctor to each question.

Again, no cross-examination.

At about the time Dr. Mann was telling the court about the causes

124

of death, a nineteen-year-old girl in old cut-off blue jeans and a raggedy blue blouse was washing the breakfast dishes in a small kitchen on Lanier Place. Brenda Foster's boyfriend came in and pointed out two familiar names in the morning newspaper. Brenda Foster put down the dishrag and dialed the police. Within half an hour she was telling them how she knew that Ray Smith and Pierre Pettiford were guilty.

One other aspect of the background had to be drawn before the Government's case could shift the jury's attention from the killed to the killers. Obviously the jury would assume that physical evidence had been gathered from the scene and subjected to scientific analysis. None of that evidence implicated Smith or Pettiford, Shuker knew, and the jury was entitled to know that fact. If the Government did not produce the results of those examinations, the defense lawyers surely would. They had received copies of all scientific reports prepared by the Government in connection with the case and could be expected to make good use of them. Perhaps the impact of those tests could be blunted if the Government itself, rather than the defense, introduced them. That way the tests might appear to the jury more like nonevidence, suggesting neither guilt nor innocence, than like evidence affirmatively demonstrating Smith and Pettiford's innocence. Shuker decided the Government would present the facts to the jury.

It was long and tedious testimony presented by the police who had collected the items from the Carwash and the F.B.I. technical experts who had examined them. After several hours the jury learned that although the Carwash had been thoroughly dusted for fingerprints, the porous nature of most of the objects resulted in less than a dozen prints suitable for comparison; that only one of the usable prints had ever been matched positively with anyone—an employee named Lewis Banks; that the victims' nail clippings contained no hairs or fibers of significance; that a loose button found on the floor had probably been torn from John Weaver's shirt; that some loose hairs, mainly Negroid, were found on some of all three victims' clothing and throughout the locker room of the Carwash, but that unfortunately none of those hairs could be compared with the hair samples taken from Raymond Smith and Pierre Pettiford because the pigmentation of their hair, like that common to many Negroid hair samples, "is so dense that it is not possible to obtain a sufficient amount of transmitted light when viewing them microscopically to pick out the details that are necessary in order to make this type of comparison."

Certain of the items also contained blood: Weaver's fingernail clippings contained traces of type A human blood, as did a gray coat and Gloria McDowell's dickey and dress and Rosenberg's shoe and trousers and the work clothes under Gloria McDowell and the grossly bloodied pipe and the brush from the bathroom, and even the toilet seat. Other items had type O blood: Weaver's hat, coveralls from the bathroom. Several objects contained both types A and O blood: Rosenberg's jacket, a pair of socks, Weaver's jacket and pants. Other items contained blood which could not be typed: one of many boots, Gloria McDowell's slip and girdle and panties, another of Rosenberg's shoes, and Weaver's shoes and the knife and second pipe.

The jury was not really watching or listening as the technicians droned on. At the end Shuker had to ask, "Were any blood samples from Mrs. McDowell, Mr. Weaver, and Mr. Rosenberg ever delivered to you?"

"Yes."

"Were you able to type those samples?"

"No, sir."

"Why not?"

"They were putrefied."

"By putrefied, what do you mean?"

"Rotten, decomposed."

The testimony had not been helpful to the Government. None of those facts indicated that Smith and Pettiford were guilty. But that itself was a fact the jurors had a right to know, and now, if they had listened, they knew.

Cross-examination of the technicians was brief, but the defense's dual purposes could be accomplished briefly. First, they stressed that none of the usable fingerprints found at the Carwash matched the fingerprints of either Smith or Pettiford. Second, they suggested to the jury that the police had done a sloppy job. They showed that no hair samples had ever been taken from other employees at the Carwash to compare with the hairs found on the bodies of the victims. And they would not let the jury overlook the police bungling of the blood samples:

"Agent Silas," Berman asked the F.B.I. serologist, "do you have an opinion as to why the known blood samples of the three deceased were putrefied?"

"Only that it was from bacterial action of some type," the agent replied.

"And how," Berman asked, "would that occur—the handling, would that be a reason? The manner in which it is handled?"

"Well, that is rather broad," he answered. He paused. Then he said, "I—I suppose I would have to say yes, that it could be contaminated some way."

Police mishandling of potentially valuable evidence did not itself suggest the innocence of the men on trial. But when you defend in a criminal case, you try to make somebody other than your client the accused. You put another man on trial—or society, or the prosecutor, or the police—to divert the focus of the trial from the defendants themselves. Mishandling the blood samples was itself a generally negative aspect of the quality of police work in the case, police work which, after all, had eventually resulted in the arrests of Smith and Pettiford. Police mistakes in important areas might indicate they had made a mistake in arresting the men they had arrested. It did not, of course, make perfectly logical sense. But a juror is just a man, and the affairs of men do not always make perfectly logical sense.

The agents' testimony had been long, and by now several jurors were nodding inattentively. The judge declared a brief recess.

The first witness for the jury when they returned was Robert Gordon, the Carwash owner. He told them about his business.

"The carwash business is a very variable business. Some days you can wash a hundred cars and other days you can wash seven hundred or eight hundred cars, like on weekends. People who work in carwashes know about this, and if they want to get a day's work, they will come by the carwash and say, I want to work today, you know; and they will work for that day, and you won't see them again sometimes for two or three months when they will come back again and work a day."

Depending on the day, there might be one or two dozen workers scrubbing down the cars that slide through the pit. In a year there might be a couple hundred W-2 Form workers as well as a few hundred transients, men who would come and go, who would be paid at the end of the day, men whose names would be scribbled on a piece of paper in the morning and discarded in the late afternoon.

On December 10, 1968, business had not been good. It was cloudy, cars weren't coming in, and late in the afternoon Gordon had dropped by and told Irving Rosenberg to close up shop at 5:00. Later that evening he had returned, and the police were alredy there. In his office, the safe, whose combination was known only to Gordon and Irving Rosenberg, was open and empty. Missing were about $1,000 in cash, consisting of the

127

funds used to advance employees' pay, the day's receipts, and miscellaneous funds—plus any money remaining from the $807.15 payroll check Irving Rosenberg had cashed, according to his habit, to pay the workers a day early. Also missing was a green bag which generally contained some of the cash, and a white cloth bag which generally contained most of it.

On cross-examination Gordon described his part-time employees in more detail—transients, sometimes worked and sometimes didn't, no records kept, just a name to be written, paid, and forgotten all in one day—at least two hundred transients every year.

And their uniforms, donned and doffed in the locker room in which Gloria McDowell's body had been found—blue, one-piece coveralls, like jumpers.

Did any Carwash employees ever wear a white uniform, Perazich asked, white with red letters saying Mr. Wash Carwash?

"Not indicating Mr. Wash Carwash," Gordon answered. "Some men do use their own uniforms, and not all men wear a uniform. But no, the Mr. Wash Carwash uniforms were never white with red lettering."

Gordon left the stand.

In over a day of testimony, the jury had not heard the Government elicit from any witness the name Raymond Smith or the name Pierre Pettiford. Now, gradually, those names would lie at the heart of all testimony.

The Government called Miss Craig to the witness stand. She strode into the courtroom briskly, wearing the uniform jacket and pants of another carwash. When she spoke, her voice was tough, clipped, positive, assertive.

Her name, she said, was Barbara Craig. By Tuesday, December 10, 1968, she had worked at Mr. Wash Carwash for two years. Every Tuesday Irving Rosenberg would cash the payroll check to pay the workers a day in advance. On Tuesdays there would be a lot of money at the Carwash.

"Miss Craig," Shuker asked, "do you see anyone in the courtroom who you saw at any time working at the Carwash on Rhode Island Avenue in the year 1968?"

"Yes, I do." She pointed first at Raymond Smith and said, "The man sitting right there, the third man down the table with the checkered jacket on and the striped tie." Then she pointed at Pierre Pettiford and said, "The fifth man down in the dark tie and dark jacket."

Did she remember when in 1968 she had seen them working at the Carwash?

128

"Not the exact date," she said, "but about the season." And although she couldn't be sure, she recollected both men had worked there at about the same time. It hadn't been hot then, and it hadn't been cold. "Because the third man down"—again she pointed to Smith—"worked in the pit and he wore his sleeves rolled half the way up. And during that time it couldn't have been too cold because you had to still wear a jacket in the pit. Even though you had heaters on in the pit." It was around the end of summer, the change of seasons from summer to fall.

The younger Murray began the defense cross-examination. Had she worked at the Carwash in 1966? Yes. And did she remember Smith working there then? No, she said, she did not. Murray knew the Carwash records reflected that Smith had indeed worked there in 1966 and would later use them to prove it. Craig's having worked there at the same time as Smith in 1966 could explain her confusion about the year she remembered the defendants working with her at the Carwash.

How long had Smith worked there in 1968? She could not recall. Was it a matter of weeks, or months? A matter of weeks. She could not recall how long Pettiford had worked there in 1968. And when had she first told anybody about remembering Smith working at the Carwash in 1968? About two weeks ago. Almost one and a half years after the murders. Murray had no further questions.

Perazich rose to ask a few. Did she recall his client Pettiford being employed at the Carwash in 1966?

She couldn't recall. "I didn't associate with the men employees too much at that time because I really wasn't interested," she said. "I talked to the women employees and they are the only ones I knew." She didn't start making friends of the male employees until 1968. And in 1968, between summer and fall, the fifth man at the defense table—Pettiford—had been a vacuumer in the rear of the Carwash.

Then Perazich read her a string of names of employees who had worked at the Carwash in 1968, and she remembered only a few. Finally he explored with her the possibility that her feelings about the murders might be coloring her testimony. She admitted having been a good friend of Mr. Rosenberg, and being quite concerned at his death. But no, she had not been a close friend of Gloria McDowell and didn't know her personally.

"You didn't know anything about her personal life?" Perazich asked.

"No."

"She was an attractive girl, wasn't she, ma'am?"

"I would say so," Sonny Craig answered. "Yes."

When the cross-examination was over, Shuker asked the witness one last question: could she identify Carwash people more by their names or by their faces. "By their faces," she answered and left the witness stand.

She was followed there by Edith Dean, the other employee Shuker had met on his visit to the Carwash two weeks ago.

She too told the jury she had seen the fifth man at the defense table—Pettiford—working at the Carwash in 1968. She couldn't recall exactly when, but it was sometime after summer. Around October, as best she could recall. She remembered him because there had been an incident. He was a vacuum man in the rear of the Carwash, and one day he was vacuuming a cab and cut his finger. He came up to Irving Rosenberg and asked for a Band-Aid. And Irving Rosenberg had told him there was no Band-Aid around.

The younger Murray's cross-examination was brief.

"Miss Dean," he asked, "Are you and Miss Barbara Craig very close friends?"

"We were close friends," she said, "Yes."

"Do they sometimes call her 'Sonny'?"

"That is right."

"Did any other women ever go out with you all?" Murray asked.

"No."

Then it was Perazich's turn. Could she recall how long Pettiford had worked at the Carwash in 1968? No, she could not. Could she recall seeing him at the Carwash in 1966? No, she could not. And it had not been until about two weeks ago that she had first been shown a picture of Pettiford and had mentioned to the authorities that she remembered Pettiford's having worked at the Carwash in 1968.

"But I didn't need a picture," she added. "I knew him without his picture."

A luncheon recess was declared, and the crowded courtroom emptied. As he walked toward the elevator to return to his office one flight below, Shuker was called to the side by Irving Rosenberg's widow.

She'd forgotten to tell Shuker one thing all along, she whispered. For a short time in the fall of 1968—around the time Craig and Dean had just testified to seeing Smith and Pettiford working at the Carwash—Gloria McDowell had become ill, and Mrs. Rosenberg had taken over for a few days as cashier. And she now remembered, while listening in court to the two lesbians testify, that Smith and Pettiford had in fact worked there then.

130

Shuker listened without interrupting. When she was through, he told her he simply did not believe her, and the jury would not either, and he would not call her as a witness. Mrs. Rosenberg walked away, and Shuker stepped into the elevator.

When court resumed, there were some stipulations given to the jury. Both sides agreed that business records reflected that Smith and Pettiford had worked at the Carwash together during much of November and December, 1966, when Barbara Craig and Edith Dean had also worked there.

And the jury was told that the next Government witness had died a month and a half ago from "pulmonary infarction due to acute tricuspid insufficiency due to heroin addiction." Answers she had previously given under oath at a preliminary hearing would now be read to them by a court reporter. That was all the jury learned about Ruby Taylor. A white woman named Elaine Wells walked up to the witness stand with a transcript bound in blue covers, and Shuker stood at the end of his table with his copy of the transcript and read to her:

"Will you give us your name, please."

"Ruby Taylor," Elaine Wells read back to him.

"Now, Mrs. Taylor, I want to direct your attention to December 10, 1968—it was a Tuesday—and ask you whether or not on that day you had occasion to see anybody who is in this courtroom?"

"Yes."

"And whom did you see?"

"Pierre Pettiford and Raymond Smith."

"Do you see them in the courtroom now?"

"Yes, sir."

"Would you point to them for the record and tell us which one is which?"

"This is Pierre and this is Raymond." Elaine Wells, playing Ruby Taylor, did not point.

"Can you tell us approximately what time of day it was that you first saw them on December 10, 1968?"

"Well, it was in the early evening."

"And where did you see them?"

"At Raymond's house."

"Do you know where that is?"

"I think it's 67 V Street."

131

"Would you tell us what happened when you saw Mr. Smith and Mr. Pettiford at Mr. Smith's house in the early evening hours?"

"Well, just as I got there, Mr. Pettiford left to get some beer, and Mr. Smith and I had, you know, a little squabble about a personal problem. It wasn't anything, you know, important, as far as this case is concerned. Just something about, you know, him and myself."

"What happened after that?"

"Well, Mr. Pettiford left to get the beer, and while he was gone, me and Ray argued—and then—he called and told him someone wanted to see him. And I didn't see this man, I just heard his voice, you know, ask him was he ready. And he said yes. And by that time Mr. Pettiford I imagine should have been almost back, because he told me to look out the window and see if I saw him, and I did. And he told him to 'Come on, man, aren't you and that woman ever going to stop arguing? I got the heat.' "

"What did he mean when he said he got the heat?"

"Well, you know, the guns."

"Where was Mr. Pettiford when he said this?"

"Out back."

"All right. Now, what, if anything, was Mr. Smith carrying at this time?"

"Well, he had two little short jackets, I think they're windbreaker jackets, they're called, and one was yellow and one was blue, and some masks you wear when you're skiing, you know, that the eyes and the mouth are out but the rest is covered, and a pair of white coveralls with red writing on them."

"Where was the writing?"

"I think it was across the back."

"Can you remember what the writing said?"

"I can't be positive. I think it's 'Mr. Wash-Up' or 'Wash-It' or something similar to that."

"What happened after that?"

"He went on out, and put the lock on the door, and I laid across the bed and read some comics and pretty soon I went to sleep. And he woke me up when he came back in, I don't know how long, how much time."

"Who woke you up?"

"Mr. Smith. I don't know how much time had transpired between that, but when he came in he was all covered with—you know, had a lot of blood on him and some fresh gouges up in here somewhere, on his face. And I asked him how did he get all the blood, so he said he had to—well, he said

132

he had to slap a bitch, and I said, 'You don't get that much blood slapping anybody.' And he said, 'Well, if you had been slapped with what she was slapped with, you'd be full of blood, too.'"

"And then what happened?"

"Well, he asked me to clean his shoes, they had blood on them also. And I refused to do so, and in the meantime he was removing his shirt, and he had this cloth bag he kept close to him and I couldn't exactly see what was in it, but from—you know, it looked like it might have been money, but it had a little blood on it, too. He went in the bathroom, and I took some money out of his shirt pocket, what wasn't bloody I took out, and I left."

"Now, had you ever heard at any time prior to this any discussion about Mr. Carwash?"

"Yes, I had."

"Can you tell us approximately when you heard that discussion?"

"Well, I'd say it might have been about—I'll say roughly about three weeks, maybe."

"And can you tell us roughly what they were talking about?"

"Well, it seemed like they were passing the buck about—you know, about sticking the place up. One would say the other one didn't have enough heart or maybe vice versa and they would tell: 'Man, you're chicken, you're not going to do it.' You know, the conversation run something like that."

"Now, at any time did they refer to this place by name or address?"

"Well, I can't exactly say about the name or the address, you know, other than mentioning the streets."

"What street was that, ma'am?"

"Rhode Island Avenue."

"And what basis, if any, did you have for inferring that the place they were talking about was the Mr. Wash Carwash?"

"Mainly because they were arguing about the way that the tips were split. They were arguing about who got more than—you know, the other fellows, somebody didn't put enough in the cup, or something like that. And some girl didn't count it out right, she'd been cheating, or something, you know."

"Did there come a time when Mr. Smith spoke to you about what would happen to you if you went to the police?"

"Oh, Ray used to threaten me all the time about, you know, what he would do if—if he didn't get me, he would get one of my girls, and what he

133

could do if he did—you know—catch one of the kids. And one day he went so far and told me—came to my house and told me to come out, he said he had something to show me. Well, I was—you know, kind of shy of him anyway, but since my stepmother, she was home, I went out on the front porch and from there down on the street to this station wagon. It was white, I believe. And he said, 'This is how you'll be if you ever tell anything on me,' or something similar to that. And, it was a man back there, he was a white male, and he was dead."

"White—the station wagon had been what's commonly known as a hearse?"

"It wasn't made like that."

"When did this happen, about how long after December 10, 1968?"

"Couple of months, maybe a little better. I'm not exactly sure."

Shuker read, "I have no further questions," had nothing left to read, and sat down. All that was left of Ruby Taylor, all the jury could see, was a sheaf of bound papers, and a primly dressed court reporter blandly reading the words that once an unknown woman named Ruby Taylor had spoken under oath at a preliminary hearing.

Tom Fay stood and read the next series of questions to the woman playing Ruby Taylor.

"Mrs. Taylor, how long have you known Raymond Smith?"

"Oh, since 1966."

"And you've seen him constantly during that time?"

"I know him quite well. I know him as well as a wife would know her husband, just about."

"Have you seen him constantly over that time?"

"Well, quite often, I guess. Part of the time I lived with him."

"Were you living with him at the time of this offense?"

"No."

"You were never legally married to him, were you?"

"No, sir."

"Did you see him at all in the month of November, 1968?"

"Let me see, it's a little difficult to tell. Yeah. Yeah, I saw him in November, and I saw him in October. I'm trying to think of a month that I didn't see him in."

"When you say you 'saw him,' do you mean that you saw him on a regular basis or just saw him perhaps once or more?"

"I'll tell you, Ray had a habit of—he'd call me up, and I didn't want to

134

go out with him, or I didn't want to see him, make myself available, he'd come around the house, or call, and he'd have a number of little things to ask me, but he was making—fixed it so I would see him, if it was only a glance. And he would, you know, make himself available."

"Perhaps I should rephrase that question," Fay read. "Say, six weeks before this offense which is the subject of this proceeding, how many times did you see him?"

"Well, now, I couldn't exactly say. It's difficult to say, because I didn't keep a record of how often I saw him since—"

"Well, did you see him two or three times a week?"

"I saw him as often as every day. He came up that way a lot. I think he had some friends that lived back around about a block away from me, that he would take, I guess, that route home, and go by my house and maybe ring the doorbell, or he would call or something."

"And during this time he was living at 67 V Street, you say?"

"Yes."

"And was that where he returned on the date in question here?"

"Yes."

"Well, how did you happen to be present when you heard these plans being made? Did you overhear them in hiding, or was this planned in front of you?"

"No. It could be a case where I was in the next room. I didn't take notes as to what I was doing or where I was at that time. I wasn't concealed, if that's what you mean. I might have been doing something, I might have been reading, or—I'm not exactly sure what I was doing."

"Do you recall the approximate date when you heard this offense planned, the alleged offense?"

"No, I don't."

"Did you hear them talking about it more than once, or several times?"

"I would say at least three times."

"Was all this three times in one week, or over two or three weeks?"

"Over a period."

"Over a period of how long?"

"I'd say about maybe two weeks."

"And was this the two weeks preceding the offense?"

"Yes."

"And all during this time Mr. Smith was living at 67 V Street, is that correct?"

"To the best of my knowledge, that's where he was."

"Now, you stated that one of these people was wearing white coveralls—"

"No, I didn't say that."

"You didn't?"

"No."

"What clothes were Mr. Smith and Mr. Pettiford wearing?"

"Clothes is all I know. I didn't stop to see what color they were. I told you that they had a pair of coveralls, but I didn't say anything about he had them on."

"Oh. Where were the white coveralls?"

"In his hand."

"What did the white coveralls have written on them, if anything?"

"I think it had 'Mr. Washup' or 'Washing' in big letters."

"Now, when they left, what was their method of transportation?"

"I don't know."

"When they left, was there anyone with them?"

"Yes, it was a third party, but I didn't see him. I only heard him."

"Did at any time the police persuade you or influence you to testify as you've testified here?"

"No."

"What you've told us here is just what you know?"

"Yes, sir."

"Anyone promise you anything for testifying the way that you have?"

"No."

"Anyone promise to do you any favors in any way with reference to your testimony in this case?"

"No, sir."

"Mrs. Taylor, in the period within six weeks of this offense, were you taking narcotic drugs at that time?"

"No."

"On the date of these events, December the 10th, were you under the influence of any drinks, liquor or anything, at the time you say you saw them return with the blood on them and so forth?"

"No, sir."

"Do you recall the day of the week on which this offense took place?"

"It was Tuesday, December the 10th."

"Mrs. Taylor, do you recall any other events of that particular Tuesday?"

136

"I recall quite a few events of that particular Tuesday, but what really clinched it in my mind as to what had happened, by reading the daily tabloid the next day."

"You mentioned having an argument earlier that day with—with Mr. Smith—what time of day was that, approximately?"

"In the early evening."

"What do you mean by early evening? Two, three o'clock?"

"Well, in wintertime it gets dark early, so I'd say it was about—maybe about six, maybe. Maybe about six o'clock."

"Was it dark already?"

"Yes. In the winter it gets dark early."

"You're sure it wasn't closer to five? Do you recall looking at a clock at the time?"

"No, I don't. We didn't have a clock."

"Did you have a radio or television on?"

"No."

"You said you recall reading some comics?"

"Yeah, reading the comic notes."

"And you said you fell asleep? You now recall doing those things on Tuesday, December 10?"

"And another reason I remember it was a Tuesday, because I had some sewing to get out by Friday, and being locked in that room while he was going—he left the door locked—was holding me up, because I had to get it out, you know, by that weekend."

"Now, you stated that Mr. Smith and Mr. Pettiford returned with a bag. Was there anything written on the side of that bag?"

"I don't know."

"Did you see anything written on that bag?"

"I saw some black writing, but tell you exactly what it was, I couldn't do that."

"Did you ever see a green bag?"

"I said the bag was white."

"Well, on this date, when Mr. Smith and Mr. Pettiford returned, did either one of them have a green bag?"

"If they did I didn't see it."

"Did you ever state to Mr. Smith that you were going to get even with him for previous altercations?"

"No."

"Now, you said when Mr. Pettiford returned, he said he 'had the heat.' Did you ever see any weapons?"

"I don't think I said when he returned, sir. Read your notes again. That was before they left."

"Before they left, before you fell asleep?"

"Yes, sir."

"Did you ever see any guns?"

"Yes, I have."

"What type guns were they, as best you can describe?"

"Well, one of them was somewhat similar to the ones that the police officers carry now, like maybe you see on TV with the little short nose on it. And the other one was—with a long barrel, maybe like a Wyatt Earp type gun, something like that."

"And you saw these on the date of the offense? Had you ever seen them previously?"

"Yes, I had."

"Where had you see them previously?"

"Oh, maybe he'd be wiping it with kind of a greasy rag."

"You say 'he.' Who are you referring to?"

"Mr. Smith. And maybe on one or two occasions, Mr. Pettiford might have, you know, wiped it or something."

"You saw Mr. Pettiford with a gun?"

"Yes. At one time or another, and practicing a fast draw, something like that."

"Where were the guns kept?"

"I don't know."

"These times when you saw Mr. Smith or Mr. Pettiford handling the guns, were these occasions at 67 V Street?"

"They were at his home, yes."

"Did you see Mr. Smith often enough to know whether or not he was working at the Carwash at this time?"

"Yes, and I didn't have to see him to know that he—when he'd call me he told me, and he was always trying to borrow money, or to get me to borrow it from somebody for him, or crying about his rent was due, and he didn't have any money to get any food with, or something like that."

"Well, was he working or was he not working at the Carwash? I am not clear from your answer?"

"At this time I knew he was not working."

"He was not working?"

138

"No, sir."

"Had he ever worked at the Carwash?"

"Yes, sir. He had. He got fired, and I think they were away from there for about maybe two weeks. And then Pierre went back first, and then I think he must have talked to the people and then they let Ray come back to work."

"Both Pierre Pettiford and Raymond Smith both at one time had worked for this Carwash?"

"Yes, sir. Yes."

"This was in the summer of 1968? That they were working at the Carwash?"

"I couldn't say exactly for the whole summer. Just say a portion, maybe a portion."

"Now, 67 V Street, did Mr. Smith rent the whole premises there, or did he have an apartment?"

"He had a room."

"Where was the room located?"

"Second floor back."

"And were you in this room at the time you say you saw Mr. Pettiford returning with the guns, on the date in question?"

"I didn't tell you that Mr. Pettiford returned with the guns. I don't think I told you anything about the guns upon their return concerning Mr. Pettiford. I told you about Mr. Smith, how he was covered with blood. I was in his room when he returned."

"You said Mr. Pettiford went out, and came back; this was before the offense. Is that correct?"

"Yes. He went to the store to purchase some beer."

"Now, you stated that Mr. Smith came around and saw you after this offense, and threatened you? Is that correct?"

"Yes."

"He was driving a white station wagon?"

"Yes."

"And what did you say was in the station wagon?"

"A body of a dead man."

"Where was this in the car?"

"It was in the back, stretched out in the station wagon. See, it's only one place it could be, would be in the back stretched out."

"Are you telling the court that Mr. Smith was driving around with a body in the car?"

139

"I think that was his job at that time, to—you know, pick up."

"Did the white station wagon have any writing on the side of it to indicate it was connected with any operation or funeral parlor business, hospital, or D.C. Morgue, anything of this type?"

"Bernardo's."

"Bernardo's Funeral Parlor?"

"Yes, sir."

"Was this body in a casket or in a sack or anything of this sort?"

"It was covered—it wasn't in a casket, definitely, but I couldn't say it was in a sack. It was just straight, the legs were straight. I happened to just see the two feet and a portion of the legs. The upper part was all covered up with a blanket, so I couldn't tell whether it was encased in something or not, you know."

"How did you conclude this was a white male?"

"From the lower portion of the legs, perhaps from maybe midway of the leg down. It looked like to be a white man."

"I have no further questions," Fay read, and sat down.

Then Berman stood in front of the jury to read with Elaine Wells.

"Ma'am, this station wagon, did it have windows on the side, or only in the back?"

"It had—I think it had windows at the side, maybe with—I'm not certain whether it was curtains or maybe venetian blinds; I'm not too sure on that, because it is not every day that someone drives up and shows you a body in a car or station wagon. So, I can't recall."

"Was your vision into the rear of the station wagon obstructed by anything?"

"No. He opened a—I think he let one portion up and the other portion down, of the back."

"Opened up part of the station wagon for you to see?"

"Yes, sir."

"Do you recall what month this occurred in, that you saw this?"

"No, not offhand, I don't."

"Well, was it after Christmas?"

"Yes."

"Can you just give us a rough estimate of when this was?"

"I know it was after—it was after New Year's. But just to say exactly what month, or what week, I'll say—close as I can come to it would be maybe around—I'll say between February and maybe April."

"And this was 1969?"

140

"Yes."

"Can you describe what Mr. Smith was wearing?"

"No, I cannot."

"Do you recall what time of day this was?"

"It was—it was after lunchtime and before three o'clock, because my kids hadn't come home from school yet."

"Your stepmother was sitting on the porch at this time?"

"I said my mother was in the house, my stepmother."

"Did you discuss this incident with your stepmother right after it occurred?"

"Yes."

"Did she, to the best of your knowledge, observe the white station wagon?"

"Yes, she saw the station wagon, but she didn't come down in the street to look at the body. But she saw the station wagon, and she told Raymond to carry it back where he got it from."

"She talked to Mr. Smith that day?"

"Yes."

"Was she present at the time the alleged threats were made?"

"No, she would have not been able to hear, because we were on the sidewalk, and she was in the house."

"Now, you stated that on the 10th, Mr. Pettiford, sometime in the evening, around six o'clock, went out to get some beer, and this is when you had an argument with Raymond Smith. Had they been drinking prior to their leaving the V Street address?"

"Yes."

"What had they consumed?"

"Oh, it would be difficult to tell, since he had quite a few empty bottles and beer cans, so it's difficult to say exactly what they had consumed."

"Approximately how long had you been there then?"

"I think I'd been there about, maybe—I'll say roughly maybe—not quite a half hour."

"Were Mr. Pettiford or Mr. Smith drunk?"

"No, they weren't drunk, but it would be difficult if you were to judge it by voices, because at times Mr. Pettiford stammers anyway, but they weren't drunk, no. Perhaps maybe just feeling good, because they were just loud and laughing, but then Mr. Smith laughs a lot anyway, regardless of what he is drinking."

141

"Was there any difficulty on their part in walking, or were they unsteady on their feet?"

"No, sir."

"When Mr. Pettiford left to get some beer, were there any discussions as to where he was to go to purchase the beer?"

"No, but it's two stores, one facing the house and one right behind the house, and I assumed he went to the one behind the house. If you live in the area, you know one is a little cheaper than the other."

"Now, what time did Mr. Pettiford return with the beer? Was it five or ten or fifteen minutes, that he came back?"

"Oh, very swift; I mean he didn't take very long. So, I'd say maybe five minutes, ten minutes, something like that."

"Was there a third party present at this time, or did you just hear his voice?"

"I just heard his voice and no more."

"Did Mr. Pettiford come back with any beer?"

"I assumed that was what he had in a paper bag."

"Did you ever observe them taking anything outside of the paper bag?"

"Not at that time, no."

"Did Mr. Pettiford ever come back into the room again?"

"Just to the door."

"Now, was it at this time when you heard this third voice speaking?"

"Oh, let me see. I don't know whether it was before he went to the door or after; anyway, he didn't come in. He was waiting apparently on the outside, or either he could have been waiting down in the lower hall. I don't know which."

"At the time that Mr. Smith returned with the bag with the blood on it, was Mr. Pettiford with him?"

"No, sir."

"Was anybody else with him at this time?"

"No, he came in the room all alone."

"Did you overhear anyone else talking in another room at this time?"

"No."

"So at this time, Mr. Pettiford was not at 67 V Street?"

"No, not on the premises, no."

"Did you at this time observe Mr. Smith with a ski mask?"

"I didn't see any of those items that they left with. Just the bag with the—you know—"

"Just the white bag?"

"Yes."

"At that time did you not hear or see Mr. Pettiford?"

"Yes, I heard him, but to tell you who he was talking to, I couldn't say positive, because—"

"But after you woke up you heard Mr. Pettiford?"

"Yeah."

"Well, when you heard him, could you tell from hearing where he was?"

"Oh, he was—I'll say he was from—maybe passing from back of Ray's house, possibly, or was in his house, because you could see his house from Ray's window."

"Did you see him at any time after Mr. Smith came back, when you testified about the bag, the white bag?"

"No, sir."

"How many previous times have you heard Mr. Pettiford's voice?"

"Many times."

"And you're sure it was Mr. Pettiford's voice that you heard at that time?"

"Yes, sir."

"Did Mr. Smith ever say anything to Mr. Pettiford after he'd come back into the room with the bag?"

"Ray yelled something to Pete, but exactly—"

"Pete? Who is Pete?"

"Pierre. Words were said, but I couldn't say exactly what it was."

"But you heard Raymond Smith call out to Pierre?"

"Yes, that's the way it was, but I don't want to say anything, because I'm not certain; I do know he called out to him."

"What is your best recollection of what was said?"

" 'Put it in its usual place,' or 'put them in their usual place,' or 'put it away,' or—anyway, it had something to do with putting something away. Just what it was, I don't know."

"When Mr. Smith came back, with the blood on him, did you observe a gun?"

"No."

"Was there blood on his hands?"

"To the best of my knowledge, I think he had blood on his hands. But he had blood—I'll just say blood all over. Just looking at him, it would be strange that he wouldn't have any on his hands, and in so many other places."

143

"You don't actually recall?"

"No, sir."

"When he returned, was he wearing one of the jackets that he had left with?"

"No."

"Well, from that time to today, have you seen that jacket?"

"No."

"Did you ever see Mr. Pettiford with any blood on him?"

"No."

"Did Mr. Smith, when he returned, make any statements to the effect that he had gone to the Carwash?"

"No, he didn't say that he had been to the Carwash. He told me that he had slapped a girl, so I said that 'You don't get all that blood just slapping somebody.' And he said, 'Well, if you had been slapped with what she was slapped with, you'd be bloody, too.' "

"Now, ma'am, you stated that Mr. Smith locked the door as he left. Was this locked from the inside or from the outside?"

"The outside."

"And you could not get out the door?"

"No, sir."

"Do you recall what time Mr. Smith returned?"

"No."

"At that time did you own a wristwatch?"

"Yes, but I didn't have it on."

"Can you make a rough estimate as to how long you were asleep?"

"No, I can't."

"Can you tell us how many comic books you read before falling asleep?"

"I don't think he had over two or three."

"And did you fall asleep right after reading these comic books?"

"I don't know, sir. I might have fell asleep on the last page, but I had finished two of them."

"On direct examination, you testified that when Mr. Smith came back, with blood all over him, he had a gouge above the lip. Do you know if on December 10, 11, or 12, any of those days, he ever went to a doctor or any hospital as a result of that gouge?"

"I wouldn't know. I don't think it was bad enough to require a doctor, unless it might have been a little tiny kid that would be afraid of the blood or something."

144

"Is the reason that you don't know because you weren't with him on the 10th, 11th, or 12th?"

"I wasn't with him on the 11th or 12th."

"O.K. Did you talk to him on the 11th or 12th about his going to a doctor?"

"No, I did not."

"Did you talk to him on those dates about anything else?"

"No, I didn't."

"Did you see him on those dates?"

"No, I didn't."

"When was the next time after December 10 that you saw Raymond Smith?"

"I couldn't say offhand."

"Well, was it within a matter of days, or weeks? Was it before January 1st?"

"It's difficult to say, because he—I didn't see him, but he called. He called me several times—many times."

"Did you see him before Christmas?"

"No, sir."

"Well, did you talk with him before Christmas?"

"Yes, I talked to him before Christmas. Only briefly."

"Do you recall how many times, roughly?"

"No, I don't."

"Could it have been more than five?"

"It's difficult to say. He was making a nuisance of himself; it's down on the records, the police records, that he was. I mean he—he just kept calling, and I was trying to—my stepmother was trying to get him to stop calling. Maybe two or three days we wouldn't hear anything from him. Then about three o'clock in the morning the phone would ring and it would be him."

"And this was every two or three days?"

"I mean, I just couldn't say whether every two or three, to be exact about it. I mean, he'd—you know, call quite frequently, and then he would stop for a while and then start again."

"So then you are certain that from December 10 to—let's just use the cut-off date January 1—that he called you roughly at the very most every three or four days?"

"Yes."

"And did you talk to him at these times?"

145

"Not all the time. If I answered the phone, I would—but all the time I didn't answer the phone."

"You didn't answer the phone?"

"No. Sometimes my stepmother or my sister might answer it. Or one of my kids."

"Ma'am, you said that you heard discussions some three weeks prior to December 10 about sticking up some place. Did they actually mention Mr. Wash Carwash?"

"Didn't mention it by name, no."

"You said they just mentioned Rhode Island Avenue, is that correct?"

"Yes."

"Do you recall where you were at the time you overheard these conversations?"

"At Mr. Smith's house."

"Who was present at the time that you overheard this?"

"Mr. Smith, Mr. Pettiford, and myself."

"Was anyone else present other than the people you've named?"

"No, sir."

"Were these conversations at night or during the day?"

"At night."

"Is there any way that you can best estimate exactly when they were?"

"No. I can recall that they were in the latter part of the season."

"The 'latter part of the season,' meaning—?"

"It was in November, but as for the date, I can't be sure."

"You also testified on direct examination that Mr. Smith asked you to clean his shoes. Have you seen those shoes since December 10?"

"I told you I hadn't seen any of those garments or anything pertaining to that date since."

"You said that he took off his shirt. Do you recall what the color of that shirt was?"

"Oh, let me see; I think it was—maybe it might have been a gray, or faded."

"Was this a long-sleeve or short-sleeve shirt?"

"Long-sleeve."

"Were there two pockets or one pocket?"

"It's two pockets."

"And was the money—"

"I don't know which pocket."

"All right. How much money did you take out of the pocket?"

146

"About forty-some dollars. I don't remember the exact amount, but I know it was over forty and less than fifty."

"What denominations? Were they tens, fives, ones?"

"I think I had one twenty, and a ten, and a five, or two fives. I can be sure about the twenty and the ten."

"Do you recall seeing a lot of singles?"

"Like I said, I didn't count it. And I had taken a few ones myself, that didn't have blood on them. I know there wasn't too many."

"Ma'am, on direct examination, you stated that you heard them talking, or arguing, about the way tips were split, and some girl being pointed out that she cheated. Did they mention any girl's name, specifically?"

"It might have been they did, but I don't—I couldn't say offhand what the name was."

"When Mr. Smith returned, carrying the white bag with the blood on it, was he wearing the same clothing that he had left in that night?"

"Yes."

"Now, at that time, did Mr. Smith know where you lived?"

"Yes, sir."

"Were you ever shown pictures of Pettiford and Smith by Officer Mosrie?"

"Yes."

"And did you identify these pictures as either of these two?"

"Yes, I did."

That was the end of Ruby Taylor's transcript, and Elaine Wells left the witness stand. To assist the jury in evaluating Ruby Taylor's credibility, Perazich then read to them a stipulation agreed upon by the Government and the defense: that on July 15, 1969, Ruby Taylor had been arrested and charged with a felony for which she would have received a mandatory five-year sentence if convicted; that at the time of her arrest she was using heroin five or six times a day, and was in acute withdrawal; that within a week of her arrest she implicated Smith and Pettiford in the Carwash case, and two days later the felony charge was dismissed and replaced by two misdemeanors; that the following day she testified before the grand jury in connection with the Carwash case and was released on personal bond. Subsequently the misdemeanors had been dismissed, and an attachment previously issued in connection with Ruby Taylor's probation had been withdrawn.

With Ruby Taylor's testimony over, Shuker was ready to disclose, at last, the nature of the corroboration to which he had vaguely but pointedly referred during his opening statement. He approached the bench with defense counsel to announce that the Government's next witness would be Robert Coleman and that, pursuant to its obligation, the Government would now provide copies of Coleman's criminal record to the defense.

Perazich asked the judge to allow examination of Coleman outside the presence of the jury before allowing him to testify. There might, he argued, be testimony Coleman would give which would be inadmissible, and all such questions should be resolved before the jury became inadvertently exposed to inadmissible evidence.

In fact, ordering Coleman to testify initially out of the jury's presence would serve other defense purposes as well. With the exception of his grand jury testimony and sketchy notes made by the detective who had first interviewed him in jail, Coleman's statements had never been reduced to writing; nor had he ever spoken with any defense investigators. The more statements a witness has given, the more likely he is to be inconsistent when he finally testifies before the jury, and the easier the job of impeaching his credibility—whether or not he is telling the truth. Shuker realized the collateral consequences of having Coleman testify outside the jury's hearing, and avoided these consequences by stating to the judge and counsel the substance of what Coleman would say. It was the first time they learned the substance of Robert Coleman's testimony, and everything would be admissible. Then, of course, the jury would decide whether to accept it or reject it.

The third day of trial was almost over, and the defense made one last attempt to get further information from or about Robert Coleman. At the bench Berman asked Shuker to agree to allow the defense to speak with Coleman in Shuker's office one flight below the courtroom that afternoon. Shuker, under the law, could not instruct Coleman to speak with them, or not to speak with them. He could only explain to Coleman that the choice was his, and make his office available for whatever questions Coleman chose to answer.

This Shuker agreed to do. Before the lawyers left their whispered conference at the bench, however, the judge had something to tell them all.

"Since everybody is at the bench at this point," she said, "I don't want to read about this in the paper tomorrow, from anybody—from whatever

148

source. We assume it is heard right here only. And I don't wish to see that this man's name is brought forth in tomorrow morning's newspaper." And one more thing she wanted Shuker to ensure: that Robert Coleman be provided protective custody overnight. Nobody disagreed.

Other technical issues remained concerning the proposed testimony of Robert Coleman, issues best argued outside the presence of the jury and the public. Counsel would assemble tomorrow morning in the chambers of Judge Green before testimony began.

The jury was dismissed for the evening.

There were a couple of meetings held in Shuker's office late that afternoon when court recessed. First, Coleman and the lawyers for the defense entered and sat down by themselves. It was a short meeting. Coleman said he would really rather not talk about the case with them.

And when the defense lawyers left and Coleman walked away in the company of a detective, Shuker entered and picked up his telephone messages. Brenda Foster, Ruby Taylor's daughter, had called. She had already given a statement to the police. Shuker dialed her number and told her to be at his office early the next morning.

At which time Shuker met a tall, tan, pretty girl, neatly dressed, who was introduced by the policeman with her as Brenda Foster. Then Brenda told Shuker about her mother, Ruby Taylor, and her mother's ex-boyfriend Ray Smith.

She told him Ruby first met Ray Smith in the spring of 1966, when he moved in with Brenda and her mother in their place on Wyoming Avenue. Brenda didn't much like the bully who cuffed her around whenever he pleased and used to beat Ruby pretty often—with his hands, with his fists, with a chair, a table, anything he could get his hands on. And she also knew his friend Pete Pettiford from the meetings Pettiford, Smith, and a third guy used to have in the Wyoming Avenue apartment when they'd plan the dozens and dozens of holdups they would pull. Brenda would be listening from the bedroom. Most of the time Ruby'd just be sitting and reading or knitting while they did their talking. Only sometimes Ruby would butt in, like when she once told them that if they went ahead and robbed the carwash they worked at, they'd be recognized and caught.

But that had been on Wyoming Avenue in 1966, over two years before the triple murder, and Shuker considered such testimony inadmissibly remote. Anyway that was not why he had told the police to drive Brenda Foster to his office early in the morning on the fourth day of trial. Time was short, and he got her to the point.

Brenda Foster could not be sure of dates in the abstract but used her two little girls as calendars. When her younger daughter was a month and a week old, she said—which would be toward the latter part of July, 1969 —Brenda had a strange meeting with Smith. He came up to her in front of a discount store in downtown Washington and asked where Ruby was. Ruby was back on her habit at the time, and Brenda Foster didn't know the answer. Then Ray said something very strange that Brenda couldn't understand. He said, "You tell your momma that if she knows what I know, she will keep her mouth shut." And then he walked away.

Brenda did not really know what it all meant, she told Shuker, until that Christmas, when she saw her mother for the first time in half a year. Ruby was at the hospital at the time, in pretty bad shape because of drugs. One of the things they talked about was Raymond Smith's comment to Brenda on the street. Ruby explained to Brenda about Smith and Pettiford leaving to rob the Carwash, and Smith coming back covered with blood, and Ruby taking a little of the money. But because of Ruby's condition, Brenda simply hadn't known whether or not she was just talking. Ruby said she hadn't told the police about it, so Brenda thought it might not be true. After all, Ruby had said some strange things that afternoon, like claiming that Ray had out a contract for her and was trying to kill her in a way that would look natural.

Only when she'd read yesterday's newspaper did Brenda learn her mother had eventually gone to the police, and when Brenda added it all up with what she knew about Raymond Smith, she realized Ruby had told her the truth that cold winter day at the hospital.

Shuker asked about other times Brenda Foster had been with Raymond Smith. She told him of a few, always dating the occasion by the age of her two babies. Shuker noted one occasion in particular, when Smith had come by to see Ruby, and Ruby wasn't in, so Brenda let him sit awhile to wait. That would have been, said Brenda, when her older daughter was ten or eleven months old—sometime around November of 1968. And that, Shuker knew—and knew Brenda couldn't know—was around the time the two lesbians had claimed Smith and Pettiford were working at the Carwash—during the time between Smith's leaving Durham for Washington in the fall and his returning to Durham after the murders.

One other thing he knew. He knew Brenda Foster would make a good witness. An honest, sincere girl who had suddenly realized that her junkie mother had been telling her the truth, a young girl who admitted not liking Smith because of the way he used to beat her and her mother and who didn't try to hide her dislike; a calm, soft-spoken girl who simply had some truth she wanted to tell. For nearly two hours Shuker grilled her, and never did he doubt a word she had to say about the two men who always used to brag to her about all the jobs they'd got away with. She even confirmed Shuker's impression of Emma Roland, her grandmother, sadly telling him that Mrs. Roland seemed to be getting slightly senile, as well as being unwilling to get involved in this case.

It was almost ten o'clock, and time to go to court. Shuker left Brenda Foster sitting with a policeman.

The lawyers met that morning in Judge Green's chambers. They sat in a semicircle around her desk, with the court stenographer recording every word.

Shuker explained Coleman's work as a narcotics informant to the judge and defense lawyers. He told them that Coleman's release on bond following his arrest on a bench warrant in August, 1969, had been arranged so he could return to the street to make narcotics buys from major sellers. Infiltrating the narcotics underworld to make purchases from wholesale suppliers is a dangerous business, and the secrecy of Coleman's activities was still intact because none of the cases he had made had reached trial yet. Consequently, Shuker would be unable to show the jury the real reason underlying the leniency; to introduce that testimony in open court would endanger Coleman's life, the life of a man who had come forward to work for the Government at substantial risk to himself. He therefore asked Judge Green to exclude questions revealing the leniency given Coleman.

The defense urged Judge Green to allow the widest scope of cross-examination, arguing that it would be naïve to suppose that Coleman could divorce the two matters in his mind.

She agreed.

The lawyers were ready to return to the courtroom to begin the day's testimony, but first Shuker told them and the judge about Brenda Foster. He told them she had called, and when and what she had said, and that

151

until her call Brenda Foster had not been known to the Government. Now he proposed to call her as a witness.

Perazich immediately objected, on the grounds of her absence from the capital list. But if he wished, Judge Green offered to postpone her testimony to allow the time he would have had to investigate her if her name had appeared on the capital list. He waived the postponement, and his objection to her testimony was overruled.

"I am sure that we are all seeking the same thing here, and that is the truth," the judge told the lawyers as she ruled. "We certainly don't want these people to be convicted if they are innocent. On the other hand— equally so—all of us must be concerned to not have all of the information against them if they are guilty. I think the truth is the most important thing that we can possibly have, with the greatest latitude offered to the defendants to explore it and make sure that it does hold up in the light.

"It isn't a game, certainly, that is being played on each side. It can't be. And so we can't say this doesn't meet this criterion, and we are all surprised, so it can't be heard. You don't want it this way and neither does the court. If there is anyone who can throw any light on the situation, I say let them come forward, and then, if they are fabricating anything, I expect you competent defense counsel to be able to show that, for whatever reason or basis there is."

The lawyers rose and returned to the courtroom. Moments later the judge returned, and then the jury. Finally Robert Coleman entered the courtroom, placed his hand on a Bible, swore to tell the truth, and sat on the witness chair.

Shuker stood and walked to the defense table to give them a transcript of Coleman's grand jury testimony. Then:

"Sir," he began, walking to the end of the jurors' box so Coleman's eyes would be focused in their direction, "Would you speak directly into that microphone and in a good clear voice so we can all hear you, tell us your name."

"Robert Coleman."

Shuker's examination of Coleman would be short. The facts about which he would testify were few, and if the jury believed him, Smith and Pettiford would be convicted. In a jury's eyes, a witness is often more impressive under the hostile attack of cross-examination than during the friendly questions on direct. Coleman had been thoroughly prepared for that during the last week. Now, before Coleman met the test of cross-examination, the only thing for him to do was tell his short but deadly story.

The courtroom was absolutely still.

"Mr. Coleman," Shuker asked quietly, "I want to direct your attention back to the date of December 10, 1968, a Tuesday. As of that date, did you know a man by the name of Raymond Smith?"

"Yes, sir," Coleman answered, bending forward slightly to speak into the microphone in front of him, looking directly at Shuker's face.

"Did you know a man by the name of Pierre Pettiford?"

"Yes, sir," Coleman answered.

Shuker asked him if he would point out in the courtroom the men whose names he had just identified. Without hesitation, but in no particular hurry, Coleman stepped down from the witness stand, walked coolly across the courtroom to the defense table, looked at and pointed with one finger to each of the two black men seated there, and stated, "Mr. Raymond Smith." A pause. "Mr. Pettiford."

Smith and Pettiford looked down blankly at the table in front of them. Coleman walked back to the witness stand.

Shuker resumed his questions.

"Mr. Coleman, did there come a time on December 10, 1968, when you had occasion to see Mr. Smith and Mr. Pettiford?"

"Yes, sir."

"And where did you see them, sir?"

"In the vicinity of Fourteenth and U Street."

"Do you remember about what time of day that was?"

"Approximately eight o'clock at night."

"At the time you saw them, what if anything did you do?"

"Pettiford had called me and I stopped for him to get up with me."

"Was Pettiford alone?"

"No, sir."

"Who was with him?"

"Raymond Smith."

"Mr. Coleman, will you tell us in your own words what happened then?"

"I stopped to wait for Pettiford and Smith to catch up with me and Pettiford asked me about some money, so I said I didn't make it a policy of giving away money like that unless he had something to offer. So he said he had a watch. And I asked him what he needed the money for

153

and he said he needed the money for his friend Raymond. And Pettiford asked me was there any place that we could talk about it, you know. He said, Raymond's in trouble. So we went to an apartment at 1337½ U Street. That's an apartment building where we went on the second floor to a back apartment which I was familiar with and—as we got in the apartment Pettiford asked me about some drugs and at this time I noticed he had been drinking and I stated that I didn't think he needed any. So he asked me again and when I went to get the drugs, I stayed maybe three or four minutes, and acted as though I was going to get him some, so I came back and told him I couldn't get any. And at the time I was almost at the room I heard an argument among themselves about—"

"Among whom, sir?"

"Pettiford and Smith."

"Did you hear what they were saying?"

"Yes sir. Pettiford said, 'Well, you beat the gentleman like a damn dog.' And—well, Raymond said, 'Well, you did that to the bitch.' Pettiford said, 'Well I had to kill the damn bitch.' And through the conversation Raymond was saying that he needed an alibi. I pried in the conversation a little bit and I asked Smith what about an alibi, you know. I said, well, that I wasn't going to say anything about it and—he said that this took place at a carwash where they worked at. So I said, well, I didn't have but a little bit of money, and I gave Pettiford $12 that I had and he gave me a Timex watch. Raymond said that if he could get to North Carolina that he would have a pretty good alibi because his family was there and that he could get a job, and it was somebody else that he could go and get a few dollars from to help him out. I think that is all I can remember about that."

"Did Mr. Pettiford say anything about what he was going to do?"

"Yes, that he would stay here and keep his nose clean."

"Mr. Coleman, was anything said about why the man was beaten like a damn dog?"

"I do remember that it was about somebody could identify somebody, somebody was familiar with—and it was some name called but I don't recall what it was. A nickname or something."

"At this time do you remember whether or not you heard any other conversation at that time, at that place between those two people?"

"Yes, sir. I also remember that it was about a—about that they was going to somebody's house to change clothes and one was living there, was familiar with somebody that was there, and I think it was—it was a lady and she didn't like one of the fellows because they had a conflict or something but I don't know which one it was."

"I have no further questions," Shuker announced, and sat down. He thought Coleman had done well so far: his answers had been firm, he had not claimed to know too much, he had not appeared overeager to see Smith and Pettiford convicted, he had thought before each of his answers. But that, of course, was the easy half of Coleman's examination. Now the collective skills of five defense lawyers would test him.

Before cross-examination could begin, however, several matters concerning Robert Coleman's background had to be resolved at the bench. Judge Green ruled that the defense could impeach Coleman by bringing to the jury's attention the fact of his 1963 conviction for housebreaking. She repeated her ruling that his most recent charges, and their resolution, could be explored. Disclosure of his criminal background was to be circumscribed, however, when it happened also to involve the defendants: Shuker agreed to caution Coleman against testifying that he had in fact spent several years in jail with Pettiford. Of course, that kind of association might make Coleman's testimony of Pettiford's alleged statements on the evening of December 10 somewhat more credible than if Coleman and Pettiford had simply met from time to time in country courtyards. Yet the possible prejudicial impact of the jury's learning that Pettiford was in fact fairly familiar with the inside of jail cells rendered that testimony inadmissible. Or at least the court ruled that it was inadmissible. If it were erroneously excluded and Smith and Pettiford were acquitted, the Government would of course have no right to appeal, because of the defendants' constitutional protection against being placed twice in jeopardy for the same offense. But if it were erroneously admitted and a conviction resulted, an appeal would follow, the matter might then be raised as one of the appellate issues, the conviction could be reversed, and the defendants might be granted a new trial.

The possibility of appellate review of convictions hovers threateningly over big criminal trials in Washington. The jury would not be told of the previous relationship between Pettiford and Coleman.

Before the jury left for lunch, juror number seven, who had sent word to the court of a personal health problem, was excused from service. Alternate juror number one was instructed to take her seat following the luncheon recess. Alternate number one—now juror number seven—

155

was the man who had served earlier that month on the jury which had convicted a man of five robberies in a case Shuker had prosecuted.

The elder Murray stood, glanced at the jury, and began the cross-examination of Robert Coleman. The courtroom was filled and quiet. In the last row Vic Caputy, the tough old guy who for days had grilled Coleman in mock cross-examination, sat quietly now, listening.

"Mr. Coleman," Murray began, "do you expect any favor or benefit for the testimony you are giving today against these defendants?"

"No, sir." Robert Coleman was either lying or still did not trust the Government to help him out.

"When did you first give any statement to the police?" Murray asked.

Coleman thought for a moment, then looked up at Murray. "It was in the month of September. I don't know the exact date." Judge Green interposed to ask what year. 1969, Coleman told her.

Murray continued. "Were the police the first individuals you ever told about this matter after its occurrence on December 10, 1968?" he asked.

"Let me see if I understand you now," Coleman said after a moment. "Would you repeat that again?"

Murray rephrased the question. Coleman testified he had not told anyone of his conversation with Smith and Pettiford until he had gone to the police last August. To emphasize his point, Murray turned toward Coleman and repeated: "So that you kept this thing secret to yourself for ten full months, correct?"

"That is correct," Coleman answered.

"When you finally did talk," Murray asked, "what was your status? Were you outside or in jail?"

He had been in jail, Coleman answered.

If Coleman and Ruby Taylor had independently accused Smith and Pettiford of the killings, one's testimony would buttress the other's. Murray tried to show that at the time Coleman implicated Smith and Pettiford, he already knew of the offenses with which they had been charged.

"Raymond Smith was down there at that time, wasn't he, at the jail?" Murray asked.

Coleman answered, "Yes."

"He was held on a murder charge, right?" Murray continued.

"He was arrested for it, yes."

156

"You knew that, didn't you?"

"Yes," said Coleman, without expression.

"What part of the jail were you committed to when you were arrested?"

"I was in Cellblock Number Two."

"Was Raymond Smith in Cellblock Number Two, too?"

"Yes."

"Was Smith the first person you talked to about his own murder charges since December?"

"No, I haven't talked to him about it."

"You did not talk to him?" Murray asked. "Did you see him down at the jail?"

"Yes, I seen him."

"Did you talk to him there about anything?"

"No."

"Did you get close to him, within speaking distance at any time?"

"In the jail, I was on one landing and I don't know what part of the landing he was at," Coleman answered.

"I am asking you if you came close enough to him at any time to engage in conversation with him," Murray persisted. "You did speak?"

Coleman nodded yes.

"Did you speak about the case?"

No, said Coleman. They would only pass one another occasionally and would say hello. Coleman thought hard before every answer and could not be led to acknowledge any conversation with Smith in jail concerning the night of December 10, 1968.

Murray switched topics. He would explore Coleman's relationship, if any, with Ruby Taylor, again to demonstrate that Coleman had gone to the police only after learning that Smith and Pettiford had already been accused of the killings.

"Do you know Ruby Taylor?" he asked Coleman.

"Vaguely."

"Vaguely," Murray repeated. "How long have you known her vaguely?"

"I guess about two years."

Murray repeated slowly, as if to himself: "About three years."

"Two, he said, counsel," the judge corrected.

"Two years," Coleman calmly repeated.

"Two years, pardon me." Murray moved on quickly: "Did you know her to be reputed as a user of narcotics?"

"Yes, sir."

"Did you ever have any dealings with her in regard to narcotics?"

"No, sir."

Murray returned to the meeting Coleman claimed to have had with Smith and Pettiford the night of the murders.

"Was she the person to whose house these two were supposed to go and change clothes?" Murray asked.

An affirmative answer by Coleman would neatly connect his testimony with Ruby Taylor's, corroborating hers with his own.

"I don't have no knowledge of that," Coleman replied.

Coleman was deliberate in all his answers, and Murray found himself repeating some of them.

"You have no knowledge," he said. "Where was Ruby Taylor living at that time, if you know?"

"I don't have no knowledge of that either."

"Did you know where she hung around?"

"No," said Coleman. "I do not."

"In this conversation—" Murray began, and then cut himself short. "Pardon me, let me withdraw that and take you back to where we were." He redirected the focus of his questions.

"Did Smith indicate to you at any time in the jail that he knew you heard this conversation between him and Pettiford?"

Coleman furrowed his brow for a moment, then looked up at Murray. "I have to ask you to repeat that again," he said.

Murray rephrased the question.

"No," said Coleman, "we never had a conversation about anything like that."

Murray went on. "But did he show any resentment at you in regard to the matter?" A pause; then, Murray: "I am sorry, I don't want to confuse you. I am mixed up myself. You have stated you didn't say anything about this conversation."

It was not a question, but Coleman responded: "All we had in common was, Hello."

Murray returned to the topic of Coleman's greatest vulnerability as a truth-teller in the case: the motive to help himself by testifying for the Government. Coleman did not deny that he had divulged the information linking Smith and Pettiford to the Carwash killings only after he had himself been arrested for second-degree burglary and sale and possession of narcotics, and that even as he was answering Murray's questions, those

158

charges were still pending; that four bench warrants had been issued for his failure to appear in court as required; and that a short time after relating his conversation with Smith and Pettiford to the police, he had been released on bond. His own interests had clearly been served by his providing information to the police. Having been confronted with those facts, perhaps Coleman's story of meeting the defendants on December 10 could now be shaken.

Coleman had not approached the police until nine months after Tuesday, December 10, 1968. Was he—could he be—certain of the date?

Coleman told Murray he was sure. Tuesday, December 10, 1968.

How could he be so sure?

He had read the newspaper the following day, and recognized the name of Gloria McDowell. He had met her a few years earlier at Ben's Chili Bowl, and seen her a dozen times since. In fact, she used to date a friend of Coleman. Murray pried further.

"When was the last time before December 10, 1968, that you had seen either Smith or Pettiford?"

Coleman thought a moment, then said, "Would you repeat that again, please."

"Are you having difficulty hearing me up there?" Murray shot back.

"I want to make sure that I understand what you mean," Coleman answered quietly.

The question was rephrased. Coleman testified he had seen Smith several times that summer, during which time Smith had been employed, though Coleman could not say where.

And when had Coleman last seen Pettiford before December 10, 1968? Perazich beckoned Murray over and cautioned him in a whisper that Coleman's answer to that question might reveal the fact that Pettiford had previously been in jail. The question was withdrawn.

Murray asked some more questions about the circumstances of Coleman's meeting with the defendants the night of the killings, and Coleman provided some more details: they had met shortly after 8:00 P.M.; the streets were dark; Coleman had just left his own apartment to catch the racing results when Smith and Pettiford came up to him. Smith had told him he was going to Durham that night to build an alibi, and Coleman described the building in which the conversations had occurred.

Then Murray approached the one aspect of Coleman's direct testimony that seemed most open to contradiction by Ruby Taylor's own transcript:

"How were these men dressed when you first saw them?" he asked.

"I haven't the slightest idea."

"Was it cold that night?"

"I presume it was."

"Why do you presume that?"

"I don't have any knowledge of how they were dressed and the temperature or the weather."

"I believe you said there was some talk of changing into—changing their clothes?"

"That is right."

"They were going to somebody's house?"

"Yes."

"Some lady's house?"

"That is right."

"They didn't indicate who it was?"

"No."

"Was Smith full of blood?"

"Not that I saw."

"He had no trace of blood on him?"

"Not that I saw."

"Did he have a cut on his lip?"

"Not that I saw."

"Did he have scratches on his face?"

"Not that I saw."

"You do remember distinctly that they were going to change clothes, right?"

"Right," said Robert Coleman. Murray asked only a few more questions, then announced that his cross-examination was over. Coleman's last few answers had been strange indeed: if Smith and Pettiford had killed Rosenberg, McDowell, and Weaver that night in the Carwash, and had not yet changed clothes, they would have been bathed in blood when Coleman met them. Shuker jotted it down on his yellow pad as a subject for clarification on redirect examination.

Perazich rose to cross-examine on behalf of Pettiford. He began by inquiring in detail, again, about the building in which Coleman claimed to have heard Smith and Pettiford discuss the Carwash murders. Again Coleman described the premises: a two-story building, restaurant on the first floor, four rooms on the second floor, conversation in the rear room, which contained a bed and two chairs. Coleman described the house in detail, and Perazich shifted to surer grounds.

160

Had Coleman ever known Pettiford to use narcotics—Pettiford, whom Coleman claimed had asked for narcotics that Tuesday evening? It would have been a dangerous question, of course, an easy one for Coleman to lie about, but Shuker had told Perazich eariler that morning what the answer to the question would be.

"No," said Coleman.

"But that night he wanted narcotics?" Perazich argued.

"That is correct," said Coleman.

Again Perazich forced Coleman to outline his considerable list of pending charges: second-degree burglary, with a possible maximum sentence of fifteen years; inciting to riot, with a possible maximum sentence of a year; several counts of narcotics violations, with possible maximum sentences as high as twenty years.

"They are still pending in this court, aren't they, sir?" said Perazich, his voice clearly audible throughout the courtroom.

"Yes, sir," said Coleman.

The judge instructed the jury that no one is penalized until found guilty. Perazich shifted again to the conversation of Tuesday night, December 10, 1968.

"What do you come out at eight o'clock to do normally, sir?" he asked.

"I come out generally to catch results of the races."

"Isn't it a fact, sir," said Perazich, raising his voice, "that you come to the U Street area to sell dope?"

Coleman answered calmly into the microphone: "I come out generally at eight o'clock to get the results of the races."

"Isn't it a fact, sir, that you have sold narcotic drugs?"

"I have," said Coleman.

"Are you an addict, Mr. Coleman?"

"No," he answered, "I am not."

"But you sell."

"That is correct."

"You have sold in the past?"

"I have."

"You have?"

"Yes."

Perazich again turned to the night of the murders. He asked a few more questions, but again Coleman's description of the circumstances surrounding his meeting Smith and Pettiford could not be shaken. Finally

161

Perazich asked point-blank why Coleman had disclosed his information to the police. Point-blank, Coleman answered that he wanted their help on his pending cases. But although he hoped for favorable consideration in his own cases, no promises had ever been made to him, no promises at all.

"Mr. Coleman," Perazich asked, "are you the same Robert Coleman who in 1963 was convicted of housebreaking?"

Coleman answered that he was.

"No further questions, Your Honor," said Perazich. The cross-examination of Robert Coleman was over.

Shuker rose to clarify one point.

"Mr. Coleman, was it your testimony that you heard Mr. Smith and Mr. Pettiford say something about changing clothes?"

"Yes."

"Now, from what you heard, were they saying that they had already changed clothes or that they were going to change clothes after they saw you?"

"That they had already changed clothes."

Counsel on both sides asked a few more quick questions, and Robert Coleman was excused.

The end of the fourth afternoon of the trial was drawing near, and the Government called its last witness of the day. Detective Mosrie testified that on one occasion he and Detective Kennedy had driven out to the address Ruby Taylor gave on V street, that the address she had given as 67 V Street did not appear to match the description she had given; that they had picked up Ruby and driven her there, and she had immediately pointed out the house by sight instead of number. And that the correct address was 137 V Street, not 67.

That finished the testimony for the day. When the trial recessed, Perazich passed Vic Caputy in the corridor and told him that Coleman had been a tough witness to break down.

Shuker had one more job to do before returning to his office. He called aside the newspapermen who had been attending the trial regularly and asked them please not to print the name of Robert Coleman.

Perazich, meanwhile, sent an investigator to check out the premises at which Coleman claimed to have heard Raymond Smith and Pierre Pettiford discuss a triple murder.

The first witness the following morning was Brenda Foster. She walked

162

to the front of the courtroom in her white blouse and dark skirt, swore to tell the truth, and sat in the witness stand. Her words came soft and nervous as she looked at the man asking the questions.

"My name is Brenda Foster," she said in answer to Shuker's first question.

In July of 1969, did she know a lady named Ruby Taylor?

"Yes, I did. She was my mother."

In July of 1969, did she know a man named Raymond Smith?

Yes, she said, she did. The Negro man at the far table, wearing a checkered jacket and striped tie. She had known Smith since 1966.

"In July of 1969," Shuker asked her, "did there come a time when you saw the defendant Raymond Smith?"

"Yes," she replied. "It was about a month and a week after I had my baby. That would make it somewhere around the 24th of July." He had come up to her on the sidewalk at 7th and F Streets, just outside Bargaintown. He had been alone, and she had been alone.

"I was looking at the displays they had in front of the store and when I got ready to go into the entrance I saw Mr. Smith. And he was smiling and, you know, he asked me about the baby and I told him it was a month and a week. He asked me, you know, how was my momma doing and I said I didn't know, so he asked me, you know, he asked me—he told me, 'When you see your momma you tell her that if she know what I know she will keep her mouth shut.'

"He went on to say that—had she told me anything, and I said No. So then, you know, I asked him why and he said, 'Well, never mind,' you know. He walked on to the bus stop."

Raymond Smith's body trembled slightly in his seat, his forehead became wet, and his eyes became watery. He turned his head toward Fay, and whispered that Brenda Foster was a liar.

Shuker had no further questions. The younger Murray and Berman had some.

There was a time, she answered Murray, when Smith had lived with her mother and herself. "Would you say," Murray asked, "that you like or dislike Mr. Smith?"

"I don't particularly care for him, if that is what you mean."

Shuker asked to approach the bench. There he informed Murray that among the reasons for Brenda's dislike of Smith was an occasion when he had assaulted her. Shuker advised Murray that further questions along that line might expose Smith to testimony suggesting assaultive conduct in addition to the Carwash killings. The lawyers returned to their places, and Murray continued his questioning on other subjects: the corner on which the conversation had allegedly occurred; the length of time; previous conversations. Brenda Foster remembered, and gave Murray the answers. One thing she could not remember was whether or not it had been raining. She had not related the conversation with Smith to Ruby Taylor until December, when she visited her mother in the hospital.

Murray had one last matter to inquire into.

"When was the first time you notified any of the authorities about this conversation?"

"Well, when I read in the paper Friday."

"The first time you notified anybody about this was Friday?"

"Yes." To the defense it was an astounding answer.

Suddenly Berman introduced a strange name—

"Who is Emma Roland—did Ruby Taylor ever refer to her as her stepmother?"

"Yes"—

and dropped it. Then he tested nineteen-year-old Brenda Foster's recollection in another area.

"Prior to December of 1968, what was the first time that you knew your mother to use narcotics?"

"During the riots." That would be around April, 1968.

"How do you happen to recall that?" he asked.

Brenda Foster paused for a moment, then looked up at Berman. Then she said sadly, "You don't forget that."

Berman pursued the question: "Well, is there a particular incident that occurred during the riots that you recall this by?"

"No," she answered. "That's when she started acting different."

"What do you mean by acting different?"

"Well," she answered, "sleeping."

"How about the way she talked," Berman asked. "Did she talk different?"

"No," said Brenda Foster, "she talked the same."

"Did she ramble on?"

"Did she what?"

"Ramble on and say strange things."

"No."

There was no further cross-examination.

164

The crowded courtroom was silent as Brenda Foster stepped down from the witness stand and walked through the swinging gates to the rear. Then Shuker stood and announced, "Your Honor, the Government rests."

Generally, when the Government announces that it has rested its case, another ritual of the criminal process occurs, often just "for the record." Outside the presence of the jury, lawyers for the defense submit oral motions for judgments of acquittal, asking the judge to rule that the evidence produced by the Government is not sufficient to warrant a reasonable finding by a reasonable jury that the defendants are guilty beyond a reasonable doubt. The standard for the judge to follow in ruling at that juncture is not whether the judge believes the defendants guilty, but whether enough evidence against the defendants has been introduced to allow a jury to so conclude. In applying the standard, the judge must view the evidence in the light most favorable to the Government. It is a standard which the Government usually satisfies, but the ritual has a reason. On an appeal following a conviction, certain allegations of reversible error which the defendant may make will not be considered unless the defense moved for judgment of acquittal at the conclusion of the Government's case, and at the conclusion of the defense case. It is a musty old rule honored much in the breach, but the possibility that the dust may one day be blown off and the rule followed results in regular compliance. Often the motion is sufficiently frivolous that the defense attorney will offer it without argument, or with just a few words. Often the Government will simply state its opposition.

When Shuker rested the Government's case, the jury was excused briefly from the courtroom. On behalf of Raymond Smith, the elder Murray rose, moved for judgment of acquittal, without argument, and sat down. On behalf of Pierre Pettiford, Perazich rose, moved for judgment of acquittal, argued for a few minutes, and sat down. Shuker rose, stated his opposition, and sat down.

The judge ruled immediately.

"The court denies the motions," she said. After a brief recess the defense case would begin.

During the recess Berman spoke with Pettiford in the cell block behind the courtroom. Couldn't he possibly recall where there might be some W-2 forms showing where Pettiford had been sometime, any time, in late 1968, which might refresh Pettiford's recollection about his activities during that period. It was a question Berman and Perazich had been asking ever since

165

they'd met him eight months ago. As always, Pettiford thought for a moment. Then, he told Berman yes, maybe there was somewhere Berman might look. He used to keep a little plastic bag with a bunch of papers. If Berman would go around to his old place, Pettiford's roommate, an old alcoholic, might let him in, and Berman might find the forms. And one thing more. Berman might come across an old newspaper clipping about the Carwash crimes. Pettiford wasn't sure whether or not it was there, but sometimes he used to cut out an article when it was about a person or people he knew.

For the first time since Pettiford had flunked the lie detector test, Berman thought he might be guilty.

CHAPTER SIX

R AYMOND SMITH was the key to the defense, and he would testify first.

The usual practice in presenting an alibi defense is to put the alibi witnesses on the stand before calling the defendant himself, thus allowing him to hear what they have to say in court, to attune himself to the prosecutor's style of cross-examination, and—occasionally—to tailor his story to theirs, to iron out any minor wrinkles that develop. But that is a tactic juries sometimes see through, and one the prosecutor may persuasively bring to their attention in summing up the case at the end, and it was important that Raymond Smith be believed when he told the jury his alibi. Since Pettiford claimed not to recall his whereabouts the night of the murders, his fate as well as Smith's would ride on Smith's performance. Raymond Smith walked slowly across the front of the courtroom to the witness stand, swore to tell the truth, sat down in front of the microphone, and answered the first question put to him by Fay:

"My name is Raymond Smith." It was the first time Shuker had heard the voice say anything but "not guilty." It was a steady voice.

The claim of Smith's activities during the months before and following the Carwash killings unfolded fact by fact as he answered each of Fay's questions:

He had lived in Washington until September of 1968, he said, last residing at the Park Towers and last working at Curtis Chevrolet in Washington. In the middle of September, he had moved from Washington to Durham, North Carolina. Shortly after arriving in Durham, he began working at the Holiday Inn there, leaving that job after a week or two at the most. That was his last job in Durham, though he later hunted around there for other jobs at the Jack Tarr Hotel, The American Tobacco Company, the Durham Sun-News, S & W Restaurant, and several other

167

places, many of the names by now forgotten. On December 12 he had applied for unemployment compensation and welfare in Durham.

When he had first arrived in Durham in mid-September, Smith said, he lived for two or three weeks with his stepfather, Claude Smith, on Dowl Street. He had then moved to Ruth McCallum's place on Fargo Street, where he lived for about a month. By then, he said, December had come, and he rented a room from Viola Fuller on Mangum Street. On December 10, 1968, that was where he lived—on Mangum Street in Durham, North Carolina. After nearly a month there, he moved back in with his stepfather on Dowl Street, where he stayed for a couple of days until, on New Year's Eve, he returned by bus to the District of Columbia. From mid-September until New Year's Eve, he had been in Durham; he had not returned to Washington a single time during that span; it was as simple as that.

Shuker noted everything Smith said. He noted especially that one month was missing from Smith's recitation of his addresses in Durham.

Fay handed Smith two small colored tickets and asked whether Smith could identify them. Yes, said Smith, he could. They were tickets his brother, Claude, Jr., had given to him in Durham for a Thanksgiving dance to be held on November 22, 1968. The dance was scheduled for the Square Club, in Durham. Smith had not been able to attend.

Then Fay handed him an Employment Security Commission card and book. Smith identified both as his and read aloud the two dates of his appearances marked inside: December 12, 1968, and December 19, 1968.

"Do you recall anything that occurred in Durham December 10, 1968?" Fay asked him.

Smith answered calmly, "No, I don't."

"When did you first become aware that you were a suspect in this case, Mr. Smith?"

"Well, it was one morning after I got off of work, and I happened to call a young lady that I was going with. And she told me that the detectives had been there, torn her house to pieces, and they were looking for me. So she told me—"

"Let me rephrase the question," Fay interrupted. "When was this, as far as the month and year if you don't recall the exact date?"

"This was in August."

"Of which year, sir?"

"1969."

And what had he done after the young lady had told him he was wanted?

"I went down and gave myself up to homicide."

That was Smith's defense. That was where he had been when Irving Rosenberg, Gloria McDowell, and John Weaver had been slaughtered, that was where he had been for months before, that was where he had remained for weeks after. And when he learned he was wanted, he gave himself up.

Finally Fay asked some questions about Ruby Taylor and Robert Coleman, and about their testimony.

Smith said he had known Ruby Taylor, had met her and lived with her for a few months in 1966, had seen her once on 14th Street in 1967, and had not seen her since. He had never lived with her at 67 V Street—in fact, he had never lived at 67 V Street—and he had never lived with her at 137 V Street—in fact, he had not lived at 137 V Street at any time in 1968. As for Robert Coleman, he had met him for the first time in his life while in jail in connection with this case. Never before had he so much as seen him or talked with him.

It was all so simple that Fay didn't even bother asking whether, on December 10, 1968, Smith had committed the Carwash killings. He told the court he had no further questions and sat down.

Cross-examination of an accused murderer is different from the way it occurs on television. Accused murderers do not confess dramatically on the witness stand. The prosecutor knows this, and goes about his job accordingly, eating away at the man's story piece by piece. The questions, their sequence, the timing will be aimed toward less direct methods of eliciting a "confession." He will try to develop significant inconsistencies in the defendant's story, try to demonstrate that aspects of the alibi are fiction, try, perhaps, to elicit a spark of insolence from the defendant. For the courtroom is a deceptively calm and sterile place, with an atmosphere of propriety which almost belies the possibility of human passion and savagery. Sometimes, when you examine a defendant—if you are skillful, or lucky, or both—you can draw a touch of fire in the man's answer and that, really, is all a jury has to see. Of course, you must always be in command. You must probe, and probe, and probe, until you get the truth; and you must pin down a man's evasive answers. If he is slippery, the hook must go through cleanly.

You also have a reason for cross-examining any witness, a reason for

169

asking any questions at all. If a witness has testified honestly, in your judgment, and has not given particularly harmful testimony, and knows no facts particularly helpful to your side, you may choose not to cross-examine. You will not try to make an honest man look dishonest, but may show him to be inadvertently wrong. But when you believe the witness is lying, you try to show him to be lying. Raymond Smith could not be inadvertently inaccurate in claiming to have been in Durham, North Carolina, at the time of the Carwash killings. He was either honest and innocent, or lying and guilty.

Shuker realized, however, that records established Smith's presence in Durham before and after the crucial date of December 10, 1968. He theorized that Smith had worked for a while in October at the Holiday Inn, had left that job and spent some time applying unsuccessfully for others, had run out of money and returned to Washington for a time, had committed the robbery and murders, and had immediately returned to Durham to establish an alibi—just as he had told Coleman he would do.

Shuker rose to cross-examine.

"When was it that you left for Durham, North Carolina, Mr. Smith?" he began.

"I left for Durham in the year of 1968."

"What month?"

"What month? I think it was in September."

"What part of the month of September?"

"Well, about the first week in September."

"The first week in September?"

"That is right."

"Are you pretty sure of that?"

"Yes, I am."

It is not quarrelsomeness that makes a good trial lawyer force answers to questions that apparently have been answered already. It is just a way of cementing a man's recollection. Smith had now sworn that after the first week in September, he had left Washington for Durham. But Shuker had the records and knew the witnesses for Curtis Chevrolet in Washington would prove that Smith had been employed there until October 4, 1968. Raymond Smith's first demonstrable falsehood.

"How long after you got to Durham did you get employment?"

"I would say from two to three days."

"And that was at the Holiday Inn?"

"The Holiday Inn."

170

"How long did you work there?"

"Approximately about two weeks."

"Could it have been as little as a week?"

"It is a possibility."

"Now, did you work at the Holiday Inn at only one time or did you work there more than once?"

"One time."

"Two to three days after you got to Durham?"

"That is right."

"Mr. Smith, could that have been in the latter part of October, 1968?"

"No, it could not have been."

"How many days passed from the time you first got to Durham and the time you got your job at Holiday Inn?"

"Well, I would say it was about three to four days before I went to work."

"It couldn't have been as long as four weeks?"

"Yes, I am pretty sure."

Pretty sure. Not definite enough. Shuker pinned him down:

"Could it have been as long as four weeks?"

"Impossible," said Raymond Smith.

But Shuker had the records and the witnesses from the Holiday Inn, which proved that Smith had worked there from October 23 through October 31. It was strange, Shuker thought, that Smith would fabricate testimony in areas in which documents would expressly disprove his allegations. Perhaps it was his anxiety to accommodate and rebut the testimony of Misses Craig and Dean placing him at the Carwash in the fall.

In a lengthy cross-examination, not every question pierces to the marrow. Sometimes you ask questions when you know the answers will amount to something you can later disprove. Sometimes you ask some easy questions to let the man get just a little too confident. Those answers, though not spectacular themselves, may provide threads you can weave neatly into the fabric of your case.

Shuker asked some questions about Smith's occasional visits to Durham. None of the questions was difficult. How often had he gone to Durham in the past; how had he got there; how did he get there on his last trip in 1968. Always Smith had taken a Greyhound bus. And how long is the bus ride from Washington to Durham? Six and a half, maybe seven hours. If Smith had committed the Carwash killings on December 10, he could have been in Durham early the next morning. A point for the jury

171

to consider. He could have begun establishing an alibi in Durham on December 11, 1968.

Shuker asked Smith to retrace his living quarters in Durham. First, two or three weeks with his father on Dowl Street in the beginning of September. Then to Fargo Street, in a room rented from Ruth McCallum. How long had he stayed there?

"I would estimate two to three weeks, maybe a month," Smith answered.

"Now, during this period," Shuker asked, "this two to three weeks or a month, what month was that?"

"It would have to be the month of November."

"November?" Shuker asked, incredulous.

"Yes."

"What happened to October?"

Smith paused for a moment. Then he said he couldn't be too sure about dates. Then Shuker asked him:

"Where were you in October?"

"In Durham, North Carolina," said Smith.

Where in Durham? Shuker asked.

"There is a possibility I could have been staying on Fargo Stret. I don't know the exact date."

"Well, two or three weeks you stayed with your father, is that right?"

"Yes," said Smith. Then he added: "Or more."

"Or more?"

"Yes," said Smith, "I don't know the exact date."

"Did you work at the Holiday Inn about the first week of September?"

"I worked at the Holiday Inn. I don't know whether it was the first week."

"But it was September?"

"Yes, it was."

"Between then and December 12, did you work anywhere else?"

"No, I didn't."

"Between the time you worked at the Holiday Inn and December 12, 1968, did you go to the unemployment office at any time?"

"No, I didn't."

"But you had no other jobs?"

"No, I didn't."

At the Holiday Inn, Smith had been paid no more than $1.60 per hour,

172

hardly enough to tide him over until the time he had finally applied for unemployment compensation. He had applied at other places, Smith testified, sometimes filling out forms and sometimes not, but couldn't get a job because the companies told him they didn't want to hire or fire anyone around the time for Christmas bonuses. He had even gone a few times to a place called The American Tobacco Company, filling out a form the first time he went, though he was unable to recall the precise date.

"Did you get money from any other source other than your work at the Holiday Inn?"

"Yes."

"Where?"

"I used to gamble," said Raymond Smith.

"Is that the only other source of money you had?"

"And I have family there. Actually," he added, "I didn't have too much money after I was there for a while, to be truthful."

"When you went to the Employment Commission in Durham," Shuker went on, "you filled out some papers, didn't you?"

"Yes, I did."

"That was on December 12, 1968?"

"That is right," Raymond Smith said.

Shuker asked the courtroom clerk to mark two pieces of paper as Government exhibits for identification. He looked down at the papers, then up at Smith. Did Smith remember telling the people at the Employment Commission about his previous jobs?

Yes, he had told them.

"Do you remember telling them that you worked at Curtis Chevrolet in the District?"

"Yes," said Smith, "I think I mentioned it. It is a possibility."

"Do you remember telling them that you worked there in November of 1968?"

"No, I don't remember telling them that."

Shuker glanced down at the papers in his hand again, then again at Smith.

"Could you have told them that?" he asked.

"Yes," Smith admitted, "I could have."

"Well," said Shuker, "did you work there in November of 1968?"

"No," Smith insisted, "I did not."

The document was one of Shuker's aces. Not only did it establish that

173

Smith had previously admitted to being in Washington until considerably after early September, 1968; the card was important for some information it did not contain.

Shuker showed it to Smith, and directed his attention to the list Smith had provided of his previous employment.

"You listed Hagner Management Corporation, three and a half months in 1968, before Curtis Chevrolet, it that right?"

"That is right."

"Government Services, Incorporated, two months in 1968?"

"That is right."

"The Army and Navy Club, three months in 1965?"

"That could be right."

"Rinaldi's Funeral Home, two months in 1967?"

"It is a possibility."

Shuker paused for a moment, then looked straight at Smith, and said slowly, "But you didn't list anything for 1966, did you, Mr. Smith?"

Smith turned his eyes toward the ceiling and said nothing for a moment. He put one hand to his face. Then he said very softly, "No, I didn't."

"You worked at the Carwash in 1966, didn't you, Mr. Smith?"

A little more quickly this time, Smith answered, directly into the microphone: "Yes, I did."

Shuker put the application form down deliberately, to let those answers sink in. Two days after the Carwash murders, Smith had listed employment ranging back to 1965 but had not listed his jobs for 1966, the year in which documents irrefutably showed he had worked at the Carwash.

"When did you get to Durham," Shuker went on, "in September or December?"

"I don't understand your question," said Smith.

"Well, you said in this application that you filled out that you worked at Curtis Chevrolet to November 1, 1968; you identified your own handwriting, didn't you?"

"Yes."

"When did you get to Durham," Shuker repeated.

"I arrived in Durham in September," Smith said. "I could have put anything on there," he said, pointing to the documents. "That ain't nothing."

"You could have put anything on there?"

"Yes," said Smith, "because I didn't want the employment office to know that I hadn't been looking for a job."

174

Shuker moved to another subject. He knew by now that Smith's Durham relatives and acquaintances would testify as alibi witnesses, placing Smith in Durham around the time of the murders. Even before they took the stand, he wanted to show that the alibi witnesses had reason to testify in Smith's behalf. In addition, the fact that Smith had known of their presence in Durham in December of 1968 would have made Durham a natural place for him to seek an alibi after committing the murders.

"Your stepfather lived in North Carolina, is that right?" Shuker asked.

"That is right."

"And your brother?"

"That is right."

"Does any other of your family live there?"

"Not that I know of."

Shuker stared at Smith in disbelief. "No relatives at all?" he asked.

"Not that I know of."

How about Vera Bullock, Shuker asked, who lived in Durham; had Smith first met her in the fall of 1968?

"She is my sister."

"Then you do have other relatives there, don't you?"

"Oh, yes," Smith said quickly. "I thought you said sisters and brothers." In fact he had another sister living in Durham. And yes, he had known Ruth McCallum in Durham for several years.

Sometimes when you are cross-examining, you switch purposely from one subject to another, and then back again. Often, if you ask the questions in chronological order, it is easy for a witness to testify he was at one place, then moved to another, and then to a third. But if you scramble the dates and places, if you spread them out, if you take them out of order, and if the witness is dissembling, you may trip him. Of course, you may even trip an honest witness or lose the jury.

Shuker switched again to Smith's residencies in Durham. Where, he asked, had Smith lived before moving back with his stepfather just before New Year's? On direct, Smith had answered Mangum Street, where he had rented a room from Viola Fuller.

On Moline Street, Smith now answered, where he had stayed for two or three weeks, or maybe longer, with a woman whose last name he could not recall. He had moved there, he said, from Viola Fuller's house on Mangum Street, where he had been living on the day he went to the Employment Commission, two days after the murders. It was the first time Smith had mentioned the Moline Street residence to the jury.

175

Another inconsistency. Again, Shuker returned to the date Smith had originally left Washington. How long had Smith been living at his last Washington residence?

"It must have been about—I left there about the last part of September, something like that."

"The last part of September?" Shuker asked.

"No, I mean. You say what part of September. I don't quite understand you."

Shuker moved to another topic.

Did Smith have any friends or associates with whom he had socialized in Durham between September and New Year's Eve, 1968?

A lady named Cary, Smith said. He had met her in September at a bootleg house she owned and had seen her once or twice a week through December, but could not recall her last name or address. And although he had met her friends, he could remember no names. He would also see Sarah Magnum almost daily from the time he met her just before Thanksgiving until New Year's Eve. There were also her friends. "But I wouldn't know their names," Smith said. "I never got too familiar with them."

Smith had also seen his brother twice a week, he stated, and his stepfather also, in November and December. Shuker tried to pin him down. Had he seen his stepfather the first week in December? "No, I didn't. I don't know." Had he seen his stepfather the second week in December? "I don't know that I have, sir." The third week in December? "I imagine I seen him between that time, yes. I would say that I did."

"You say your father saw you maybe twice a week, but you don't remember whether he saw you the first three weeks in December?"

"That's right," Smith answered.

And Smith's sisters, Vera Bullock and Cora Young—he used to see them quite often, too. Used to see Cora Young two or three times a week during November, 1968, in fact.

Shuker had interviewed Claude Smith, Sr., a week ago, and believed the man would tell the truth when called by the defense. And as for Smith's sister Cora Young: On September 4, 1969, shortly after 5:20 P.M., Cora Young had told homicide detectives visiting Durham that she had not seen Raymond Smith much after October, 1968, because he had not returned to her home after stealing two of her guests' wallets.

Where had he been living just before moving back to his stepfather's house in late December?

176

"I was staying at Mrs. Fuller's house."

"That is Viola Fuller?"

"Yes."

"That is on Moline Street?"

"No—well, I stayed there in Mrs. Ruth McCallum's house."

"Was it not your testimony before," Shuker said, "that the last place you lived in Durham was on Dowl Street with your stepfather?"

"That's right—the last place I lived in Durham, yes."

"And the place you lived before that was where?"

"Was on Moline Street," Smith admitted, correcting his error. "Yes, you are right."

And when his father would visit him in Durham in November, where was Smith living?

On Fargo Street.

"Did you live on Fargo Street all of November?"

"I lived—I think about all of November, I can't remember. I am pretty—I am not too sure all of November."

Smith's words were no longer flowing as easily as they had when he had first taken the stand. But he swore to certain facts without doubt: he had not worked at the Carwash after 1966, not even for a day, though he had known Irving Rosenberg when he worked there in 1966, and might have known Gloria McDowell and John Weaver; he had not so much as seen Pierre Pettiford, whom he had known for six years, or Ruby Taylor, throughout 1968; he had not lived at 137 V Street since 1966; he had never in his life seen Robert Coleman until they met in jail in 1969. And although he could not remember exactly where he had been, or with whom, in the late afternoon and early evening hours of December 10, 1968, he had been somewhere in Durham, North Carolina.

And what about Brenda Foster? Smith had in fact seen her, he testified, in late August, 1969, not far from where she had testified earlier to having seen him. But the conversation, he said, had been quite different from the way she recalled it. Brenda Foster, whom he had not seen for two years, had asked him for money.

"Brenda Foster asked you for money?" asked Shuker in disbelief that Brenda Foster, though she was on welfare at the time, would ask Raymond Smith for a loan.

"Brenda Foster had always constantly asked me for money," Smith responded. And, coincidentally, just after he had walked away from

177

Brenda and proceeded up the street, he met Ruby Taylor, whom he had not seen in about two years. "She acted like she saw a ghost," Smith remembered. And the next day he had been arrested.

When you are cross-examining, you like to begin on a high note, and to end on a high note as well—you like to hit one point you've been surrounding. Shuker had saved one last pair of documents to question Smith about. Holding them, he asked:

"You went to the North Carolina Department of Public Welfare, did you not, in December, 1968?" he asked

Yes, said Smith, he had gone on December 31, to get funds to return to Washington.

"You were interviewed at that time, weren't you?"

"Yes, I was."

December 31 was not the first time he had been to the Department of Public Welfare in Durham, was it? No, said Smith, it was not.

The first time was December 12, two days after the murders, correct?

"I don't know if that was the date I went there or not," Smith answered.

"But you were there once before?"

"Yes," said Smith, "I am pretty sure I was."

And on December 12, 1968, when he had first gone to the Department of Public Welfare, hadn't he in fact told his interviewer that he had just arrived from Washington, D.C.?

"It is a possibility that I did," said Smith.

And on December 31, his second trip to the Department of Public Welfare, hadn't he told them that he had come to Durham only a month ago?

"I don't know," said Smith. "I could have."

"You could have said that?"

"I could have," said Smith. "I don't know."

Was it true that on December 12th he had just arrived in Durham?

"No, it isn't true."

"But you did tell them that?"

"It is a possibility that I did."

"And is it true that on December 31, 1968, you had only been in Durham about a month?"

Smith hesitated. Then he said: "Would you rephrase that, please?"

178

"Is it true that as of December 31, 1968, you had only been in Durham one month?"

"It is possible I said that."

"Did you say that or not?"

"I don't know exactly what I said, but it could be possible that I did say this, yes," said Smith.

"Had you been in Durham just one month?"

"No," said Smith.

"Did you also tell them on December 31, 1968, at the Welfare Department, that you had been living with your brother?"

"Yes, I think I did do that," said Smith.

"But you were not living with your brother, were you, Mr. Smith?"

"No."

Shuker believed he had made his point. "No further questions," he said, and sat down.

The defense simply asked permission to recall Smith later on to identify some documents. That was an unusual procedure, but permission was granted without objection from the Government, and Smith stepped down from the witness stand.

The younger Murray thought the strategy of not providing Smith with documents or dates had paid off, that Smith had appeared as a sympathetic witness trying to recall as best he could events long past, a man who had not contrived an alibi. Shuker thought Smith had seemed like a liar. So did Berman. The jury, of course, had not seen Charlie Murray speaking with Smith in jail and telling him simply to rely on his own memory of the dates and events in Durham, to never mind the facts that appear on the documents, and just to have some confidence in his lawyers.

The defense planned to pursue several courses to support Smith's alibi. They would specifically disprove material aspects of Ruby Taylor's testimony, and they would corroborate material aspects of Raymond Smith's.

First, the comptroller of a private business, Government Services Incorporated, took the stand, stated that official business records showed Raymond Smith had worked there from April 1, 1968, through May 7, 1968, and stated that Smith's home address had been listed as 2440 16th Street, about a mile from the V Street address to which Ruby Taylor had

179

referred. His testimony was read from official business records, and Shuker saw no point in cross-examining.

Then the defense called the official representative of a company that operated the Dorchester House, who testified that Raymond Smith had worked there from May 20, 1968, through July 26, 1968, and that Smith's home address was listed as 2440 16th Street, about a mile from the V Street address to which Ruby Taylor had referred. Again the testimony was read from official business records, and Shuker chose not to ask any questions.

The manager of Curtis Chevrolet took the stand, testified that official business records showed that Raymond Smith had worked there from August 27, 1968, through October 4, 1968, and stated that Smith's home address had been listed as 2440 16th Street, about a mile from the V Street address to which Ruby Taylor had referred. His testimony too was read from official business records, but this time Shuker rose to emphasize a point:

"October 4, 1968?" he asked slowly, glancing at the jury.

"That is correct," said the witness.

"That is not September of 1968, is it, sir?"

"No, sir," said the witness. Raymond Smith's own witness proved that Raymond Smith had not left Washington until at least early October, 1968. Shuker had no further questions. He sat down and scrawled some words onto a yellow pad, a thought to call to the jury's attention at the end of the case, when he would sum up: what had Smith been doing between October 4, the end of his job at Curtis Chevrolet in Washington, and October 23, the beginning of his job at the Holiday Inn in Durham—the first day his presence in Durham was recorded? That would be the period of time Craig and Dean remembered seeing him at the Carwash. The dates fit. But would—could—the jury remember?

The testimony of those three witnesses had not taken more than half an hour in all, but the defense had established Raymond Smith as a man with fairly stable employment in 1968, who would apparently not need to pick up a few days' pay at a local and familiar carwash. And they had established that during most of 1968 he had lived at a fixed address and that that was not the address at which Ruby Taylor claimed to have heard Smith and Pettiford discuss the Carwash crimes. If the discussion had not occurred there—if, indeed, it could not have occurred there

180

because Raymond Smith was not living there on December 10, 1968—what was the likelihood that it had occurred at all?

That brief testimony had been gained at some risk, however: the jury now knew that Smith had not been telling them the truth when he told them he was in Durham, North Carolina, in September of 1968. Perhaps Raymond Smith had not been truthful. But had he killed?

When you are driving a key point home to a jury, you use all the evidence you have. The records of Smith's three employers concerning Smith's address contained only information which he himself had supplied while working for those companies. Though he would not have had any apparent motive for falsely stating his address at the time, the defense would leave no room for doubt. A representative of the Park Towers apartments, the building located at 2440 16th Street, testified that the address Smith had given to his employers had been his true address. His lease had begun there in February, 1968, and his apartment had not gone to another tenant until October 9, 1968.

To eliminate all doubt, Murray called Ennis Wilkins, an elderly man wearing an old suit, who walked slowly to the stand. He was the landlord at the ramshackle house that stood at 137 V Street, the building in which Ruby Taylor had claimed to have been with Smith and Pettiford the day of the murders. He rented out the rooms there, and he had once rented a room to Raymond Smith, a small room in the back of the house, upstairs. He didn't recall exactly when that was, but it was certainly not in the second half of 1968, he testified. On cross-examination he conceded that he was testifying from memory. Though he did keep records on his rentals, he said, he was simply unable to find the record showing the exact dates of Smith's occupancy.

Since moving out, though, Smith had visited the place. Ennis Wilkins could not remember exactly when, though he did recall having seen Pettiford at the old house also. In fact, Pettiford had come to visit Smith. The old man could not recall exactly when. Maybe it was in December, 1968, he said, though maybe it was not. No, his memory did not seem terribly keen, but he insisted he had not rented out the room in some time—certainly not after the first half of 1968. How long had it been vacant? As best he could remember, two years. And did anybody now rent the room in which Raymond Smith had lived, the room in which a woman now dead had been locked up reading comics while Smith and

181

Pettiford had, perhaps, been bludgeoning to death three people they vaguely knew, but who might have recognized them?

Nobody, said Ennis Wilkins. "I use the room for my closet now," he said.

If those witnesses had proved Ruby Taylor wrong about the address at which she claimed to have heard Smith and Pettiford plan to rob the Carwash and to have seen Smith return after the job was done, they had not proved that she had not heard the planning at all or seen Smith return bloodied from the scene. To that end the defense called a series of witnesses to corroborate Raymond Smith's story that he had been in Durham, North Carolina, on December 10, 1968.

That had not been a particularly noteworthy day in Durham, and because the defendants had not been charged with the murders until nearly nine months later, it would be difficult, if not impossible, for anyone to recall having seen Smith in Durham on that precise date—or to recall that Smith had not been in Durham on that precise date. But if the defense could show that around that time of year Smith had been in Durham—if his presence there had been observed by a lot of people—the cumulative effect of that testimony might persuade the jury that he had been there on December 10.

Viola Fuller took the stand and testified that she operated a sports shop on South Mangum Street in Durham, and that in late 1968 Raymond Smith had rented a small room from her in the back of the store. She kept no records but could make a pretty good guess at the dates: her sister had been in an automobile accident on November 13, and Smith had rented the room about three weeks afterward. She had never seen him before he stopped by to rent the room. He had stayed for three weeks, not paid for the last two, and left during the Christmas holidays. That would mean that on December 10, 1968, Raymond Smith had been renting a room several hundred miles from Washington, D.C., just as he had said.

Could it have been, Shuker asked, that Smith didn't rent that room until Christmas? No, Mrs. Fuller said. Or could it have been that if he had moved in before Christmas, it had been only two weeks before—or sometime after December 10, 1968? "No, it was approximately three weeks," she answered, "because he was there about three weeks."

Sometimes, when you cross-examine a witness whose testimony is

182

as helpful to the other side as Viola Fuller's, you let him be really helpful. You slacken the rope and let him pull however much he wants. Nearly seventeen months after the fact, Viola Fuller even remembered that Raymond Smith had moved in on a Monday.

On Wednesday, September 3, 1969, Viola Fuller had told homicide detectives visiting Durham that Raymond had moved in for three weeks beginning around Christmastime, 1968.

Then Sarah Magnum took the stand. She had met Smith in November of 1968 in Durham. And she remembered visiting him at Viola Fuller's sports shop once when the snow was on the ground. That, she said, would have been in December. And she had seen him almost every day in early December.

It was that brief. How do you show that it is not the truth, if you believe it is not the truth? You ask about specific dates, and maybe she will be demonstrably wrong, or maybe she will claim to remember what she could not possibly remember. Or maybe her testimony will sound generally artificial, or memorized, or maybe she will appear overly determined to establish an alibi for Raymond Smith.

When, asked Shuker, had she first seen Smith? In November. When in November? She couldn't be sure, but around Thanksgiving. How often would she see him? "I can't say every day but I saw him regular." Where? Mainly at her home. How frequently in November? Two or three times a week. And in December?

"Well, sometimes I would see him twice a day and again once a day."

"Did you see him once or twice a day every day in December of 1968?"

"Well, very seldom he would miss a day coming."

"Do you remember seeing him in the first week in December of 1968?"

"I can't say the first week but very seldom he would miss coming to my house in December."

"Do you remember any particular days that you saw him in the second week of December?"

"Well, I can't say exactly what day but very seldom he would miss coming to my house."

Other questions. Then again:

"Most every day he was visiting you in December?"

"Very seldom he would miss a date coming to my house."

"Do you remember what days, if any, he did miss coming to your house?"

"I wasn't paying that particular attention but very seldom he would miss a day."

On Wednesday, September 3, 1969, Washington homicide detectives interviewing Sarah Magnum in Durham had written into their notebooks, while she was answering their questions, that a friend of hers named Bill had been arrested for rape on the last day of November, 1968, and that from that day on she had not seen Raymond Smith until Christmas. Sarah Magnum testified to the jury that she had told the police no such thing.

Then Vera Bullock, Smith's sister, took the stand. She had first seen her brother in Durham around mid- or late October, she said. And she had seen him a few days later. Before New Year's she had seen him eight or ten times, mostly when he would visit her home. She had bumped into him once, outside on Fargo Street. That had been in late November or early December, she recalled, a little over a week after a particular birthday she knew. It was the last time she had seen him until after Christmas.

Shuker's questioning was brief. Between that last time in late November or early December and that first time after Christmas, could she recall having seen her brother in Durham?

"I can't say that I do," she answered. "I don't remember."

That was all.

The next witness for the defense, Raymond Smith's father, walked slowly to the stand. He spoke softly, with a quiet, unhappy air of dignity; he was the sort of man you see wearing clothes that are always old and always clean.

"What is your occupation?" Murray asked him.

"I work as a janitor."

"Are you also a minister?"

"I am, sir."

Shuker had spoken to the man a week ago and had detected no reason to doubt his integrity. When you have no reason to doubt him, you just listen and try to make a witness for the other side work for you.

When, asked Murray, had Reverend Smith first seen his stepson in late 1968? Around the middle or latter part of October, he said. Raymond Smith's stepfather was contradicting Smith's own testimony of having moved in with him in Durham in early September. Raymond had lived with him that first time in October for a couple of weeks, and then moved out when he had got some kind of job. Mr. Smith had seen him several times afterward. He hadn't seen him much in November, but Raymond

184

had moved back in right after Christmas, just before returning to Washington.

How many times, Shuker asked on cross-examination, did Reverend Smith actually recall having seen his son in Durham in November? Maybe not at all, he said, though it may have been a couple of times. But he had seen Raymond regularly when Raymond had moved in during October? Yes. And he had seen Raymond regularly when Raymond had moved back in around Christmas? Yes. And before Christmas, how many times in December had he seen Raymond? Two or three. And how much before Christmas had those occasions been?

"Maybe about two weeks."

"Two weeks before Christmas?"

"Yes."

"Do you remember whether or not you saw him on Tuesday, December 10, 1968?"

"No, sir, I don't remember that."

"Or Monday, December 9?"

"No."

"Or Wednesday, December 11?"

"No, sir."

Raymond Smith's father, then, really could not corroborate what Raymond Smith had said.

Incidentally, Shuker asked, did Reverend Smith still live in Durham? Yes, he did. And how had he come up for the trial? By bus. And how long had the ride taken? About five and a half hours. The Government had no further questions.

The trial was now in the late morning of its sixth day, and the jury had heard much testimony about numerous facts from many witnesses. Among the principles underlying the jury system is that each juror will, after hearing all the testimony, distill fact from fiction, and that that distillation will be further refined when the twelve men and women comprising a cross section of the community discuss the case after all the evidence is in. Would they be able to recall which witness had said what about whom at what time? Could they compartmentalize different witnesses' statements about Moline Street and Mangum Street and Sarah Magnum and Ruth McCallum and Fargo Street and Dowl Street, and when Raymond Smith was alleged to live at each, and by whom, and in what month, and for how long? Was it important that they make those distinctions?

185

Following the testimony of Raymond Smith's father, Judge Green declared a brief recess. As Shuker stepped outside to light a cigarette, he chatted briefly with some courtroom observers who had been stopping by daily to watch the trial. Then he strolled by the witness room, where prospective witnesses who had not yet testified awaited their turn. He noticed an unfamiliar white face.

Throughout the trial, Shuker had expected a surprise. The attorneys for the defense had seemed more confident than one might suppose with possible death penalties facing their clients if convicted. And the opening statement for Smith had referred to documentary proof of Smith's innocence. In fact, it had been after that reference that Shuker had issued a forthwith subpoena to the one Durham company that Smith had mentioned to the police but which had never responded to previous requests to produce records. Now he recalled that that forthwith subpoena had never been returned.

Shuker approached the stranger in the witness room and asked him whether he was a prospective witness for the defense. The man said his name was Charles Rich, he was associated with the personnel department of The American Tobacco Company in Durham, North Carolina, and he was present to testify that on December 10, 1968, Raymond Smith had applied there for employment, hundreds of miles from the scene of the murders of Irving Rosenberg, Gloria McDowell, and John Weaver. He even showed Shuker a document which, he said, proved it. Shuker looked at the piece of paper Rich handed him, but before he could ask any further questions, one of the courtroom marshals hurried into the witness room and told him the judge was back on the bench. Shuker hurried in thoughtfully. Smith and Pettiford and their lawyers were already seated at the defense table. Shuker sat down at the Government table, the jury was brought back into the courtroom, and the elder Murray stood and announced: "I call Mr. Rich, please." Charles Rich walked into the courtroom with his piece of paper.

Murray asked the preliminary questions to identify to the jury Charles Hampton Rich, employed in the personnel division of The American Tobacco Company in Durham for many years, interviewer of job applicants for the company.

"Have you brought with you an application made in the month of December, 1968?" Murray asked.

"Yes," said Rich. "Let me make sure." He reached into his folder and,

186

indeed, the application was there. He handed Murray the single piece of paper, a printed form filled out in pencil, bearing no erasure markings.

"Mr. Rich," Murray asked, "would you know the applicant if you saw him today?"

"No, I would not."

"Did you personally interview the applicant, whoever he was?"

"Yes."

Murray then handed the piece of paper back to Rich, who testified that it was an application for employment made out by a man named Raymond Smith, with the same social security number as the Raymond Smith on trial.

"When did that applicant make that application for employment?"

"December 10, 1968."

Smith whispered to the younger Murray: "I knew you had something." Pettiford stared steadily at the witness. The questioning continued.

"Do you know the time of day that he made it?"

Rich did not.

"What were the office hours of The American Tobacco Company at that time?"

"Eight A.M to four P.M.," said Rich.

The defense now had in evidence an application of Smith dated the day of the murders, filled out hundreds of miles away from the scene. Murray had no further questions.

Shuker rose to cross-examine.

"Mr. Rich," he began, "do you see anyone in this courtroom you remember interviewing for a job?"

"No," he answered, "I do not."

"Mr. Rich, do you have any personal memory whatsoever of the interview this paper is a record of?"

"No, I do not."

Who fills in the information requested on the application, Shuker asked.

"The applicant," said Mr. Rich.

"There is a line there for a date, is there not?"

"Yes."

"Normally, who puts the date in?"

"The applicant."

"The applicant?" Shuker emphasized.

187

"Yes," said Rich.

"He fills out the date on there?"

"Yes."

"Do you remember whether this interview took place on December 10, of your own recollection?"

"Not absolutely." Shuker was about to sit down, with no further questions, when Mr. Rich added, "But I don't see how it could be otherwise."

"Why?" said Shuker. "Because the date December 10 is on there?"

"Right."

"And who put that date on there?"

"The applicant, I assume," said Mr. Rich. "He is supposed to have. It's been so long I don't know." Now Shuker had no further questions.

There was no way to predict how the jury would consider Smith's application—whether they would acquit both defendants on the strength of it alone, or would consider it a self-serving piece of paper Smith had predated after murdering, with Pettiford, three human beings. To be sure of one thing, Shuker submitted the application that afternoon for comparison with known exemplars of Raymond Smith's handwriting. The police department expert reported back that Raymond Smith had filled it out.

It was now time to put on Pierre Pettiford's defense. Although his attorneys announced that Pettiford's case would now begin, the next series of witnesses was really no more his than Smith's. They had simply been investigated and interviewed before trial by Pettiford's lawyers, so Pettiford's lawyers would do the questioning.

Berman had arisen early on the morning Pettiford was scheduled to testify and by 6:30 A.M. was picking his way past the garbage leading to Pettiford's old basement apartment and somewhat fearfully knocking on the door. A dirty old alcoholic dressed only in his undershorts answered, and Berman explained that he was looking for Pete's plastic folder, and why. The apartment was actually one room divided by what had probably once been a curtain, hanging gracelessly from the ceiling. There were two old cots, a caseless pillow, some old army blankets, a toilet bowl, and now, in the old alcoholic's hand, Pierre Pettiford's old plastic envelope. It contained a load of papers: a photograph of Pettiford with his old jail basketball team, his report card from jail with B grades in arithmetic and

188

Negro history, and dozens of unrelated items. But no W-2 forms for late 1968. And to Berman's relief, no newspaper clippings on the Carwash case.

Pettiford's defense began with Lieutenant Bernard Crooke of the Metropolitan Police Department, who, as a homicide detective in September, 1969, had been the first member of the squad to speak with Robert Coleman—since Mosrie and Kennedy were in Durham at the time, checking out Smith's alibi. His notes of the initial conversation with Coleman had been turned over to the defense by Shuker.

Crooke was an experienced witness, and a good man to begin Pettiford's defense: no juror would suspect a policeman of lying in favor of the defense. He was called to establish certain inconsistencies between Coleman's original statement to him and Coleman's testimony at trial: that Coleman had told him of having first spoken with Smith and Pettiford a day or two after the crime, not the night of the crime; that Coleman had told him he had in fact spoken with Smith and Pettiford in the D.C. Jail following their arrests; and that Coleman had told him that in their conversation in the apartment near 14th and U, Pettiford had told Coleman "they"—rather than Smith alone—were leaving for North Carolina.

Shuker's cross-examination was aimed not at establishing the falsity of the witness's testimony but the circumstances under which Coleman's statements had been made. Had Coleman in his discussions with Crooke fully detailed his conversations with and observations of Smith and Pettiford the night of the murders? No. He had seemed to be holding back at the time; he had been coy; he hadn't at the time wanted to say very much. And had a statement of the interview been typed up for Coleman to read, sign, and thus affirm as true? No. Had Crooke ever spoken with Coleman thereafter? No. Had Crooke been the man who had gone over in detail with Coleman his alleged conversation with Smith and Pettiford? No, it had been Detectives Mosrie and Kennedy who had dealt with Coleman afterward; Crooke had not been specifically assigned to the case, he had just been around the homicide office and helped out one day.

Next Perazich called to the stand the investigator he had sent to 1337½ U Street the afternoon of Robert Coleman's testimony— to check out the address Coleman had identified as the building in which he had listened to Smith and Pettiford discuss the murders and which he had described physically under cross-examination. The investigator had reported to Perazich that in fact no such address existed, although one block away—

at 1437 U Street—stood a building that matched Coleman's description. Perazich hoped nobody would think to elicit the latter fact. His own questions elicited only that neither 1337½ U Street nor 1337 U Street exists, that neither existed on December 10, 1968, and that the closest buildings to the address Coleman had given were a theater and a warehouse.

Shuker, though, had found time himself, while preparing the case, to visit the scene of the conversations Coleman had related, and realized what was now occurring in court. He looked for a moment at Perazich, then stood, asked the investigator whether he had bothered looking one block away, got an affirmative reply, and told the witness to describe for the jury the premises at 1437 U Street—which the witness did, and which matched Robert Coleman's description. Shuker glanced again at Perazich, said, "No further questions," and sat down.

The defense next called an old lady they considered one of their strongest witnesses, Ruby Taylor's stepmother. Wearing a shabby old print dress, Emma Roland walked unsteadily, slowly, across the courtroom to the witness stand. Berman tried to put her at ease:

"Mrs. Roland," he began when she had finally sat down, "I want you to speak up in a loud clear voice so the ladies and gentlemen of the jury and myself can hear you. Speak into the microphone. Would you please provide your full name and address?"

Emma Roland. Been living at 1709 Lanier Place the last six years.

Shuker had not known Emma Roland would testify for the defense, but he had spoken with her on an earlier occasion anyway. She had struck him as perhaps senile, unresponsive, perhaps slow-witted, certainly slow to answer questions; and her recollection of the last few years had been weak. He had not thought she could provide believable testimony helpful to either side. She had simply not seemed like the kind of witness whose credibility you would want to vouch for, and certainly not the kind of lady whose credibility you would want to attack. Today he would have to cross-examine her.

Berman continued his questioning:

"Do you know a gentleman by the name of Pierre Pettiford?"

"No, I don't."

"Do you know a gentleman by the name of Raymond Smith?"

"Yes."

"Do you know a lady by the name of Ruby Taylor?"

"Ruby Taylor is my stepdaughter."

And now she would be asked those few questions designed to show

190

that her stepdaughter had lied to the authorities about the events surrounding December 10, 1968.

"On December 10, 1968, or at any time after that date, did Ruby Taylor live with you?"

"No."

"Did you ever live with her after that date?"

"No."

"Did you ever visit her at her apartment after that day?"

"No, I didn't."

"Did you ever see Raymond Smith with a white hearse and a dead body after that date?"

"No, I didn't."

"Did Ruby Taylor ever live with you?"

"Yes, she did."

"When did she live with you?"

"I think it was between 1966 and 1967."

"Did you ever see Raymond Smith go out with Ruby Taylor when she lived with you?"

"No, I didn't."

Berman had no further questions. In his judgment she had already materially impeached Ruby Taylor's testimony about her relationship with Smith, her meetings with Smith, and the threat she had allegedly received from Smith.

Shuker did not believe she could honestly recall all that.

"Mrs. Roland," he began, "where were you living when you were living with Ruby Taylor?"

"I never lived with Ruby Taylor," Mrs. Roland answered slowly, quietly, into the microphone. "She lived with me."

"Do you know where Ruby Taylor went to live after she moved out of your place?"

"Summit Place, the street right back of me."

"Right behind you?"

Yes, Mrs. Roland said. Less than a block away.

"Did she ever come over to your house?"

"She didn't visit," Emma Roland answered.

"Never at all?" Shuker pressed gently.

"No, she never came to visit. She came to my house just to stop by."

"Just to stop by?"

"Yes," Emma Roland reaffirmed, "not to visit."

191

"Can you tell us when that was?"

"I really don't know."

When had she last seen Raymond Smith, Shuker asked.

"I couldn't tell you definitely, but Ray did stop by to say hello one day, not a long visit, but he was passing and stopped." He had been on foot, she recalled, but she did not know how he had got there, or from where.

Shuker thought that might be around the time of the threat to which Ruby had earlier testified, around February or April of 1969, and asked if Mrs. Roland might estimate when.

"I really don't know the exact time, but—just a minute," she said. "Let me get myself together." Again she hesitated. "It had to be the first part of 1969—that summer, you know. It was nice weather."

"Nice weather?"

"Yes," she said. "I was on the porch."

"You were on the porch that day?"

"Yes," Mrs. Roland answered. "He stopped and said hello." Still, she could not recall the exact month. That was understandable. Perhaps she could identify with the present time of year—early spring. Could it, he asked, have been in the spring, like today?

"Right," said Emma Roland, "because I wouldn't be sitting out there in the winter."

Had Smith told her anything but hello?

"Now, if a person don't stop by, they don't come to say more than hello. What he said I don't remember. We had a little conversation, but I don't remember what we were talking about."

Had she, in fact, seen Smith at other times in 1969?

"I don't know," she said. "I don't remember that."

And did she recall whether she had seen him in 1968?

"I don't remember that," she said, "because it didn't interest me that much to pay attention to what time he came if he came, but he didn't visit my house that much. He stopped by, because I only knew him through Ruby. I met him through Ruby."

She had remembered enough for Shuker, and he stopped questioning. For the defense nobody rose to ask any more questions. Emma Roland lumbered off the witness stand.

Now it was time for Pierre Pettiford, who had told his lawyers and the police that he could not recall the events of the day on which three

192

heads had been smashed, to tell it to the jury. Before calling him to the stand, however, Perazich asked to approach the bench.

Perazich naturally expected that because of Pettiford's inability to recall specifically where he had been on December 10, 1968, much of Shuker's cross-examination would be designed to pin Pettiford down to any one specific date he could recall around that time, and probe forward or backward from there. But Pettiford, Perazich reminded the judge, had been arrested for petit larceny on December 28, 1968, and had remained in jail for about a month. That fact, if brought to the jury's attention, would prejudice his case unfairly in this trial. In addition, Perazich informed the court that previous to Thanksgiving of 1968, Pettiford had been unable to hold a series of jobs for more than a short duration. That fact, said Perazich, would also prejudice Pettiford in the eyes of the jury, by showing him to be shiftless. The defense was therefore asking the court to rule that Shuker's cross-examination of Pettiford be confined to the time period between Thanksgiving and December 28, 1968.

Shuker readily agreed not to elicit testimony from Pettiford concerning his month in jail for petit larceny, realizing it might present arguable grounds for reversal of any conviction that the jury might return and fearing that the jury might conclude the Government was seizing small straws. But he realized also that confining cross-examination to a two-month period would defeat several objectives of his questioning. In the first place, a man like Pettiford, with his spotty employment record over a considerable period of time, would be precisely the type of man who would have worked for a couple of days at the Carwash to pick up some cash in the fall of 1968. Furthermore, by questioning Pettiford about his activities and whereabouts over a long span of time, Shuker could either force him to admit remembering his whereabouts on certain days around December 10 or show the jury that Pettiford was plainly exaggerating his inability to recall his whereabouts and was hiding at least some events he could in fact recall. If Pierre Pettiford were hiding the truth of his activities on and around December 10, 1968, perhaps the jury would remember the testimony of Ruby Taylor and Robert Coleman in considering his motive for hiding that truth.

The defense motion to limit cross-examination was denied, though the Government would not be allowed to elicit testimony concerning Pettiford's arrest in late December of 1968. To be certain no reversible error would be injected inadvertently at this late stage of the trial, Shuker asked

Perazich whether Pettiford had been in jail at any other time in 1968, in order to avoid mention of such an arrest. Perazich excused himself for a moment from the bench conference, conferred briefly with his client, and returned to the bench.

"Your Honor," he reported, "it is Mr. Pettiford's recollection that the only time in 1968 that he was in jail, although he is not sure, is that period we indicated."

Pierre Pettiford could not even remember for certain when he had been in jail in 1968. Shuker smiled faintly and suggested that if Perazich would simply caution his client not to volunteer any such information, he would not be asked about it. The lawyers returned to their tables, and Perazich stood and announced: "The defense calls the defendant Pierre Pettiford." Whereupon Pettiford walked to the witness stand, swore upon a Bible to tell the truth, the whole truth, and nothing but the truth, and sat down to tell it.

"When were you arrested in this case?" Perazich asked as soon as Pettiford had given his name and last address.

"August 28, 1969."

"Directing your attention, Mr. Pettiford, to the period between Thanksgiving, 1968, and Christmas, 1968, do you recall where you were living?"

"Yes."

"Where were you living, sir?"

"I was living at two places. First I was residing with my aunt, and then I moved and I resided at 1344 Harvard Street."

"Where were you living with your aunt, if you recall?"

"2132 Flagler Place."

"Do you recall when you left 2132 Flagler Place?"

"Yes, right after Thanksgiving."

"1968?"

"1968."

"In about this time period, sir, that is, Thanksgiving to Christmas, 1968, where were you employed?"

"I was working for Mr. Smith. I was doing odd jobs really. I was helping a man by the name of Mr. Smith."

"Daniel Smith, sir?"

"Yes, sir. Daniel Smith."

"Again, sir, in this time period, between Thanksgiving and Christmas

1968, if you can recall, what people did you see that you know, your friends, family, or anything else?"

"I saw a number of people."

"Could you name some of them, if you can recall, who saw you in that period?"

"My aunt, Miss Cora Green, and my sister."

"Did you see anybody else outside the members of your family around the holidays of 1968?"

"Yes."

"Who else?"

"Ralph Sullivan."

"Anybody else, sir?"

"Yes, his brother June."

"Is there anybody else that you can think of that you saw around that time?"

"Raymond Jones."

"Is there anybody else that you saw about that time, sir?"

"I am trying to think. It has been so long."

"Did you see Mr. George Sanka?"

"Yes."

Unimportant facts, perhaps, but facts designed to show simply that Pierre Pettiford had been living a normal life with normal people.

"Mr. Pettiford, you have heard the testimony in this courtroom regarding the Carwash at 616 Rhode Island Avenue, haven't you, sir?"

"Right."

"Did you ever work at that Carwash, sir?"

"Yes."

"Would you tell Her Honor and the ladies and gentlemen of the jury when you worked at the Carwash?"

"I worked at the Carwash in 1966."

"Do you recall how long you worked at the Carwash in 1966?"

"Approximately five to six weeks."

"Did you work at that Carwash in 1967?"

"No, I didn't."

"Did you work at that Carwash in 1968?"

"No, I didn't."

"Did you work at that Carwash in 1969?"

"No, I did not."

195

"Mr. Pettiford, at the time you were at the Carwash in 1966, did you come to know an employee by the name of Gloria McDowell?"

"No, I did not."

"Did you come to know an employee by the name of John Weaver?"

"No, I did not."

"Did you come to know an employee by the name of Irving Rosenberg?"

"Yes, I did."

"How did you come to know Mr. Rosenberg?"

"He was the manager of the Carwash in 1966, when I was an employee."

"Mr. Pettiford, do you know the co-defendant in this case, Mr. Raymond Smith?"

"Yes, I do."

"How long have you known Mr. Smith?"

"Approximately ten to twelve years."

"Did you see Mr. Raymond Smith in the period between Thanksgiving and Christmas, 1968?"

"No, I did not."

"Did you see Mr. Raymond Smith prior to the period of Thanksgiving, 1968, within the year 1968?"

"No, I did not."

"Did you see Mr. Raymond Smith in the year 1967?"

"I might have."

"But you didn't see him in the year 1968?"

"I did not see him in 1968."

"Did you see Raymond Smith in the year of 1969?"

"Yes, I did."

"Do you recall when you saw him in 1969?"

"I would say March—late February or March. Along that period. Spring."

"Did you know a young lady by the name of Ruby Taylor?"

"Yes, I did."

"How did you know Mrs. Taylor?"

"I knew her through Raymond Smith."

"Did you see Mrs. Taylor at all in the year 1969?"

"No, I did not."

"Did you see Mrs. Taylor in the year 1968?"

"No."

"Did you see Mrs. Taylor in the year of 1967?"

"No."

"When, if at all, did you ever see Mrs. Taylor?"

"I saw Mrs. Taylor in 1966."

"Did you see her frequently in 1966?"

"Somewhat. Five or six times, I would say."

"Do you know Robert Coleman?"

"Yes, I do."

"How long have you known Mr. Coleman?"

"Four years."

"Did you see Mr. Coleman in the year 1969?"

"Yes, I did."

"Where did you see him, sir?"

"When I was incarcerated at the D.C. Jail."

"On these charges, sir?" The jury must not be led to think Pettiford had any other alleged criminal activities beyond the Carwash case.

"On these present charges."

"When was this, if you can recall?"

"Approximately early September."

"1969?"

"1969."

"Did you see Robert Coleman in the year 1968?"

"No, I did not."

"Did you see Mr. Robert Coleman in the year 1967?"

"No, I did not."

"Mr. Pettiford, were you at the Carwash at 616 Rhode Island Avenue, on the date of December 10, 1968?"

"No, I was not."

"Were you with Raymond Smith at all on December 10, 1968?"

"No, I was not."

"Did you see Ruby Taylor on December 10, 1968?"

"No."

"Did you see Mr. Robert Coleman on December 10, 1968?"

"No."

That was what Pierre Pettiford told the jury.

In the last year Shuker had been the prosecutor assigned to over seventy cases and had lost only twice. One of those had stayed fresh in

197

his mind: a trial in which the man's defense was one of the most difficult defenses for a prosecutor to attack on cross-examination. The man had been arrested four months after the crime and claimed not to recall his whereabouts on the day of the crime.

When you cross-examine a man who is lying, you can sometimes seize on a fact the witness has alleged to be true and show it to be false. But if the man does not claim to have been anywhere—if he cannot recall where he was, or with whom, or for what purpose—there is no fact to contradict or to rebut. So you try to force him to remember—something, anything, at any proximate time. And then you show that if he remembers that time, he must remember a nearby time, and you progress forward or backward until you reach the day in question. Or you show the fact he claims to be true is not true. Or you show circumstances suggesting a high likelihood that the man does in fact recall where he was. But if the man still claims to remember absolutely nothing, over a period of time in which he should—must—remember something, he must be hiding something. You try to show that his lack of memory is itself a lie. And if his lack of memory is a lie, you hope the jury will believe his denial to be a lie as well.

Shuker began.

"Who did you see on December 10, 1968, Mr. Pettiford?" he began.

"The time has been so lengthy, I can't recall who I saw on that particular date."

"Where were you on December 10, 1968?"

"I don't know where I was on December 10, 1968."

"Did you work on December 10, 1968?"

"I could have worked on December 10, 1968."

"Did you?"

"I don't know. I said I could have."

"You don't know?"

"No, I do not know."

"Who were you working for as of December 10, 1968?"

"I do not know precisely."

"Were you working for anyone on December 10, 1968?"

"Yes, I was working. Yes, I was working infrequently doing odd jobs."

"For any particular person?"

"Yes."

"Who?"

"Daniel Smith."

"Well, is that who you were working for as of December 10, 1968?"

"Not on a regular basis. I said infrequently."

"What do you mean by infrequently? How often?"

"Not every day."

"How often?"

"Well, two or three times a week, perhaps."

"Every week two or three times a week?"

"Not necessarily, no."

"Would there be weeks when you didn't work for Daniel Smith?"

"No, there wasn't."

The judge interrupted: "You are dropping your voice so we are having a hard time hearing you," she advised the witness.

"How many days a week?" Shuker continued.

"As I said before, two or three days a week."

"Every week?"

"Two or three. One time I worked a whole week."

"One time you worked a whole week?"

"Yes."

"When was that?"

"I don't know precisely. It was a long period."

"In December or November?"

"I do not know."

"Was it before Christmas?"

"Yes, it was before Christmas."

"Was it before Thanksgiving?"

"No, it wasn't before Thanksgiving."

"It was either in late November or December before Christmas, is that right?"

"Right."

"Where did you work?"

"I worked—he was the janitor of the apartments on Hobart Place."

"When you worked for him, would you always work in that apartment house?"

"Yes."

"What kind of odd jobs did you do for him?"

"He was somewhat old. I would help him take the trash out, you know, and small things of that sort, you know."

"On any one of the days when you would work helping Daniel Smith, how much of a day would you work helping him?"

"Three or four hours."

"Was that usually in the morning or afternoon?"

"Usually in the morning."

"One of those days when you would work for Daniel Smith, what time would you wake up?"

"I would say 7:30 or 8:00."

"What time would you arrive for work?"

"Between 8:00 and 9:00."

"How far was it from where you were living to where you worked?"

"Three and a half blocks."

"Would you walk?"

"Yes, I would walk."

"Would you go anywhere before you would go to work?"

"No."

"Let's make this a four-hour day—what would you do when you got off work at one o'clock?"

"Sometimes I would stay around there for a few hours."

"Doing what?"

"Might be drinking some beer or something."

"With whom?"

"With the whole family there, you know."

"Which family?"

"Daniel Smith's."

"So, you might stay there for how long?"

"I might spend a couple hours around there."

"Then what would you do?"

"I might go up around my old neighborhood."

"Where is that?"

"First and Rhode Island Avenue."

"Would you see anybody in that neighborhood?"

"Like I said before, I grew up in the neighborhood."

"This is one of those days. Who would you normally see?"

"I would see a lot of fellows on the corner that I might have grew up with."

"Who?"

"Any great number of people around there that I know."

"How long would you usually stay there?"

"No particular time. I might just pass through or I might stay around there also."

"Let's say you passed through. If you just passed through, how long would you stay?"

"It is hard to say."

"An hour or less than an hour?"

"If I was passing through it would be something like fifteen minutes."

"What would you do next?"

"I would go home."

"This would be about four o'clock in the afternoon?"

"I don't know anything about time."

"What time did you usually get home on one of these days when you worked half a day?"

"I had no reason to rush home. I might do anything. I might go to the movies. I might walk somewhere."

"Go to see Raymond Smith?"

"To see Raymond Smith? What for? No."

"What time would you usually get home if you didn't go to a movie?"

"I would get home about 10:30 or eleven o'clock."

"If you didn't go to a movie?"

"Yes."

"What would you have been doing from the time that you buzzed through your old neighborhood until 10:30 or eleven o'clock?"

"I know people. I might go by somebody's house to visit people."

Perazich had not subpoenaed Daniel Smith to corroborate Pettiford because Daniel Smith, in a pretrial interview, had said he'd only seen Pettiford about three times in his life and didn't very much like him.

"Now, what about one of the days when you didn't work—one of the four or five other days of the week? If you weren't working, what time would you get up?"

"I got up about the same time—woke up anyway."

"What would you do on that kind of day?"

"Nothing in particular."

"Did you go out or stay at home?"

"It all depends."

"You just don't know?"

"No, I don't."

"In December, 1968, on the days that you weren't working, or the days that you only worked three or four hours, what did you do with the whole day if you didn't work, or the rest of the day if you did work? What people did you visit?"

201

"Well, June Sullivan. I stopped by his house."

"Every day?"

"Not every day."

"How often?"

"I used to be around him a lot, you know."

"No, sir, I don't," Shuker said.

"They would come by my house sometimes and I would come by their house sometimes," Pettiford explained.

"In December of 1968, how often did you see this person?"

"Quite frequently."

"As often as once a day?"

"Not that often."

"How often?"

"I would say every other day."

"About what time of the day?"

"It didn't make any difference what time. It wasn't early or wasn't late. It was mostly during the day or early evening."

"Where?"

"At his residence."

"Where was that?"

"1341 Euclid Street."

"Who else were you seeing during that period of time?"

"His brother Ralph."

"How often did you see Ralph?"

"About the same amount of time."

"Did they live together?"

"Yes."

"Well, did you see him at 1341 Euclid Street, too?"

"From time to time. He wouldn't be there all the time. Both of them wouldn't be there together all the time."

"Where else would you see him in December of 1968?"

"He used to come by my house sometimes."

"Where?"

"1344 Harvard Street."

"From Thanksgiving in November, 1968, until Christmas of 1968, other than the two brothers you have mentioned, is there anyone else that you were spending a significant amount of time with?"

"I would be around George Sanka."

202

"George Sanka?"

"I have been around him a considerable amount of time."

Perazich had not subpoenaed George Sanka to corroborate Pettiford because Sanka, in a pretrial interview, indicated he didn't much like or trust Pierre Pettiford because he was a no-good shiftless drunk.

"When in the summer did you start living at Flagler Place?"

"I can't pinpoint the precise date."

"The beginning of the summer or the end of the summer?"

"It could have been spring. I know it was warm. It could have been spring."

"Were you living there alone?"

"No, with my aunt."

"Had you lived there before?"

"I had."

"How often had you lived there?"

"I have lived there off and on all my life."

"Did there come a time near the end of 1968 when you moved out of Flagler Place?"

"Right."

"When was that?"

"That was after Thanksgiving."

"How soon after Thanksgiving?"

"A couple of days after Thanksgiving."

"What day of the week did you move out?"

"I don't know."

"You don't know whether it was a weekend or a day in the week?"

"I don't."

"Where did you go?"

"I moved to 1344 Harvard Street."

Perazich had not subpoenaed the Harvard Street landlord to corroborate Pettiford because the landlord, in a pretrial interview, had claimed not to remember anyone named Pierre Pettiford, and, anyway, coming down to testify for him at trial would be an awful imposition.

"Going back to the times when you weren't working for Daniel Smith during the period of November and December, 1968, the times from noon on the days you did work, and the whole days on the days you didn't work, who else did you see?"

"I saw a lot of people that I knew."

203

"Who were you seeing most frequently at that time?"

"I couldn't say anyone that frequently because—like I said, June and Ralph Sullivan."

"What about the whole rest of the week? What would you do with your time?"

"I don't know. This happened, I guess, ten or eleven months ago. I can't recall everything that I did."

"Think back," Shuker suggested.

"I have tried to think about it ever since I have been locked up for this," answered Pettiford.

"You don't know what you were doing with your time?"

"No, not the particular date."

"I am talking about a whole two-month period."

"I told you in general the things I did."

"Yes, sir, except for the four hours you would work every two or three days, you saw two people, is that right?"

"I used to paint also."

"In November and December of 1968?"

"No, I didn't say that. In the fall of 1968."

"Let's go back then. How long did you work for this Daniel Smith?"

"Several weeks, total."

"Well, how many weeks do you mean by several?"

"It could be two. It could be three."

"A total of two or three weeks?"

"I said several."

"More than two or three?"

"No."

"Two or three weeks then?"

"Right."

"Now, how much of November did you work for Daniel Smith?"

"I can't remember the months."

"Were you working for him at the time of Thanksgiving?"

"No."

"Did you start working for him after Thanksgiving?"

"A couple days after Thanksgiving."

"Did you start working for him on a Monday?"

"I don't know the day of the week."

"Did you have any other jobs while you were working for Daniel Smith three or four hours a day, two or three days a week?"

"No, I can't recollect of any. There were jobs earlier during the summer, you know."

"Right before the day you started working for Daniel Smith, were you working?"

"No, I was seeking employment then. I couldn't find employment because it was so near Christmas."

"When was your last job before you started working for Daniel Smith?"

"It had to be painting, I guess."

"When was it?"

"I think it might be either September or October."

"Were you working at all in November up until the time you started working for Mr. Smith?"

"No."

"Nowhere at all?"

"No."

"Were you taking any kind of day work—work maybe one day?"

"I was mostly seeking employment. I might have helped Mr. Matthews. This is a man that owns a truck, and he does light moving, you know."

"What about October, did you work then?"

"I might have worked then."

"You worked in October?"

"I said I might have. I am not sure."

"Where did you work, if you might have worked in October?"

"Painting."

"Painting houses?"

"I was painting rooms, really."

"Were you working for anyone else or for yourself?"

"I was working for another gentleman."

"Who was that?"

"Mr. Truesdale."

"How long did you work for Mr. Truesdale?"

"I know I worked there at least a week."

"What is the longest it could have been, as far as your memory is concerned?"

"A week."

"That was what month? Either October or September?"

"Right."

"You don't know which one?"

"No."

"Did you have any other jobs in September and October of 1968?"

"I can't recollect any."

"What is the next job that you remember before September or October of 1968, when you worked about one week?"

"I did maintenance work in a building at 18th and M Streets."

"When was that?"

"I don't know."

"Was it in the summer?"

"It was kind of warm."

"How long did you work there?"

"I don't know, but I became ill on the job."

"How long was it? Do you remember?"

"No."

"Was it more than a month?"

"I don't know how long it was."

"Now, in September and October you worked one week as a painter, is that right, sir?"

"Yes, something near that."

"In November you did not work until after Thanksgiving, and then you worked two to three weeks for Daniel Smith, is that right, sir?"

"That is right."

"You would work two to three half-days a week for Mr. Smith, is that right, sir?"

"Yes, but I did some more work."

"When?"

"Nearing Christmas I did some work for the resident manager. I stripped and waxed the floors, you know, of the basement corridor for the resident manager."

"How long did you work on that particular job?"

"That took up an entire day."

"A whole day?"

"Yes."

"Now, in that four month period, September, October, November, and December, up to Christmas, when you weren't working, what were you doing?"

"I wasn't doing anything in particular."

"Did you go around to try to find day work?"

"No, I mostly was seeking out companies, and I wasn't too successful at that."

"Mr. Pettiford, did you work at any carwashes in September, October, November, and December?"

"Of course not."

"None at all?"

"No."

"You did work at a carwash in 1966, didn't you?"

"I most certainly did."

"You worked and were on the payroll then?"

"Yes."

"When you worked there in 1966, were you aware of the fact that people came in and worked only one day sometimes and then would drift off—that there was day work available?"

"I am not particularly aware of that."

"You are not?"

"No. Why should I be?" said Pettiford.

"How long have you known Raymond Smith, Mr. Pettiford?"

"Ten to twelve years."

"And he started working at the Carwash the same time you did in 1966, didn't he?"

"Yes, sir. I think that might be correct."

"Now, in 1966, when you were working at the Carwash, would you see Mr. Smith off the work premises?"

"Yes, I would see him from time to time, yes."

"Did you socialize with him then?"

"We used to socialize."

"In 1967, did you see Mr. Smith at all?"

"I think I saw him in 1967."

"What about in 1968?"

"I didn't see him in 1968."

"You didn't see him at all in 1968?"

"Not at all."

"Never even bumped into him on the street?"

"No."

"Nowhere at all?"

"No."

"But, you did see him in 1969, is that correct, in the spring?"

"That is correct."

"Did you bump into him on the street then?"

"I was seeking employment then."

207

"That was the first time you had seen him since 1967?"

"Since 1967."

"Did you see Ruby Taylor in 1966?"

"I did."

"When you did see Ruby Taylor in 1966, where would you see her?"

"I would see her with Raymond."

"Whereabouts?"

"Maybe in the street where he used to reside at."

"137 V Street?"

"I don't know the address."

"You lived on Flagler, didn't you?"

"I did."

"At any time that you lived on Flagler, did Raymond Smith live right around the corner from you?"

"Yes, he did."

"On V Street?"

"On V Street."

"Did you ever visit him there?"

"I did."

"Did you see Ruby Taylor there?"

"I might have seen her once or twice."

"Did you see her in 1967, Mr. Pettiford?"

"I think I did."

"Did you see her in 1968?"

"I did not."

"Did you see her in the spring of 1969?"

"No, I didn't."

"Now, you said that you know Robert Coleman."

"I do."

"Was it your testimony that as of today you have known him for four years?"

"That is correct."

"So, you saw him in 1966?"

"I did."

"Did you see him in 1967?"

"I don't know. I am not sure."

"Did you ever socialize with Mr. Coleman?"

"No, I did not."

"Did you ever see him on the street at any time?"

"I might have."

"Did you? Do you remember seeing him on the street?"

"I am not sure. I have seen many people on the street."

"I am sure of that," said Shuker, "but I am asking if you saw him on the street, if you remember."

"I saw him on the street from time to time. I can't pinpoint the years, the months, or dates."

"Did you see him on the street in 1968?"

"No."

"Never?"

"No, I didn't see him in 1968."

"Did you see him on the street in 1967?"

"I might have."

"You don't remember?"

"I am not sure."

"Did you see him on the street in 1966?"

"Yes, I did."

"When you would see him on the street, would you speak to him?"

"Yes, I would speak to him."

"Did you ever see him when you were in the company of Raymond Smith?"

"No."

"Never?"

"No, unless you are referring to the jail."

"Were you at 14th and U Streets at any time on December 10, 1968?"

"No."

"No?"

"No."

"Do you remember that you weren't on 14th and U Streets on December 10?"

"No."

"You don't remember? Which is your answer, Mr. Pettiford?"

"I don't remember."

"You could have been there?"

"I could have been there. As far as I know I wasn't, you know. I could have been there."

"Mr. Pettiford, isn't it a fact that at about eight o'clock on December 10, 1968, at 14th and U Streets, you said to Mr. Raymond Smith, 'You didn't have to beat that man like a damn dog.'?"

"No, it is not a fact."

"Isn't it a fact that you said you had to kill the woman because she recognized you?"

"No, it is not a fact."

"In October of 1968, or September of 1968, did you at any time work at the Carwash, 616 Rhode Island Avenue?"

"No, I did not."

"Any time before Christmas in 1968, any one of the days in December, do you remember where you were?"

"Any day?"

"Up until Christmas in 1968—a day in December, 1968, any one of those days that you can remember specifically where you were?"

"I can remember being home."

"On any particular day?"

"I can't remember back that far. I can't remember any particular date. Nothing outstanding happened."

"Christmas happened in 1968, didn't it?"

"Yes, it did."

"Do you remember where you were on Christmas Day, 1968?"

"No, I do not."

"Christmas Eve, 1968—December 24?"

"No, I do not."

"You don't remember anything about it at all?"

"No."

"Or any other day in December?"

"No."

It was by now clear to Shuker, and he hoped to the jury too, that Pierre Pettiford was being deliberately evasive, deliberately short of memory, deliberately unable to recall specific events for fear of being trapped in a lie. "Your honor," he said, "I have no further questions."

Perazich had just a little more to ask, to emphasize the entire thrust of Pettiford's defense.

"Since August 28, 1969"—the day of Pettiford's arrest for the murders—"have you thought as to where you were on December 10, 1968?"

"Yes," said Pettiford. "I have tried and I have tried every day since I have been here, but I just don't know."

Then Pierre Pettiford was allowed to leave the witness stand and return to counsel table. Forgotten was a small notation by now deeply buried in the hundreds and hundreds of pages comprising police files, a notation the jury never learned of, dated August, 1969, when detectives were checking out Ruby Taylor's story: "Contacted Mr. Hudson of National Press Club who stated that Pettiford had worked there from July 21 to July 31, 1969, as a dishwasher. He had been fired for being drunk and had almost broke bad when he was fired. He listed past occupations as 'Carwash, Rhode Island Avenue, Irving Rosenberg' with reason for quitting, 'too cold.' He also indicated on his application that he had worked at the Carwash from January, 1967, to June, 1968."

The defense ended its case with two more brief witnesses. The first was an official from the U.S. Marshal's Office, who testified that on a dozen different occasions during the half-year before her death, Ruby Taylor had been given a $20 witness payment for each of her appearances in the courthouse—a standard fee for a witness appearing under subpoena. The defense believed the fee had constituted in Ruby Taylor's mind a payoff for helping out the Government.

Finally Fay recalled Raymond Smith to identify the document now known as Defense Exhibit 10, the application for a job at The American Tobacco Company in Durham, dated December 10, 1968—recalled him because when Smith had originally testified, his attorneys had intentionally withheld the fact of their possession of the application, even at that late stage. Yes, said Smith, that was his signature at the bottom, and Mr. Rich had been the man who had interviewed him. And after a brief cross-examination—

"That is your handwriting on there, isn't it, Mr. Smith?"

"That is my handwriting."

"You filled this out, didn't you?"

"Yes, I filled the application out."

"All of it?"

"Yes, I did."—

the defense rested.

Pursuant to the ritual, defense counsel asked to approach the bench for a moment after resting their cases. In a sentence and without arguing the point, each moved for judgment of acquittal. Their motions were summarily denied.

After the defense rests in a criminal case, the Government is allowed to present rebuttal witnesses to attack points made by defense witnesses.

211

The defense, if it chooses, may then call its own witnesses to rebut points made by the Government's rebuttal witnesses. The process continues until both sides have covered all points of rebuttal.

Shuker called several witnesses to try to refute the defense case.

First he called Henry Hayes, the Durham detective who had accompanied Washington detectives Mosrie and Kennedy in September, 1969, after they had driven down to freeze the testimony of Raymond Smith's potential alibi witnesses. At Shuker's request Hayes had been in Washington throughout the trial. There was no way to predict whether any conversations he had witnessed in Durham over half a year ago might become important, but in a big case you don't take chances.

Sarah Magnum had told the jury she had seen Smith almost daily, sometimes twice a day, in the first few weeks of December. Henry Hayes told the jury that on September 3, 1969, he had personally witnessed Washington detectives interviewing Sarah Magnum, and that she had told them that between November 30, 1968, and Christmas, 1968, she had not seen Raymond Smith. She was certain of the date, she had said, because her friend Bill had been arrested on November 30 for rape.

Cross-examination was brief. Shuker had contemplated, but now decided against, calling Kennedy and Mosrie to corroborate Hayes's impeachment of Sarah Magnum. Hayes, he reasoned, had been an impressive witness, an obvious professional with no conceivable interest in the outcome of the trial There was, of course, the possibility that the jury had by this stage forgotten who Sarah Magnum was, what she had testified to, and whether or why it had been important. But no amount of rebuttal could cure that.

Next Shuker called the Director of the Durham County Department of Public Welfare for authentication of documents that had previously been referred to. He had brought from Durham the records pertaining to applications from Raymond Smith. From those records, filled out by the case-worker interviewing Smith, he testified that on December 12, 1968, Smith, when applying for food stamps, had stated that he had just come to Durham from Washington. And on December 31, when applying for funds for transportation back to Washington, Smith had stated that he had come to Durham only about a month ago.

Cross-examination concerning the application of December 31 was geared to show that Smith, to get the funds to return to Washington, needed to establish that he was a resident of Washington. But as for the entry of December 12, there was very little cross-examination at all.

212

Shuker then called a supervisor in the Employment Security Commission in Durham to authenticate some other documents. He too testified from official records: an application for unemployment compensation dated December 12, 1968, and one dated December 19, 1968.

"Who puts the dates on there, sir?" Shuker asked.

The interviewer. The rest of the form is completed by the applicant himself. The witness's attention was directed to Government Exhibit 9—an application filled out by Raymond Smith on December 12, 1968, on which the applicant had furnished his employment history for several years back. To Shuker, and he hoped to the jury, two facts in that history were important. First, the applicant named Raymond Smith had stated that he had worked at Curtis Chevrolet in Washington into early November. More important, he had listed a number of odd jobs he had held in 1968, and in 1967, and even back in 1965. But for 1966, the year he had worked at the Carwash, Raymond Smith had not listed a thing.

This time, there was no cross-examination.

Next in rebuttal, Shuker announced a stipulation that all counsel had agreed to because of indisputable documentary evidence: that Raymond Smith had worked at the Holiday Inn in Durham from October 23, 1968, through October 31, 1968, and at no other time, and that on October 30, when he had rented a Hertz which he returned five days later with a balance due, he had given a Washington home address. That, Shuker theorized, would be about the date when Raymond Smith had returned to Washington.

Shuker called his last rebuttal witness, Brenda Foster, the one witness he thought could honestly and believably place Raymond Smith in Washington in late 1968, between the time he had worked for the Holiday Inn in Durham and the time he had left Washington after the murders to establish a Durham alibi. When she had first spoken with Shuker in his office early before the third morning of the trial—at a time when she could not possibly have known the trial significance of what she was saying—Brenda Foster had told of meeting Smith in late '68. She had been sure of the season because of her children: they were Brenda Foster's calendar. And when she had testified in the Government's case-in-chief concerning the veiled threat Smith had made through her to her mother, Brenda Foster had been an excellent witness, the kind you like to end your case with.

Had she, Shuker asked when she resumed the stand, seen Raymond Smith in Washington in 1968? Yes, she said, Smith had come to the Summit Place house she shared with her mother, had asked for Ruby

213

Taylor, and had sat awhile to wait for her. When had that been? It must have been around the last part of November, 1968, Brenda Foster said. Because her older daughter was ten or eleven months old, and anyway she and her mother had not moved to Summit Place until November, and their things were still in boxes when Smith arrived. Direct examination was that brief, and Shuker sat down.

The younger Murray began the cross-examination:

"Where had you moved from when you moved over to Summit Place?"

"Lanier Place."

"Are you indicating, Miss Foster, that you lived at Lanier Place at some time during 1968?"

"No. I didn't say that."

"When did you move from Lanier Place?"

"Well, it had to be in November."

"Of what year?"

"It was 1968."

"So you did live at Lanier Place sometime in 1968?"

"Yes," Brenda Foster explained. "You said 'indicated.' I wasn't indicating. I was just saying. You said I was indicating. I wasn't indicating. I was just telling you."

"At Lanier Place, you would be living with Mrs. Emma Roland, isn't that right?" Murray asked.

"Yes."

"Are you certain you lived with Emma Roland in 1968?"

"Yes," she answered, "and 1967 too."

"And your first child was born when you were living with Emma Roland?"

"No," she said. "I was living with my mother."

Murray paused for a moment. "Where was your mother living?"

"On Summit Place."

"All right. Your first child was born when?"

"In January, 1968."

"Where were you living in January, 1968?"

"I just told you," she said.

"Where were you living in January, 1968?" Murray insisted.

"Lanier Place. November I moved to Summit Place."

"Now, your baby was born in January, 1968, isn't that right?"

"Yes."

"And at that time were you living at Lanier Place?"

214

"No."

Several jurors squirmed. Murray paused again, then continued:

"Let's back up. Where were you living when your first baby was born?"

"Summit Place."

"And when was your first baby born?"

"January, 1968."

"So you were living on Summit Place in January, 1968?"

She hesitated for a moment, then squinched her face up. Then she said "No." Then she shook her head rapidly and looked down, and the judge told her to think it all through before answering, because this was very important.

Murray began again:

"When your first baby was born in January, 1968, you were living where?"

"In Summit Place."

"And how long had you been living at Summit Place when your first baby was born?"

"Well, two months."

"And you had moved to Summit Place from Lanier Place, hadn't you?"

"Yes."

"So you moved to Summit Place two months before your baby was born?"

"Yes."

"Is it fair to say then that you were at Lanier Place in October or November of 1967, and then you moved to Summit Place?"

"What do you mean by is it fair?" Brenda Foster asked.

"Is that accurate?"

"Yes," she answered, "I would say I didn't move out of there until November."

"Of 1967?" asked Murray.

"Yes."

"Not 1968?"

"No, 1967."

Murray's cross-examination was over.

It had been effective, a bad note on which to send the Government's case to the jury. Slowly, Shuker rose and asked Brenda Foster just a few more questions. He put them simply, and made certain everyone could tell he was putting them simply.

She told him a long time had passed, she couldn't really recall exact

215

dates or exact months. But she reckoned time by her children. She had reckoned the approximate date of the threat from Smith by the age of her second daughter. And she could reckon by the age of her other daughter the approximate date when she had let Ray Smith wait inside the house for Ruby Taylor. That daughter had been ten or eleven months old when Smith had come by her place to wait for Ruby. To her place on Summit Place. And that would make it November, 1968. And even though she had lived at that apartment for a year, several boxes still did remain unpacked. "We didn't have the room to unpack everything, you know, so we had things in boxes." It had been November, 1968, though, when Ray Smith had come to her apartment in Washington.

She was the last witness for the Government. The defense had no further witnesses. The testimony was over.

The jury was temporarily excused from the courtroom, and for the last time defense lawyers made the ritual motions for judgment of acquittal on each count of the indictment. This time, to their satisfaction and Shuker's shock, the motions were granted in part. In addition to armed robbery and robbery, the indictment had charged each defendant with six counts of murder, three counts alleging homicides committed "while perpetrating and attempting to perpetrate the crime of robbery," and three counts alleging killings "purposely and with deliberate and premeditated malice." Each is a type of first-degree murder and a capital offense. Now, Judge Green ruled that the jury could not consider the counts alleging premeditated murder.

She ruled even more. In a trial for premeditated first-degree murder, the court, if it deems the evidence insufficient to support a finding of premeditated murder, may allow the jury to return a verdict of second-degree murder, or an intentional killing committed with malice aforethought but without premeditation or deliberation. Judge Green would not even allow the jury to consider a possible verdict of second-degree murder. The ruling might have little practical effect, for if the jury believed that Smith and Pettiford were responsible for the Carwash killings, they would doubtless convict of felony-murder. But if—if—the jury believed that Smith and Pettiford had killed three human beings on December 10, but had not done so during commission of the robberies, the law would now require them to return verdicts of not guilty of homicide.

Before the jury returned to the courtroom, the judge and counsel discussed briefly the instructions to be given to the jury. The judge told

216

counsel how she planned to instruct, and granted or denied several instructions they requested. The jury was called back to the courtroom and excused for lunch. When lunch was over, and everyone was back in the courtroom, and the spectator seats were filled again—at 2:00 P.M. on the seventh day of trial—Robert Shuker rose to deliver the summation for the Government.

CHAPTER SEVEN

"Ladies and gentlemen, the time has come when this case is about to be argued to you," he began. "Let me remind you that in arguments counsel for the defendants and myself are relying on our own memories, but it is your memories that govern; that is, if you find either of us states something that does not agree with your memory, then you are right and we are wrong."

And he began to detail the evidence they had heard, from the beginning.

He reminded them of Lewis Banks, who had left the Carwash on December 10 at 5:05, when only Irving Rosenberg, Gloria McDowell, and John Weaver remained inside. He reminded them of Phyllis Chotner, waiting in the street for an uncle who never arrived, and the call to the Twelfth Precinct. He reminded them of the police finding three dead bodies, and hair and blood and human tissue on the walls and floor, and the bloody knife and the bloody pipes. Then he paused for a moment and lifted one of the heavy iron pipes from the long table in front of him. Gently he touched the pipe against the edge of the table. It made a very quiet thud. You could tell that if swung just a little harder, it would make a very loud thud, and that you could probably smash apart the table with no trouble at all.

Shuker put the pipe down and recalled for the jury the testimony of Robert Gordon, owner of the Carwash, who had told the jury of the hundreds of dollars stolen after closing time from a safe whose combination only he and Irving Rosenberg knew. And that much of the stolen money had been in a white cloth bag, the same kind of bag Ruby Taylor had described. And that anyone who had worked at the Carwash would have known on Tuesday, December 10, 1968, that Tuesday would be a good day to find lots of money there.

"Now, ladies and gentlemen, let me ask you this," he said. "After that testimony, is there any doubt that there was a robbery at the Carwash on December 10, 1968, of at least eleven hundred dollars, maybe more? And is there any doubt that the deaths of Irving Rosenberg, Gloria McDowell, and John Weaver took place during the commission of that robbery? In other words, ladies and gentlemen, is there any doubt that the deaths of Irving Rosenberg, Gloria McDowell, and John Weaver constituted the offense of felony-murder, murder committed in the commission of a felony, robbery?"

That, he hoped, would minimize, perhaps eliminate, any risk to the Government of prejudice caused by the judge's dismissal of all homicide counts but those charging felony-murder.

Then he reminded them that records kept by the Carwash proved unquestionably that Smith and Pettiford had worked there for five or six weeks in late 1966. And he reminded them of the testimony of Barbara Craig and Edith Dean, who had testified that Smith and Pettiford had returned to the Carwash to work for a spell in the fall of 1968—between the time in early October, when Smith had quit his Washington job with Curtis Chevrolet, and October 23, when he had started work at the Holiday Inn in Durham. And that the robbers had obviously fled more suddenly than they had anticipated, leaving behind them hundreds of obvious dollars in Gloria McDowell's pocketbook and John Weaver's wallet.

Shuker's eyes moved from one juror to another, his voice steady, intense, certain.

"At that point," he asked, "what did we have? A felony-murder, an armed robbery committed at the Carwash, no prints of any value whatsoever. There were only three witnesses to the crime. They were dead. No eyewitnesses. A perfect crime? Maybe. It could have been, but Ruby Taylor knew Raymond Smith. Ruby Taylor saw Raymond Smith and Pierre Pettiford. Ruby Taylor heard this robbery planned. Ruby Taylor saw Smith leave his apartment with two masks, two ski masks, two jackets, coveralls. Ruby Taylor heard Pettiford, who had returned downstairs, say 'I have got the heat,' and they left. She also heard them come back, and she saw Raymond Smith when he walked into the apartment.

"And what did she see? She saw a man covered with blood. She saw a man carrying a white bag with money in it. She said, 'What happened? Why are you so bloody?' And Raymond Smith said, 'I had to slap a bitch.' And Ruby said, 'Well, you don't get bloody from slapping someone.' And he replied, 'If you hit her with what I hit her with, you would be bloody, too.'

"And she heard Pierre Pettiford. She didn't see him, she heard his voice. She knew him. She said he lived right around the corner on Flagler. And he called to the window, and Raymond Smith went to the window and said to Pettiford, put it, or put them, in their usual place.

"And she told you through the testimony you heard here, testimony under oath, testimony that had been cross-examined, she told you how Smith took off his clothes, asked her to clean his shoes, which were also covered with blood, and went into the bathroom. And she told you how at that point she looked into the pocket of his shirt and she saw some money and it was covered with blood, but she looked a little closer and some of it wasn't. She took the money that wasn't covered with blood, about forty dollars, and she left.

"That was December 10, 1968. The same day, about eight or eight-fifteen in the evening, you heard how Robert Coleman was in the vicinity of 14th and U Streets when he saw some people he knew, one of whom he had known for about six years, one of whom he had known for about eight months. They were together. He saw the people in this courtroom. Do you remember how he identified them? Mr. Coleman walked off the stand, and he said, 'This is Raymond Smith right here, and that is Pierre Pettiford.

" 'They came up to me, and Pettiford said they needed some money.

" 'And I told him I am not in the habit of giving away money. Have you got anything to offer?'

"And Pettiford said, 'I have got a watch and need some money for Raymond.' And Raymond was right beside him.

"You heard Mr. Coleman describe how they went to an address which he identified at that time to the best of his memory as 1337½ U Street. He described the building for you, a store downstairs, rooms upstairs.

"They went up. They used the back room for their discussion. When they got inside, Mr. Pettiford said he would like Mr. Coleman to get him some narcotics. Mr. Coleman told you that he had never known Mr. Pettiford to use narcotics before this date. He appeared to be drinking. Coleman didn't think it was a good idea to mix narcotics and alcohol, but he went out to comply with his wish. But as he thought about it more, he decided he would not do that, that it was not a good idea.

"So he came back. He came back to the same room, and as he walked in, an argument was going on between Smith and Pettiford. And he told you what he heard.

"Mr. Pettiford said, 'You beat that man like a damn dog.'

220

"Mr. Smith replied, 'Well, you did the same thing to the bitch.'

"And Mr. Pettiford replied, 'I had to kill her. She recognized me, somebody recognized me.'

"And they mentioned the place, a carwash, and they mentioned the fact that they had worked there.

"And then Mr. Smith said that he was going to get out of town, that he was going to build an alibi, that he was going to go to Durham, North Carolina, because he had friends and family there and he could get himself a job and make himself an alibi.

"Mr. Coleman remembered something else. He remembered one other thing there that had been said. There was a discussion between the two of them, Smith and Pettiford, about the fact that when they had changed clothes, there had been a woman around, the woman didn't like one of them, something about that. That is all he could remember.

"Now you saw him on cross-examination, too. You saw Mr. Coleman. You heard the probing that was done. It was lengthy cross-examination. It went on for a couple of hours, and you heard his answers to those questions, each and every one of them.

"He told you what he remembered, and he told you what he had done. And was he shaken? Was he shaken at all? That man who walked into this courtroom, looked at the two people he was accusing of this crime, stared them in the face, and told you in public here, ladies and gentlemen, these people are the murderers.

"And you also heard from Ruby Taylor how she had been threatened on more than one occasion. And you heard the testimony of Brenda Foster concerning July of 1969, when she met Raymond Smith at Seventh and F Streets. And he said something to her, something she didn't understand. He said, 'Have you seen your momma lately? Well, if you do, you tell her if she knows what I know she better keep her mouth shut.' "

And why, Shuker asked, had a felony become a triple murder?

"Why were these people killed in that room and why wasn't the money taken from them? You know the money was taken from the safe. Why? What happened?

"Isn't this what happened? You remember what Mr. Coleman told you. He heard them say 'somebody recognized us,' in spite of those masks. Before they could search either Mr. Weaver or the contents of Mrs. McDowell's purse, somebody recognized them. And that ignited a fuse. 'I had to kill her. Somebody recognized us.'

"You remember Mr. Gordon's description of the locker room. It has no windows. It is a good place to leave people. They can't make noise that anybody will hear. Concrete walls, no windows.

"And a pipe was picked up, and Gloria McDowell's head was beaten in, and John Weaver's head, and Irving Rosenberg's. And the panic at this point was so great that the robbery was dropped—'got enough loot, let's get out of here.' In their haste, $240 and another $75 was left behind.

"What have you heard, ladies and gentlemen, to refute that?

"You heard Pierre Pettiford, who doesn't remember one day for 125 days, from September 1 to Christmas of 1968. 'I don't remember. I don't remember. I don't know. I don't know.'

"What did he know? For 125 days all he knew was this: that he may have worked in either September or October for one week as a painter; that some time around November or December of 1968, he had worked either two or three weeks, two or three days per week, half a day per day, for somebody named Smith, as a maintenance man. What did he know? That sometime, and he didn't give you the dates, that sometime in 125 days he worked about eight to eleven days.

"Ladies and gentlemen, was he at all candid with you? Does a person forget 125 days of his life? He was arrested in August, and it is now May. He has had a long time to think about it. One hundred twenty-five days— not one day, not one day that doesn't stick out in his mind. But Monday through Friday, September through December, that doesn't stick out in his mind. No time, no way, no how. 'I just don't know where I was, ever.'

"Is that the testimony of a man who is telling you the truth? Or is it the testimony of a man who is so afraid to admit one thing that he did at one time because it might pin him down to the truth, that he is not going to tell you anything?"

And then Shuker traced Smith's testimony, beginning with his statements on direct examination concerning his residencies in Durham, and how it had changed on cross-examination, and how official business records had proved he had not worked at the Holiday Inn in September or rented a Hertz car in Durham in September. And then he mentioned some other official documents. He picked up the unemployment application Smith had filled out two days after the murders.

"Mr. Smith filled out the information on Government Exhibit 10, listing the places he had worked. He listed places in 1968, 1967, 1965."

Shuker stopped for a moment, glanced back at Smith, and turned again to the jury.

" 'You didn't list anywhere you worked in 1966, Mr. Smith. Isn't that the year you worked at the Carwash?' "

Another long look at Smith. Then, to the jury:

"He said 'Yes.'

"Why didn't he list it? Why, on December 12, 1968, didn't he want to put down where he had worked in 1966? Why?"

A pause.

"He said that he also filled out some applications for public welfare—might have filled one out on December 12.

" 'Well, did you tell them that you had just come to Durham as of December 12? Did you tell them that?'

" 'I might have. I might have.'

" 'Don't you remember telling them that?'

" 'No, I might have.'

" 'Did you tell them on December 31 that you had only been there about a month looking for work?'

" 'I might have.'

" 'But that is not true, is it, Mr. Smith?'

" 'That is not true, but I might have told them that.'

"Why did he tell them on December 12, 1968, that he had just come to Durham? Why?

"Isn't the answer because it was the truth? He had just come to Durham. A little, obscure record, they will never find that. I got to get some food stamps. He slipped and it was true. Is there any other reason?"

The attorney for the Government sums up twice to a jury, the second time after the defense has argued. Then Shuker would attempt to rebut their arguments. For now, he was finished, and he sat down.

The younger Murray stood, touched his hands against the table, faced the jury, and began nervously:

"May it please the Court and you ladies and gentlemen of the jury:

"You certainly know by now I am one of the attorneys representing Mr. Smith, and I have an opportunity to speak to you about his position on this entire matter. Usually many attorneys will tell you the importance of any given case, but I won't presume to do that. I won't stand before you and tell you about the value of life or tragedy of death. All of you are older than I, and you know more about that than I."

He reminded them of the fingerprints and hair samples and clothing fibers and blood samples—all the scientific testing which had entirely failed to link Smith and Pettiford with the Carwash on December 10, 1968. And of the Government's attempt to prove the defendants had worked there at any time in the fall of 1968 through the testimony of Sonny Craig, whose time sequences were vague and awry, who had probably been confused about which year she had worked at the Carwash with the defendants. And of Brenda Foster, who had not approached the authorities until a year and a half after the killings, in an attempt to vindicate the honor of her dead mother, herself a vengeful drug addict.

He summarized Ruby Taylor's testimony, and its item-by-item refutation by other witnesses: that 67 V Street was nonexistent, that Smith had not lived at 137 V Street during the time Ruby claimed to have overheard him plot the robbery and return from the murders. And Murray recalled for the jury the testimony of Emma Roland, Ruby's own stepmother, whom the Government had not even bothered to call.

"The stepmother, of course, was called by the defense—not by the Government to show that this threat took place, not by the Government to show that Mr. Smith was harassing her, but brought by the defense— to show you that this was a fabrication—a disinterested party, the stepmother of Mrs. Ruby Taylor. Mrs. Roland came and told you that Mrs. Taylor wasn't living with her at any time in 1968, and the incident she alleged never happened and the threat never took place."

Then he spoke of Robert Coleman and the charges he faced at the time of his arrest in August, 1969, when he had told the police of the conversations on the evening of the murders:

"We would need an adding machine to tell you the number of years that that man may have faced if he was convicted of these crimes. Which Mr. Coleman do you believe? Do you believe the Mr. Coleman who told Officer Crooke that he spoke to both Mr. Pettiford and Mr. Smith at the D. C. Jail? Or do you believe Mr. Coleman when he gets on the stand and says he never talked to them? Do you believe Mr. Coleman when the very first word out of his mouth is a lie:

" 'Are you expecting any favors for your testimony here today?'

" 'No, sir.' "

He reminded them of Coleman's trying to negotiate the best possible deal for himself and of his release on bond despite his pending charges and multiple bench warrants.

"I suggest to you that all Mr. Coleman wants is to see a little bit of daylight before he dies. I suggest to you that there is pressure on Mr. Coleman; and that if he felt that what was needed was to say that Mr. Smith came up in a jelly-bean truck, he would say it.

"You can't be too hard on Mr. Coleman, and I don't intend to be; but unless we think of him too sympathetically, let's remember what he is. He is not a user, he is a seller. There are those, ladies and gentlemen, who say that a pusher is pretty low on the totem pole of human behavior, pretty low, exploitation personified.

"This is the man that the Government today asks you to believe and believe beyond a reasonable doubt. I submit to you he is not believable."

And then Murray reminded them of the testimony of the defense witnesses, so many of whom had testified that Raymond Smith had been in Durham around the time of the murders. And the testimony of Smith himself: had he scurried down to Durham, as Coleman had said, to establish an alibi?

"The Government can't have it both ways, ladies and gentlemen. They can't tell you that he was in Durham to establish a phony alibi, and then tell you that Mr. Smith forgot the alibi. They can't tell you that he falsified a date on December 10, and then tell you that Mr. Smith forgot about it. They can't tell you that he went down on the twelfth to two different offices and walked into those offices and said, 'I just came in from Washington.' Why didn't he say, 'I just blew in from Washington where I committed a triple murder'?

"Apparently somebody forgot to tell Mr. Coleman that Mr. Smith didn't need to conjure up an alibi, because he was in Durham that morning. Apparently somebody forgot to tell Mr. Coleman that whoever robbed or murdered those three people got away with $1,100, because as far as Mr. Coleman is concerned, somebody needed money and was willing to sell a watch for twelve bucks after they walked away with $1,100.

"Somebody forgot to tell Mr. Coleman that Mr. Smith had a gouge on his lip and scratches on his face, because Mr. Coleman didn't remember it. And Mr. Coleman forgot the address of where this thing happened. That is not important.

"What is important is that Mr. Smith was in Durham from the middle of October"—a month later than Smith himself had testified to—"until December 31, and didn't come home. Is there any evidence that he did?

"The Government has the burden here. The Government had the burden of proving beyond a reasonable doubt that what Mr. Coleman and what Ruby Taylor testified to is the truth.

"They failed," he said, and sat down. And then his father stood, and delivered a second, short summation on behalf of Raymond Smith:

"There never was a case," he said, "I guess there never will be a case, where you don't find disputes in the testimony and arguments by one side or the other as to what witness is worthy of belief and what witness is not. It is the rare case, and this is one of them, where you can forget what witness to believe or what witness to disbelieve.

"It is a physical piece of evidence in this case, the application of this defendant Raymond Smith, not disputed as such, a genuine written application of the defendant Raymond Smith, made by the person before whom it was filed on December 10, 1968, the very date of these murders. The time of day is not known; Mr. Rich doesn't remember. Neither does the defendant, who could have chosen to remember that it was at 3:30 P.M., a half-hour before they closed, had he been so disposed.

"There have been many instances where he told an untruth, but ironically, all those untruths on his part in Durham serve only to establish beyond any question that he was not framing a defense, framing an alibi, because if he was framing an alibi through the use of documents, he would have had intelligence enough, I submit to you, not to put obvious lies in there. Strangely enough we have a petty liar, who by virtue of his petty lying has indicated a very good reason why you are justified in finding that he is not guilty of these murders.

"And here it is," Murray stated, holding Defense Exhibit 10 in his hand, "here is that document, executed on December 10, 1968, by Raymond Smith, 250 miles away from the scene of these murders, containing possibly within this document itself some misstatements. We know others that were proven false.

"I think the issue in this case can be put in one short sentence: Does Defendant Smith's Exhibit Number 10 create in your minds a reasonable doubt that Raymond Smith is guilty of these offenses? Has this document, this undisputed and indisputable document, raised in your minds a reasonable doubt that after executing this document, Smith in some manner not shown or even so far argued got up into the District of Columbia and was able after five and a half hours to commit a murder which according to the evidence of the Government happened about 5:15 P.M.? That's an hour and fifteen minutes after the office closed. And if you give him the benefit of the doubt, you must say, it seems to me, that he made this application toward the end of the day and not at the beginning. And having arrived here, in some manner not explained and so far not argued, worked out a scheme to go into that Carwash, for what purpose even now appears uncertain, and robbed and murdered these people.

"Now, this is a horrible crime, as I suggested you would find it to be before we began the evidence. Mr. Shuker has developed with great

226

particularity the brutality. There are very few crimes you will hear of
that are as bad as this one. It was not necessary to tear these bodies the
way they were to accomplish robbery. There was some purpose that we
can only speculate why these perfectly decent people, unoffending citizens, were dispatched out of existence in the manner they were in this case.

"There are many tragedies. Those are three of them. They didn't
deserve death. They got it at the hands of somebody. You may well conclude after you have considered this paper that the person or persons—it
must have been persons—that did these murders are still on the streets.
They were known to be on the street eight months after this thing happened. The Police Department must have been under enormous pressure
to solve an unsolved triple murder—and I think the way these witnesses
were brought into court suggests that they realized the pressure they
were under and saw the necessity of shifting the burden and pressure
from them to somebody else: Mr. Shuker's office.

"But there's your question. We could argue all day long about who
was telling the truth about this and who was telling the truth about that.
But under your instructions, I suggest to you, you have only one question:
Do you have a reasonable doubt whether these two men committed those
murders? And I'm sure Mr. Shuker won't suggest that even though Mr.
Smith might be innocent, Mr. Pettiford could be guilty.

"The defense can rely upon this document, and we do, and I repeat
to you and I will not detain you further: Does this application of Raymond Smith, made in the city of Durham, 250 miles away, on the date of
these murders, raise in your minds a reasonable doubt that he committed
these crimes?

"Thank you."

Shuker sat thinking Murray had reached the heart of the case.

Now it was time for John Perazich to address the jury on behalf of
Pierre Pettiford.

He began by thanking them for the attention they had given throughout the trial and asked their indulgence for just a few minutes more while,
preliminary witness by preliminary witness and scientific test by scientific
test, he told how the Government had produced no credible evidence
connecting the defendants with the crimes. And he mentioned a list of
items which to him just didn't make sense.

Foremost was Ruby Taylor, whose pending cases had provided an
obvious motive for lying; Ruby Taylor, who testified about Smith's leav-

227

ing with Carwash uniforms which simply did not match the description of the uniforms given by the Carwash employees at trial; Ruby Taylor, whose story had been contradicted by her own stepmother and by the witnesses from Durham; Ruby Taylor, who had alleged the planning to have occurred in a house in which Raymond Smith had not been living on the day of the murders, whose daughter Brenda claimed that over a year had passed before Ruby even mentioned Smith's and Pettiford's participation to her. And some other things about the Government's case:

"Ladies and gentlemen, the Government wants you to believe that these two men, on December 10, 1968, took $1,100 or more from the Carwash. They then went to 14th and U Streets, where Mr. Pettiford tried to hock his watch for $12 to get Mr. Smith money to go to North Carolina. They also want you to believe that two days later in Durham, North Carolina, on December 12, 1968, Mr. Smith applied for food stamps—they want you to believe that. Eleven hundred dollars, and two days later he has gone down there and he is asking for food stamps. This same Mr. Smith, they want you to believe, on December 31, 1968, was down at the Traveler's Aid begging for $10 to get back to Washington.

"Is that reasonable, ladies and gentlemen? Is that reasonable?"

And what about the guns, "the heat" Ruby had said Smith and Pettiford left with on their way to the Carwash?

"The Government wants you to believe, outfitted as Mr. Shuker would characterize them, with ski masks and white coveralls with red letters and guns, they go and tear down some pipe off some wall and hit somebody with it, when they have got guns. Ladies and gentlemen," Perazich said, "that is as implausible as what they want you to believe regarding hocking this watch an hour later for $12. It just doesn't hang together. It's not reasonable. It creates, we submit, ladies and gentlemen, a very reasonable doubt."

Nor was Robert Coleman any more worthy of the jury's belief than Ruby Taylor's transcript had been. He had given the address of a nonexistent building and had claimed Pettiford had asked for drugs the night of the murder, when in fact Pettiford was not a drug user, and had given a different account of the night of the murders to Lieutenant Crooke before speaking with Detectives Mosrie and Kennedy.

"Ladies and gentlemen," Perazich argued, raising his voice, "Mr. Coleman could not testify to one fact that was independent of any knowledge he could have got of this offense from the newspaper or from talking to these men at the jail. Anything that was independent—the address, the weather, the clothes, any of those facts—he didn't know.

"What kind of person was Mr. Coleman? You heard him say he went out to hear the race results that night, a routine day in the street. Mr. Coleman very candidly admitted he was selling drugs. You have heard Mr. Murray speak about the type of people that sell drugs. You have heard Mr. Murray speak about the fact that there were six outstanding bench warrants for Mr. Coleman at various times. Yet he walks the streets of the District of Columbia on this day: he's out on bond.

"You have heard Mr. Murray make reference to the charges that are pending against Mr. Coleman. Mr. Murray stated that you would need an adding machine to determine how long Mr. Coleman might go to jail if he were convicted and given the maximum on these offenses.

"Ladies and gentlemen, I've got an adding machine in my office, and I'll tell you that is fifty-six years, fifty-six years, if convicted and if given the maximum. Think about that. And all these cases are still pending in this court. Think about that in evaluating Mr. Coleman's testimony."

And, in evaluating the testimony of Pierre Pettiford, there was just one more thing they might think about. Exactly 261 days had elapsed from the night of the murders until the afternoon when Pierre Pettiford had been arrested. Could any juror recall where he or she had been 261 days ago?

He asked that they return verdicts of not guilty, and the defense summations were over. None had mentioned that Ruby Taylor and Robert Coleman had contradicted each other about which defendant had admitted killing which victim.

Shuker rose to deliver the final argument the jury would hear, to dispel for them any lingering doubts they might have after arguments from three lawyers for the defense.

"This is a forum in which we are trying to seek the truth," he began, "and there are guidelines to use in seeking the truth from what you hear.

"Mr. Murray characterizes Raymond Smith as a petty liar. These are his words, not mine. Raymond Smith was under oath and on that stand. If he didn't tell you the truth, ladies and gentlemen, and you so find, that's not petty. And why didn't he? Why?

"Mr. Murray tells you this is a document," Shuker said, holding up Raymond Smith's Durham job application dated the day of the murders. "Ladies and gentlemen, these are documents," he said, showing them the business records introduced as Government exhibits. "These are records made in the regular course of business by a person who is under a duty for the continuation of that business to record accurately. They are dated by a person whose duty it is to make sure that they are accurate. And the man who made this record"—he held up Smith's welfare applications—"not Raymond Smith, but the man who had the duty to make this record, recorded the dates December 12, 1968, and December 31, 1968. And on December 12, the man who made this recorded the statement of Raymond Smith: 'I have just come to Durham from the District of Columbia.' And on December 31, the statement of Raymond Smith was recorded by an impartial person who had a duty to record accurately: 'I have been here about a month looking for work.'

"Those are documents. This," he added, holding up The American Tobacco Company application again, "is a piece of paper. Why is it a piece of paper? Because it is filled out by Raymond Smith. A self-serving statement by a man who went down there to create an alibi. This is just like saying, 'I tell you I wasn't here because I put it down on a piece of paper.' When? There's no time stamp on this. There's nothing on this but Raymond Smith, Raymond Smith building the alibi just as Robert Coleman heard him say he was going to do. The man who brought this paper to court doesn't remember a thing about it.

"Consider this," Shuker argued. 'At that time, the only date Raymond Smith would consider important would be December 10. 'Cover that date and I'm fine.' So on December 12 he says, 'I have covered up December 10, I can afford to relax and let something slip: the fact that I have just gotten here.' "

Shuker reminded them of the witnesses from Durham who had testified self-contradictorily about when and where Raymond Smith had been in Durham, and of how Sarah Magnum had told a different story to the police when they visited her right after Smith's arrest, and of the reasons why the scientific tests no more suggested the defendants' innocence than their guilt. And of the need to borrow transportation money from Coleman after pulling the Carwash heist: Ruby Taylor had taken the only bills not drenched in blood, and do you spend hot money that may be marked?

"Now where do you go to get money that isn't hot? Not to Pierre Pettiford, because what was he doing that gave him money? You go to one of your acquaintances, a man who may have it: Robert Coleman. The Government didn't choose the cast of witnesses in this case. They were chosen for us. They were chosen by these defendants and the kind of people they associate with. They wouldn't go to the Mayor. They would go to Robert Coleman. And they did and they got the money.

"Sure, Coleman wanted to help himself. But nevertheless, that man walked into this courtroom, ladies and gentlemen. And ask yourself this: It's comfortable, isn't it, to sit back anonymously without your identity disclosed, without having to face the people you accuse, and you can say anything. But walk into a courtroom, take an oath, face the people you accuse and say, they did it. Ladies and gentlemen, do you do that if it isn't true? Do you? Ruby Taylor did the same thing. She walked into a courtroom, she faced the men she accused, and she said, 'You did it.' And do you do that if you are not telling the truth?

"Why did she wait so long? She was threatened; she told you that. You heard corroboration of the fact. Why did she wait so long? What else did she think she could do until it became too much?

"Ladies and gentlemen, consider the very essence of the testimony of Ruby Taylor. If Ruby Taylor wanted to fabricate, if Ruby Taylor wanted to lie, she could do a good job and tell a good story, straightforward, simple: These men came back, Pierre and Raymond, and they were both covered with blood and they had a lot of money with them and they said, 'We just held up the Mr. Wash Carwash at 616 Rhode Island Avenue in the District of Columbia and we killed three people.'

"That would be the kind of testimony you would expect if you were hearing anything but the truth, wouldn't you? Not the rather involuted testimony that the truth so often is: the partial glimpse of an event that you as a witness get, and that's what Ruby Taylor got. Isn't that exactly what her testimony showed?

"And Robert Coleman: he could have added details if he wanted to fabricate, to do a good job. But he told the truth. And Brenda Foster, who didn't even know what the threat was about: you saw her on the stand. You listened to her. Was she doing anything but making every effort to recall what happened and to put it forward to you, and wasn't it the truth? And what did that threat mean, ladies and gentlemen?"

The Government asked for verdicts of guilty as charged. As Shuker sat down, Perazich thought to himself that it was the finest closing argument he had ever heard.

CHAPTER EIGHT

AFTER a brief recess it was time for the judge to tell the jury what rules to apply in deciding the case. She told them the case would soon be theirs, that they were the judges of the facts, that their recollection of the facts was of controlling significance, that they were not to draw any inferences as to guilt or innocence from various legal rulings made during the course of the trial, nor from any comments the judge might have made. The jury, and the jury alone, was to weigh the credibility and resolve conflicts in the testimony and to make its judgments solely on the basis of evidence that had been presented in court and reasonable inferences from that evidence.

She told them the defendants were presumed innocent throughout the trial, and that the burden is on the Government to prove them guilty beyond a reasonable doubt. "Reasonable doubt, as the name implies, is a doubt based on reason," she told them, glancing down at the book of instructions open before her. "It is such a doubt as would cause a juror, after careful and candid and impartial consideration of all the evidence, to be so undecided that he cannot say that he has an abiding conviction of the defendant's guilt. It is such a doubt as would cause a reasonable person to hesitate or pause in the graver or more important transactions of life. However, it is not a fanciful doubt nor a whimsical doubt based on conjecture. It is a doubt which is based on reason. The Government is not required to establish guilt beyond all doubt, or to a mathematical certainty or a scientific certainty. Its burden is to establish guilt beyond a reasonable doubt."

She explained for them certain general guidelines to use in evaluating a witness's testimony, told them about direct and circumstantial evidence, about rules concerning statements allegedly made by defendants, and about corroboration and the rules to apply in considering the testimony of an informer.

She told them about the elements of the crime charged, reading the

232

indictment for the jury and explaining the technical legal requirements prerequisite to a conclusion of felony-murder and armed robbery, each element of which the Government must prove beyond a reasonable doubt. She told them to give separate consideration to each defendant, and to each count, and not to let a finding on one defendant influence a finding on the other.

The judge had granted a defense request not to instruct the jury at this juncture concerning capital punishment but to wait until such time as the jury might return a verdict of first-degree murder. At that time, if that time in fact occurred, they could be sent back for further deliberations on the question of punishment. The procedure minimized both the possibility that the jury might use the issue of punishment as a factor in reaching a compromise verdict on the issue of guilt and the possibility that any juror might conclude that the judge, because she was instructing on the issue of punishment at this stage, had herself concluded that a finding of first-degree murder was appropriate.

The instructions took an hour, but in the end the question, if not the answer, was pretty simple: had Smith and Pettiford destroyed three lives while stealing some money from the Carwash on December 10, 1968? The law did not allow the judge to put it quite that simply to the jury.

Finally the jury was told that the verdict had to be unanimous and that if at any time they felt it necessary to ask any questions of the court, the foreman they would elect should write a note on a blank sheet of paper and hand it to the marshal who would always be waiting outside the jury room. Under no circumstances was the position of their voting to be communicated to anyone, including the judge, until they had reached a unanimous conclusion. Any notes containing tentative voting tallies were to be destroyed.

They would now be dismissed for the evening and were all to report to the courtroom at 9:30 tomorrow morning. At that time the alternate jurors would be excused, and the twelve jurors could begin deliberations. At no time until then were they to discuss the case with anyone, not even among themselves. And they were not to be influenced in any way by any media reports they might have read or heard, or which they might see or hear overnight.

At 5:18 in the afternoon, the jurors were dismissed. The lawyers returned to their offices. Raymond Smith and Pierre Pettiford were taken back to jail.

Anticipating the outcome of a jury's deliberations is as useless as it is inevitable. The following day Berman told Smith and Pettiford that the case looked good for the defense, and that even if the jury found them guilty, the trial record contained substantial appellate issues, foremost among them the admission of Ruby Taylor's testimony. But he expected the jury to return verdicts of acquittal within two hours. The younger Murray mentioned to his father that if the jury was out more than forty-five minutes, things looked bad. Shuker thought the Government's case had been presented as smoothly as the facts allowed, and expected a conviction. But that would take time.

After four and one-half hours, the door to the jury room swung open, and one juror handed a torn scrap of unlined white paper to the marshal sitting outside. He gave it to the judge, who summoned all the lawyers to the courtroom. The note, written in an uneven hand, said, "We Have A Hung Jury."

The judge called the jury into the courtroom and told them: "All counsel have agreed that you have not been out long enough with this case under consideration to announce that you are hung at this time, especially since the case lasted for the better part of a week and a half. Consequently, we will ask you to return to the jury room and continue your deliberations, with the hope that you will or can come up with a unanimous decision." Without being allowed to say a word—for a single word indicating how they presently stood would compel the judge to declare mistrial —the jury was taken back to the jury room.

The door opened again half an hour later, and another note was given to the marshal, who took it to the judge. Written in smooth script this time, the note said: "To whom It May Concern, Please let us hear Ruby Taylor's Transcrite. Foreman." Again the judge summoned all the lawyers to the courtroom.

The defense opposed granting the jury's request: isolated from its context, it would unfairly emphasize one side of the case, to the defendants' detriment.

"On behalf of Mr. Pettiford," said Berman, "we would not like that to happen."

"We would not like that either," said Fay on Smith's behalf.

"I wouldn't say that the Government wouldn't like it," said Shuker, "but I think under the rules of evidence it wouldn't be proper." At this stage there was no point in introducing another appellate issue into the record. The judge called the jury into the courtroom and told them:

"Ladies and gentlemen, we have your request for Ruby Taylor's transcript. Unfortunately, we cannot provide anything more than you have already had. Consequently, you will have to rely on your recollection of what was testified to from the transcript, just as you will have to rely on your recollection of any other witness's testimony. All I can do is to ask you to try to talk it out and reach an agreement as to your collective recollection as to what was contained in any of the testimony and all of the evidence to the best of your ability. I ask you to return to the jury room and try some more." The jurors were taken back to their room.

By late afternoon they hadn't reached a verdict, and the judge again called the lawyers and jury to the courtroom.

"Ladies and gentlemen of the jury," Judge Green said, "since it has reached five o'clock, the Court will excuse you to go home. However, we will ask you to come back tomorrow morning at 9:30 and continue with your deliberations at that time. Again, don't permit anybody to discuss the case with you while you are deliberating or at any time until you are finally excused. Don't you talk to anybody about the case, and don't in any way find anything in the way of communications about the case that haven't been presented to you in this courtroom.

"Good night."

When court adjourned, the defense lawyers told Smith and Pettiford that the longer the jury stayed out, the slimmer the chances of acquittals. Shuker thought a guilty verdict would take a good deal of time: this was an experienced jury, and the matter was one of life and death.

At 4:23 in the afternoon of the second day of deliberations, the jury sent the court another note, its first communication of the day: "Your Honor: The jury is hopelessly deadlocked. Foreman." The judge summoned the lawyers to the courtroom and stated her intention to read to the jury a standard instruction urging each juror to try, within the dictates of his conscience and duty, to reach a unanimous verdict.

The defense opposed any such instruction as being unreasonably coercive, and moved for a mistrial. If the jury had been unable to reach a verdict by now, the defense's case had obviously left a less favorable taste than the attorneys had anticipated. Shuker asked that the instruction be given. The jury was called into the courtroom, and the judge, reading from a standard instruction book, told them:

"Ladies and gentlemen, we have your note. I'd like to tell you that the mode provided for deciding questions of fact in criminal cases is by a verdict of the jury. In a large proportion of cases, absolute certainty cannot be attained. Although the verdict to which a juror agrees must, of course, be his own verdict, the result of his own convictions and not mere acquiescence in the conclusion of his fellow jurors, yet in order to bring the minds of twelve jurors to a unanimous verdict, each juror must examine the question submitted with candor and with proper regard and deference to the opinions of each other. You should consider that the case must at some time be decided. You were selected in the same manner and from the same source from which any future jury must be, and there is no reason to suppose the case will ever be submitted to twelve jurors more intelligent, more impartial, or more competent to decide it, or that more or clearer evidence will be produced on the one side or the other.

"With this in view, it is your duty to decide the case, if you can conscientiously do so. In this case, the burden of proof is upon the Government to prove beyond a reasonable doubt every element of the offense as charged. If the Government fails to sustain this burden, you must find the defendants not guilty. But in conferring together, you ought to pay proper respect to each other's opinions and listen, with a disposition to be convinced, to each other's arguments. On the one hand, if the larger number of your panel are for conviction, a dissenting juror should consider whether a doubt in his own mind is a reasonable one which makes no impression upon the minds of so many jurors equally honest, equally intelligent as himself, and who have heard the same evidence with the same attention, with an equal desire to arrive at the truth, and under the sanction of the same oath. On the other hand, if a majority are for acquittal, the minority ought to ask themselves seriously whether they might not reasonably doubt the correctness of a judgment which is not concurred in by most of those with whom they are associated in a like manner. The minority should question the weight or sufficiency of that evidence which fails to sway the minds of their fellow jurors."

And then she looked up from the instructions and looked at the jury and said: "I'd like to tell you also at this time and to remind you, ladies and gentlemen of the jury, that at this time you are not concerned with deciding the question of punishment, but the question of guilt or innocence." The jury filed out of the courtroom to continue deliberating.

As soon as they left, the defense again moved for a mistrial, this time based on the judge's last comment: they argued that in effect the judge had suggested to the jury her own view of the defendants' guilt. The motion was denied.

By 6:00 P.M., the jury still had not returned a verdict. The judge summoned them into the courtroom and dismissed them until the following morning.

Before being taken from the cell block back to jail, Smith and Pettiford had a brief talk with their lawyers, who explained that the length of the jury's deliberations indicated they had given some credit to the Government's case, and prospects for the defense did not look very good. They explained again that if the jury returned verdicts of guilty of first-degree murder, the jury would resume deliberations to decide between the two alternative punishments: life imprisonment or death by electrocution. Perazich told them he guessed that only a few jurors were holding out for acquittals, and that they could not hold out much longer: by now the jurors would all want to finish with the case, and the very nature of the crimes probably made a guilty verdict acceptable even to those jurors not convinced beyond a reasonable doubt of the defendants' guilt. The elder Murray told them the likelihood of capital punishment was extremely remote.

Pettiford just laughed weakly. Smith said, "The hell with it, so I can get the chair, who gives a damn." Then he lit a cigarette Perazich handed him and shook his head. "The people who did this should go to the chair," he said. "If the jury thinks I did this, they should give me the chair."

The younger Murray told him to try to relax, to be like Pettiford. "Yeah," said Pettiford, "take it like me, man. Who cares?" Then Raymond Smith and Pierre Pettiford were taken back to jail.

By noon on the third day of deliberations, the jury had not sent any notes to the court, and Judge Green called the lawyers and the jury into the courtroom to determine whether any useful purpose would be served by continued jury deliberations. The foreman was asked to stand, and the judge asked:

"Do you believe that more time will result in the jury's being able to come to a unanimous decision?"

Since being impaneled two weeks ago, this was the first occasion on which any one of the twelve voiceless faces would be allowed to say a word.

The foreman spoke. "I believe that—"

The judge interrupted immediately. "Don't tell us how you are voting."

"No, I am not going to. We were just getting ready to cast our ballots."

"So you feel that more time would be of some assistance, is that correct?"

237

"Yes," said the foreman, and the jury filed out of the courtroom to resume deliberations. Smith and Pettiford were again taken to the cell block.

Twenty-four minutes later, the jury informed the marshal outside their room that they had a verdict.

The lawyers were called to the courtroom. The jury was brought back to the courtroom, where they filed into their twelve cushioned seats. The foreman rose to announce the verdict. The judge asked the defendants to rise. Every juror stared at Raymond Smith and Pierre Pettiford. The quiet in the courtroom was like a deep, slow breath.

The jury is an odd concept, in a way: hard to predict, an amalgam of unknowns, twelve individuals drawn from their different homes and jobs and habits to find truth and do justice. Then, having reached their truth and done their justice, they once again become salesmen and secretaries, businessmen, laborers, and maids.

Sometimes they reach the right result for the right reasons, and sometimes for the wrong reasons, and sometimes they reach the wrong result for different reasons. Nobody else really knows what goes on when they retire behind that jury-room door—what they are doing, or talking about, or whether the job is being done well, or intelligently, or honestly. Most of the time they are just a bunch of people doing their untrained best to decide properly the future course of other people's lives.

You give your verdict, and then you go home and talk with your friends and family, and in the intimate moments when you lie awake in the quiet of a dark night, you live with your conscience, difficult sometimes, even when you have tried your best. And then you think about your vote, and finally fall asleep hoping the decision was in some sense right. And you wake up like the rest of Washington, and you don't have to read the morning newspaper past the front page to see the words that tell the rest of the people what you twelve have decreed:

2 ACQUITTED
IN CAR WASH
MURDER CASE

The two defendants in Washington's first triple-murder trial in 40 years were acquitted yesterday by a U.S. District Court jury.

The jury of four men and eight women deliberated for 2½ days and twice reported themselves deadlocked before acquitting Raymond Smith, 30, and

238

Pierre Pettiford, 29, of both murder and robbery charges.

The defendants stood with hands clasped behind their backs and seemed at first to show little emotion when the verdict came at 12:35 P.M.

Then Smith, balding and moustached, held his hand to his forehead and silently and slowly passed it over his face.

Pettiford, bespectacled and with short sideburns, showed a small wry smile after John Perazich, one of his lawyers, clapped him on the shoulder.

The Carwash case was over.